LCAAM

Qualitative
Market Research

17

Qualitative
Market Research

a comprehensive guide

HY MARIAMPOLSKI

SAGE Publications
Thousand Oaks • London • New Delhi

First published date 2001

SAGE Publications Inc.
2455 Teller Road
Thousand Oaks, California 91320

SAGE Publications Ltd
6 Bonhill Street
London EC2A 4PU

SAGE Publications India Pvt Ltd
32, M-Block Market
Greater Kailash - I
New Delhi 110 048

Library of Congress Cataloging-in-Publication Data

Mariampolski, Hy.
  Qualitative market research : a comprehensive guide / Hy Mariampolski.
    p. cm.
Includes bibliographical references and index.
ISBN 0-7619-6944-6 (c) -- ISBN 0-7619-6954-3 (p)
1. Marketing research. 2. Qualitative research. I. Title.
  HF5415.2 .M3167 2001
  658.8'3--dc21
                              2001004340

Typeset by Carolyn Winter

CONTENTS

LIST OF TABLES

Introduction

Qualitative market research practice often seems like a contest. Clients compete with consultants; field services grapple with suppliers; students are puzzled about career options; academics are astonished about the activities of applied practitioners; researchers in the global marketplace share little common currency with practitioners in other countries. The result is a miasma of conflicting claims, disappointed expectations and fruitless conflict. It is surprising sometimes that any good qualitative research work ever gets done.

This book is intended to create peace between these warring factions and meet the needs of several different audiences by creating some common ground in the applied practice of qualitative research. I had several targets in mind as I wrote this text.

First, worldwide corporate, government and not-for-profit agency buyers and users of qualitative research services and findings should be able to use this book to help plan programs and implement studies. I aim to create a resource for corporate research directors and managers, marketing directors and brand planners to help them apply best practices as they select and supervise suppliers. Clients will find many suggestions here for doing things in unexpected and creative ways as they apply qualitative approaches in their work.

Next, I expect that worldwide practitioners of qualitative research are going to see this work as both a cookbook and rule book which will help them govern relationships with clients and subcontractors. Perhaps the greatest deficiency in the discipline over the last several decades has been the need for a 'normative' work which provides sensible standards and encodes best practices derived from many years of research practice and benefits from advice shared by many different practitioners. Everyone in the field can cultivate a unique style and learn tricks, but there is still a need for a firm platform from which to soar.

Suppliers of ancillary products and services to the qualitative research industry, including field service owners/managers, transcribers, translators, videographers, etc., will also find here a resource for improving the quality of the services they deliver.

Above all, this text is meant to be an educational resource. Worldwide instructors and students of qualitative research methods at the college and university level as well as at professional seminars will benefit from its detailed guidance and numerous checklists. Unlike other guidebooks, this text situates qualitative market research firmly within its intellectual and historical context.

Finally, this book is meant to be used as an encyclopedic reference. Business libraries – corporate, association and academic – as well as personal ones will benefit from a copy on their shelves.

The structure of the book is designed to follow through a complete research engagement from the perspectives of both user/manager and practitioner. Thus, it can be used as either a continuous training manual or individual sections may be consulted to improve productivity in any specific practice area.

Qualitative market research is a field that has grown considerably in the last half century in response to the growing importance of the marketing concept (Levitt, 1983: 7) among American businesses. This concept which at its core holds that 'the purpose of a business is to create and keep a customer' has promoted a consumer focus among producers of goods and services. The marketing concept has also established itself profoundly among providers of health care services, local governments, architects and planners and others for whom the idea of the customer had been quite alien.

In other contexts, customers are also 'users' and a great deal of attention has been paid in recent years to designing all products from the standpoint of their needs and predilections (Norman, 1990). 'User needs' and 'user friendliness' have become the principal injunctions of corporate development laboratories. What better way is there to determine the match between products and their consumers than by soliciting their advice beforehand and running concepts and prototypes past them afterwards.

For late twentieth century managers, it is no longer sufficient to move products by 'pushing' them through sales techniques and incentives. On the contrary, marketers have learned to attract or 'pull' consumers to their products and services by understanding the basis of consumer opinions and preferences, and then by making efforts to meet them. This book is conceived as a guide for cultivating insights into consumers and turning these insights into effective designs and strategies.

The ideas and techniques described in this book will continue to evolve along with the inevitable changes in qualitative research practice. I invite readers – practitioners, clients, students and teachers of market research – to recommend adaptations, provide case studies, describe their own techniques and otherwise contribute to future editions. Qualitative research will only improve if we continue to share and inspire each other.

Acknowledgements

This book represents a consummation of three decades of scholarship and research practice and owes a tremendous debt not only to the published sources referenced in its pages but also to the numerous teachers, students, clients and colleagues who have been part of my ongoing dialogue over this time. Since the text has grown in successive stages representing accretions of experience and reflection, let me chart the stages of my own intellectual journey and how it became embodied in the production of this work.

I owe a debt of gratitude to Charles Winick, my teacher and advisor at the City College of New York who inspired me with examples and anecdotes derived from both his academic work and his research consulting to various advertising agencies.

My interests in qualitative research matured during my years of graduate studies in sociology at Purdue University where the incipient perspectives of phenomenology, critical theory, ethnomethodology and symbolic interactionism seemed like rebellious though refreshing antidotes to the reigning 'quantophrenia' of the time. Reece McGee, Dean Knudsen, and Walter Hirsch provided me with brilliant mentoring as well as sensitive support when I committed myself to the then rare proposition of submitting a qualitative dissertation based upon ethnographic and historical data.

After earning my doctorate, I spent several years pursuing an academic career at Kansas State University where I was privileged to teach graduate courses in qualitative research methods and community studies and became interested in applied research. The opportunity to teach a seminar on Human Factors in Architectural Design jointly offered by the sociology department and College of Architecture and cooperatively taught with Nabeel Hamdi, who remains a close friend and confidant, was an important transitional event. It inspired me to accelerate assignments as an independent consultant.

Moving to New York and formalizing the drift out of academia by setting up QualiData Research there in the early 1980s constituted another major transition. Serving as an internal research and marketing consultant to the New York City Partnership and New York Chamber of Commerce and Industry gave me a chance to hone skills and have an impact upon my home city.

In the early 1980s I also began attending regular meetings with fellow qualitative researchers at Dresner's Restaurant in Upper Manhattan. Cautious and cool at first, a core group of us became warmed by the solidarity and began imagining the creation of an association to represent our professional aspirations. The Qualitative Research Consultants Association (QRCA) grew out of these conspiratorial discussions and has continued to serve as a crucible for my intellectual development. I have been proud to serve as a regular conference presenter, board member and president of the QRCA but consider myself a net gainer rather than giver. Animated discussions at meetings and conventions have served to cultivate and clarify many of my ideas about research practice. I owe a debt of gratitude to numerous colleagues, including Judy Langer, Liz Donovan, Pat Sabena, Naomi Henderson, Bob Harris, Bill Weylock, Frank Kennedy, George Silverman, Gina Thorne, Lynn Greenberg and many others for sharing their experience and great ideas.

My association work in the late 1980s led to an invitation to become a member of the Advisory Board of the Masters of Market Research Program at the University of Georgia Terry College of Business. Since then I have been the board's voice for qualitative research in my regular guest lectures to students in the program and in semi-annual meetings with fellow board members. I have benefited from the thoughtful discussions and debates among these industry leaders representing both the clients and suppliers of research services. Regular talks with faculty members Warren French, Tom Leigh and particularly Ellen Day, who has been a strong patron of this text, have always been warm and inspiring. I admire the great work being done by the program on behalf of the market research profession.

It has been a distinct pleasure to count many MMR alumni among the clients of QualiData Research including Peter Cronin, Rob Anderson, Wendy Wilenzick, Will Hecht, Kathy Hennessey, Jeff Bowers and Chris Keenan.

In the mid 1990s, Mike Wood at the Graduate Social Research Program in the Sociology Department at Hunter College of the City University of New York invited me to teach courses on applied qualitative research and focus groups as an adjunct professor. I enjoyed the stimulation of students in the program, many of whom including Merrill Carey, Fred Neurohr and Nan Goldstein have served as associates at QualiData.

During this period, one of our clients, the Colgate-Palmolive™ Company, asked me to pull together my articles, course materials and lecture notes to create a manual on managing and conducting qualitative research for distribution to their international subsidiaries. John Hofheimer and Claudia Dusinger managed the process and offered a great deal of useful advice in producing this manual which inspired the overall structure and thrust of this textbook.

Our clients have always been a source of inspiration and challenge. Several, including Claudia Schwartz, Karen Schimpf and Bill Stack, have gone even further by being there through thick and thin.

I met two of my closest friends, Walter Dinteman and Bob Woodbury, when I was a newly minted professor and they were novices at educational publishing. We've shared many good and bad times over the years as we've gone through the vagaries of career and family transition. They have been generous with advice on developing textbooks. Bob – who has even come through as a QualiData client – was especially kind in reviewing an earlier draft of this manuscript.

A fellow qualitative practitioner rooted in academic sociology, Bob Kahle, also volunteered to review an earlier draft and provided considerate advice.

QualiData staffers Veronica Criswell and Juliana Scorza Guimaraens provided assistance and support in preparing this text. Joe Rydholm of *Quirk's Marketing Research Review*, a terrific resource for the profession, helped provide background literature. Carolyn Winter served as an effective and efficient editorial assistant in finalizing this text for publication. David Mariampolski contributed his expertise as a graphic designer in finalizing the illustrations.

My greatest debt of gratitude, however, is reserved for Sharon Wolf, my business partner at QualiData, life companion, co-parent and friend. She has been together with me for every inch of this intellectual journey and shares credit for any accomplishment.

SECTION 1

Understanding Qualitative Research

- What is qualitative research
- Philosophical foundations
- Qualitative vs. quantitative
- Organizing qualitative research
- Qualitative research applications
- Varieties of qualitative research
- Benefits of qualitative research
- Reducing bias and error
- Inappropriate uses

1.1 What is Qualitative Research

Searching for a definition

Qualitative research encompasses a family of approaches, methods and techniques for understanding and thoroughly documenting attitudes and behavior. It crosses a variety of disciplines and perspectives in the social sciences, including anthropology, semiotics, linguistics, sociology and psychology. It is applied as a research approach in a wide range of practice areas including politics, health sciences, education and marketing. Generally speaking, qualitative research seeks the meanings and motivations behind behavior as well as a thorough account of behavioral facts and implications via a researcher's encounter with people's own actions, words and ideas.

As qualitative approaches spread from the 1940s through the new millennium, they had the rather unfortunate complication of establishing themselves in contradistinction to the statistical and probabilistic methods that were also burgeoning during the same time frame. Consequently, a scent of controversy and rebellion has always attached itself both to the phrase and, indeed, to the practice of qualitative research. This controversy is a futile and unnecessary way of thinking. Qualitative research is more useful than performing studies which do not document their findings with numbers, and is a much greater tool than finding ways to establish hypotheses which are then to be 'validated' through statistical approaches. It is an orientation to knowledge and truth.

Such terms as 'naturalistic', 'humanistic', 'interpretive' and 'holistic' are perhaps better than the word 'qualitative' in expressing the scientific goals of its practitioners. Nevertheless, we are stuck with this semantic inheritance bequeathed by the disciplinary entrepreneurs of both academia and the market research industry. We are also gratuitously absorbed in a fight with 'positivism' – another perspective drawn from the social sciences of the nineteenth century which has championed the scientific approaches of the physical and natural sciences (Deshpande, 1983; Ozanne, 1989).

Enumeration is not antagonistic to the goals of qualitative research, provided that the numbers conform to the canons of probability in establishing the factuality of the researcher's assertions. Furthermore, calling something 'qualitative' is a poor synonym when the real intent is to say 'hypothetical', 'speculative' or 'unproven'. Sloppy language is often a source of disappointed expectations – not to mention the basis for false claims of social fact.

As a form of practice, qualitative methods are applied both for data collection and data analysis. To understand this properly, the word 'data' must be understood as encompassing any form of utterance or observation and not just responses to a survey questionnaire.

Data collection

Qualitative approaches rely upon personal expressions and behavioral observations either in laboratories or in the natural environment, and have a strong preference for unstructured or semi-structured questions – with a notable improvisational and interactive bent. These types of questions provide respondents reasonably unlimited opportunities to describe their feelings and behavioral peculiarities. Additionally, qualitative researchers favor examination of artifacts and traces in the physical environment as well as responses to creative challenges or imaginative types of questions, especially those which yield fanciful descriptive language and images. Current practice, for example, may challenge respondents to draw collages or imagine that a well-known brand has 'died' in order to evoke emotionally charged feelings and attitudes.

Data analysis

Qualitative researchers favor analytic approaches which are holistic, speculative and descriptive. These may include case studies exploring the range and depth of attitudes and behaviors toward a product category, analysis of various consumer types, descriptions of the decision making process involved in a major purchase, etc. Consequently, qualitative analysis may rely upon interpretation of behavioral details or respondent utterances through the lens of a theoretical perspective such as Freudian psychology or semiotics. Otherwise, it may involve creative leaps by the analyst in delivering insights into the mentality, motivations and aspirations of targeted respondents.

The importance of qualitative methods

Qualitative methods provide a necessary and complementary perspective on human behavior. When used properly, qualitative inquiry can address numerous strategic information needs, such as creative ideation for new product development, conception and evaluation of marketing or communications tactics and insights into the culturally-based preferences of various racial and linguistic minorities. In global studies, qualitative analysis provides a microscope for assessing variations in product usage based on differences in local traditions and tastes. Along with other approaches, qualitative research studies can help its users by offering both insights and explanations. A partial list of issues that can be addressed in a qualitative study would include:

- How and why do people make choices as consumers or citizens.
- How and why do consumers actually use the things that they buy.
- What are areas of either satisfaction or unhappiness with various products and services.
- What are the core mental images attached to perceptions of various brands or product categories.
- How does someone best communicate with and influence people in the market for ideas and products.
- How are marketplace preferences likely to evolve.

- What factors involved in product perception or usage are likely to enhance users' comfort, satisfaction and willingness to repurchase.

In addressing these issues, qualitative research gropes for unexpected findings and imaginative leaps. Like explorers entering uncharted territory for the first time, researchers are always challenged to make new discoveries or, at least, to envision things in new ways while overthrowing the banal, overworked complacency of received wisdom. Qualitative techniques provide competitive tools for advancing the state of knowledge and pushing insights. In fact, the value of qualitative approaches is attested to by the fact that corporate marketing research directors report that qualitative research represents 17 per cent of their total spending on external research services (Baldinger et al., 1992: 82).

Qualitative research is neither a panacea nor a magic bullet. It is not meant to replace or compete against other research approaches. Admittedly, qualitative analysis is grossly inappropriate for a variety of applications and issues best studied through other means. Estimates of market size, projections of market acceptance and optimal pricing for a product are examples of important questions which require probabilistic methods.

Qualitative methods have evolved as rigorous and systematic tools which provide users with the foundation for educated and informed decision making.

1.2 Philosophical Foundations

Qualitative research practice is both a science and an art. It combines disciplined and structured investigation against objectives with intuition and creative exploratory tools. As a profession, it encompasses a tradition that began as long ago as the 1950s.

The historical tradition

Like such innovations as radar and freeze dried foods, the birth of applied qualitative research goes back to the period of World War II when academic innovators descended from the ivory towers to support the war effort. Robert Merton (1979, 1987) and Paul Lazarsfeld's creation of the 'focussed group' was part of a push to optimize communication and the resulting mobilization of the home front. Eventually, marketers figured out that the techniques that had influenced people to buy more war bonds could also work in the burgeoning American and European civilian economies of the 1950s to entice them toward new convenience foods, automobiles and cosmetics. The new mass communications media of that period – television and general interest magazines – made it easy for advertisers to reach a wide range and substantial numbers of eager consumers with breakthrough messages. Advertising agencies of the period began to vie for the consumer's mind.

Freudian psychology went through a rebirth in the 1950s as people looked inward to gain a sense of meaning in the wake of the disastrous depression and war years and also sought guidance in rearing their abundant offspring. Ernest Dichter (1964, 1992) and Herta Herzog, who had both studied with Lazarsfeld in Vienna, hopped aboard this neo-Freudian bandwagon and challenged mass marketers with innovative research methods and shockingly fresh ways of addressing products and advertising (Bartos, 1992). Don't think of a car as a transportation machine, the 'motivational research' paradigm argued, but as an environment for living and loving.

As the complacent and secure 1950s yielded to the rebellious and confrontational 1960s and 1970s, marketers were again challenged to meet their audiences in new ways. Business was confronted and no longer regarded as the hero of the recovery. Corporations started needing to prove their social sensitivity.

Mass markets themselves fragmented into niche markets – a collection of interest groups, affiliation networks, and emerging ethnic and racial subcultures. Correspondingly, mass communication exploded as cable television and special interest publications multiplied. Young people, women and gays struggled to be heard and to advance their unique aspirations. The resumption of mass immigration, movement of peoples from Southern to Northern Hemispheres, and the awakening of ethnic consciousness began to change the look and attitude of average Americans and Europeans – challenging, in fact, the very possibility of a typical national citizen.

The explosion of 'T-groups', 'encounter groups' and 'consciousness raising' of this period led to a renewed sophistication in focus groups being conducted by an ever expanding cadre of practitioners. The ideas of Carl Rogers (1951, 1961), who advocated 'client-centered therapy' and 'unconditional positive regard', were emblematic of research innovations of this period which emphasized participatory democracy and consumer advocacy.

The booming economies of the 1980s and 1990s presented their own opportunities and challenges. The maturing of the postwar 'baby boom' generation and the decline of communist ideologies stimulated an international wave of acquisitiveness that has shown few signs of diminishing.

Demanding schedules for work, child rearing and leisure have shrunk the reach of mass media even further, correspondingly creating new opportunities for direct merchandisers who have been taking advantage of the boom in telecommunications, including rapid worldwide and cross-national delivery and computerization. Further development and proliferation of inexpensive personal computers, easy-to-use software and the Internet have added dynamism and additional marketing opportunities.

In reaction, conventional retailers have also had to go on the offensive by creating alternative models – including discount superstores, 'category killers', specialty boutiques and experiential retailing environments, like the popular Nike Towns where video, music and fantasy became tightly connected to merchandising.

The economic boom has been global in scale as traditional manufacturing centers in the Western Hemisphere and Northern Europe have shifted to the Pacific Rim and a new era of marketplace inter-connections have grown. The globalization of brands has been matched by the enlarged sophistication of worldwide consumers, particularly in emerging economies such as China and India, seeking enhancements in their families' health and well-being, opportunities for personal expression and improvements in the comforts and conveniences of daily life.

The 1980s and 1990s also witnessed the expansion of the marketing 'ideal' into almost unimaginable territories. Users of health and other professional services, participants in educational institutions, devotees of the arts and culture and even voters have increasingly come to view themselves or have become regarded by their administrators and leaders as 'consumers'. A new wave of public activation and demands for quality have yielded a public increasingly conscious of deficiencies and opportunities outside the realm of typical business affairs.

The trends of the last quarter of the twentieth century have flowered as the twenty-first century is born and struggles to release its own character. The fragmentation of markets has reached its apotheosis in ideas about 'marketing to the individual', utilizing the Internet as a sales and communications channel. Other burgeoning perspectives – such as 'guerilla marketing' and 'word-of-mouth marketing' defy traditional views of the relationship between marketing and media.[1]

The professional challenge

Qualitative research practice has responded to these challenges by becoming institutionalized and enlarging its professionalism. The founding of the Qualitative Research Consultants Association (QRCA) in the USA and the United Kingdom's Association of Qualitative Research Practitioners (now known as the Association for Qualitative Research, or AQR) in the early 1980s represented an important move from the 'heroic' era of inconsistent and sometimes wildly idiosyncratic entrepreneurs to a profession linked by standards and routine ways of conducting business.

Practitioners today are known as 'qualitative research consultants' or, sometimes more commonly, as 'moderators' who are skilled at searching for deeper truths and who have the interpersonal skills necessary to establish confidence and intimacy with respondents quickly. Accustomed to regular controversies about the meaning and utility of qualitative research, these moderators have been nevertheless profoundly responsible for the expansion of marketplace choices and the booming worldwide economies of the next millennium.

The qualitative research consultant's role stands for something greater than a mere moderator who is responsible for leading group discussions. The consultant acts as an interpreter and guide. She combines marketing instincts with an educated understanding of human behavior and motivation. Professional qualitative researchers go beyond the data to deliver insights that can inspire new product and marketing approaches that match consumer ideals.

There has been an ongoing contention between American and European 'styles' of qualitative research. The latter is characterized as notably more theoretical in its explanatory approach and more firmly rooted in the sociological and psychological principles. American research practice, in contrast, has grown up with a pragmatic stance that tends to be more receptive to management ideals taught in business schools. The Americans have championed focus groups as a core technique while the Europeans have been somewhat more catholic in their adaptation of methodological perspectives, moving toward both the psychoanalytic depth interview as well as ideas such as semiotics and ethnography drawn from anthropology.

Core goals and ideals

The field's intellectual tradition has bequeathed several goals and ideals for the qualitative orientation that underlie the daily efforts of both clients and practitioners. These include:

- *Gaining an in-depth understanding of the consumer.* Behavioral details, such as the flavor or color purchased, generally are regarded as less significant to qualitative inquiry than 'really getting under the respondent's skin'. This means gaining deep insight into the motivations, aspirations and sensations associated with a brand, category, image or phrase used in describing the product.
- *Seeing things from the consumer's point of view.* Qualitative research depends upon a dialectical balance of objective and subjective ways of confronting reality. Although good science requires some degree of distance

and detachment from the topic being studied, qualitative practice also demands a sense of identification and partisanship with the consumer's values and needs. This psychic unity helps to focus marketers' attention on their real and not imagined customers.

- *Being open to different points of view and keeping an open mind.* Qualitative research demands continuous challenge to the existing state of knowledge. This includes a reflexive examination of the researcher's own biases and predilections in confronting a product category or class of users.

- *Exploring context, conditions and change.* People are infinitely mutable and competent researchers are always challenged to explore how flexible and changeable consumer choices can be. No set of needs and values are permanent and all are subject to situational adjustment. For example, when a consumer enters a retail store or commercial web site, he or she becomes a 'shopper' subject to contextual influences. One may arrive with a need for a particular item but be swayed by a discount offer, better descriptive language, an influential sales encounter or user interface, simplicity of terms, delivery scheduling or any number of other factors.

- *Searching for the feelings and emotions behind people's behavior.* The humanistic view is a considerable advance over mechanistic and behaviorist models of behavior which view consumers as responding to a strict set of causal processes. Qualitative researchers understand that people mediate social influences through the processes of interpretation, evaluation and emotional involvement with things.

  Consumers react to product offers and marketing communications only through the lens of feelings and affect toward a word, an idea, a slogan, a picture or a design. They base their behavior not just on where they are located currently but where they see themselves moving in the future. Emotions involved in people's opinions and buying behavior may include both positive and negative feelings such as shame, anger, envy, lust, altruism and love.

- *Describing attitudes and behavior with as much relevant detail as possible.* Description is the primary currency of qualitative research and most practitioners would agree that relevant detail not only produces clarity but also yields thorough insights into consumers. Qualitative researchers develop hypotheses about behavior and use compelling evidence to demonstrate their case.

- *Understanding process in consumer behavior and motivations.* Consumer choices in the marketplace are a consequence of a lifetime of experiences and knowledge. The process of developing preferences begins with childhood socialization into specific values and beliefs, and proceeds through adulthood as people try to create and re-create their identities by linking their egos to their real and imagined consumer practices.

- *Not assuming you know everything.* Qualitative researchers are always challenged to exceed the status quo. To do this, they often have to maintain a stance of strategic naiveté and bracket their own assumptions and expectations while exploring the consumer's world. For some, this also requires a confrontational approach toward the current state of knowledge.

Absorbing an intellectual heritage

Qualitative research practice is based upon a broad and rich intellectual heritage going back to the middle of the nineteenth century. This section reviews some of the seminal ideas and thinkers associated with the birth and flowering of the approach. They represent concepts about human behavior (Freud, Rogers, Hall), social reality (Simmel, Husserl, Symbolic Interactionists), and scientific methods (Weber, Park) that lie beneath the qualitative research enterprise.

Consciously or unconsciously, many of these ideas are put into practice by researchers around the world every day. It is not our purpose here to offer a definitive review of these masters' careers and works. Rather, these thinkers' principal concepts are briefly reviewed to demonstrate how the field is built upon the shoulders of giants whose innovative ideas about human actions have established a framework for thinking about and understanding behavior in the marketplace.

Max Weber

Max Weber (1864-1920) was a German economist and social historian, known primarily for incorporating cultural elements into social science in opposition to Karl Marx's 'economic determinism'. His most famous works focused on the socio-cultural impact of world religions – for example, *The Protestant Ethic and the Spirit of Capitalism* (1904-1905; trans. 1930), as well as *The Religions of the East* series. He was also known for his provocative methodological ideas which emphasized *verstehen* – a profound understanding of the underlying dynamics and motivations behind social facts (Weber, 1949). This idea is viewed by many as the fundamental principle at the root of qualitative research.

While others conceived of societies and human action as abstract structures oriented toward productive relations, Weber's primary focus, in contrast, was on the subjective meanings that human actors attach to their actions within specific social-historical contexts.

Weber was also highly influential for qualitative analysis through his use of 'ideal types' as a manner of understanding social reality. Ideal types are concepts used to describe social and historical reality. Weber's teachings about categorizing are still useful in how we segment different types of consumers. Ideal types may represent particular historical roles such as 'the charismatic leader', or ideas such as the 'Protestant Ethic'. As abstract constructs based in concrete current or historical experience, they may be used to help understand the different ways that people behave and believe. They are useful in comparing different historical periods, describing the ways in which various beliefs or social structures have evolved and creating hypotheses about the causes and consequences of various beliefs and actions.

This organizing principle is evident in Weber's observations of the four major types of social action.

- *Purposeful or goal-oriented rational action* in which such ideas as efficiency and achievement dominate behavior.
- *Value-oriented behavior* which is oriented toward higher goals such as seeking salvation or ecological consciousness.

- *Emotional or affective motivations* which are oriented toward one's feelings and urges.
- *Traditional action* which is patterned after an approved set of symbols and action handed down as a result of religious or cultural membership.

This classification serves when making systematic typological distinctions between different types of authority, and also provides a basis for Weber's analysis of Western historical development. He believed the West had come to be dominated increasingly by goal-oriented rationality, whereas in earlier periods it tended to be motivated by tradition, affect or value-oriented rationality. He believed that such social constructions as the 'state', and 'associations' could not be understood as abstract creations outside of the actions of individuals in society. In other words, if people believe and act as though something is a fact, then it is a fact.

Georg Simmel

Georg Simmel (1858-1918), a German philosopher-sociologist, was very influential in advancing the qualitative world view and analytic structure. Like Weber, he viewed society as a web of patterned interactions, grounded in diverse historical periods and cultural settings (Simmel, 1960). However, he preferred to focus his work on the details of everyday life or what he called 'interactions among the atoms of society'.

Simmel's main contribution is his way of abstracting forms from the diverse patterns of human 'sociation'. In other words, he looked for common patterns of interaction in widely different forms of behavior. For example, he held that both war and profit-making involve both conflict and cooperation.

In 'formal analysis', as his analytic method was called, the essential features of concrete phenomena are abstracted into ideas and concepts, thereby making things observable and understandable. The forms found in social reality, however, are never pure – each contains numerous formal elements.

His analytic ideas were particularly effective in his explication of 'social types'. Probably the best appreciated of the types he described is the 'stranger' – the person who is *in* a group but not *of* it and who can, consequently, attain an objectivity about that group's reality that other members cannot reach. This perspective allows the stranger, also called the 'marginal man' by other theorists, to operate with a high capacity for self-serving manipulation and cynicism in attaining power. History provides numerous examples of 'strangers' that eventually dominated countries that were not their own. For example, Napoleon was a Corsican by birth and Hitler was Austrian.

Simmel also recognized the interaction between societies' categories and the ways people internalize their own status. His views of the poor as a social type, for example, demonstrates how poverty as a special status emerges when society assigns specific persons requiring assistance to that category. The fact that others try to correct this condition while those that accept help must acquire a negative self-image, reinforces the reality of poverty. The way out, for Simmel, is to acknowledge the individual's dual relation with society – that he exists for society as well as for himself. The individual is determined but at the same time is determining; he is acted upon but at the same time is self-actuating.

To Simmel, sociation always involves harmony and conflict, attraction and repulsion, love and hatred. He saw human relations as characterized by ambivalence. For example, those who are connected in intimate relations are likely to harbor both positive and negative sentiments. According to Simmel (1960), erotic relations equally, 'strike us as woven together of love and respect, or disrespect...of love and an urge to dominate or the need for dependence...What the observer or the participant himself thus divides into two intermingling trends may in reality be only one'.

Simmel teaches us to think beyond the easy answers and to look for the contradictions and complexities that underlie human behavior. His methodological principles were highly influential in the later work of Robert E. Park and Robert K. Merton.

Husserl, Schutz and phenomenology

Challenging and superceding Weber and Simmel, the philosophy of Edmund Husserl (1859-1938) known as phenomenology and the elaboration of these principles for the social sciences by Alfred Schutz (1899-1959) go even further in emphasizing the importance of subjectivity as a necessary methodological approach (Schutz, 1970).

The phenomenologists argue that the world can only become known through experience and ideational intuition. The essential tool for understanding the world is perception mediated through everyday experience. People then come together into meaningful groups through a process of 'intersubjectivity', according to Husserl, which is a coalition of common perceptions of the world.

Behavior in the 'life world', or our everyday reality, is grounded in a set of taken-for-granted rules – a set of assumptions that have hardly penetrated consciousness. According to phenomenology, the purpose of the human sciences – which presumably includes marketing research – is to pry beneath the surface to expose these categories and habits of mind that shape our perceptions. And, by being able to understand the foundation of our beliefs, act to change them.

Franz Boas, Bronislaw Malinowski, Margaret Mead and Edward Sapir

The work of classical anthropologists such as Franz Boas (1858-1942), Bronislaw Malinowski, (1884-1942), Margaret Mead (1901-1978) and Edward Sapir (1884-1939) remains important to contemporary qualitative research for its conceptual and methodological innovations.

Malinowski, born in Poland, spent his career teaching at the London School of Economics and at Yale. Through pioneering studies of social and economic relations among indigenous groups in the Western Pacific, he became the inventor of 'participant observation' or 'ethnography' as a method of fieldwork. Through observation and intensive analysis of field data, Malinowski was able to make sense of elaborate cultural rituals. For example, in his analysis of social exchange rituals, he demonstrated how trading shells promoted patterns of authority, hierarchy, family relationships and social solidarity among the clans that inhabited the Trobriand Islands.

Boas and his students at Columbia, such as Margaret Mead and Edward Sapir, also advanced fieldwork methods and established new and more complex concepts of 'culture' and of 'race'. Unlike their nineteenth century predecessors, Boas and Mead stressed that these two concepts were distinct and that cultural attributes acquired through social learning could not be attributed to race – a biological quality. They advanced these ideas during an era in which race, rather than cultural learning, was often held to be the primary determinant of human character. Their opposition to these ideas was futile as the Nazi movement grew in Europe, basing itself on racialist ideas, and eventually ground to its genocidal denouement.

Edward Sapir is best known for his work on the languages of native North Americans. His insights about how the grammar and vocabulary of a language structures the way its speakers perceive the world have come to be known as the 'Sapir-Whorf hypothesis' (Whorf, 1956). This innovative insight recognizes that language forms the basis of perception – that we do not really 'see' something until we know what it is called.

Ideas drawn from classical anthropology continue to influence the methods applied in contemporary qualitative research and provide the foundation of its approach to cultural norms and change.

Freud, Jung and classical psychoanalysis

The innovations of Sigmund Freud (1865-1939) and classical psychoanalysis have had a profound impact on the ways that people in the twentieth century came to see themselves. However, the relevance of these innovations for qualitative research lies mainly in their explication of the differences between conscious and unconscious thought and in their elaboration of the emotional sources of human motivation.

Freud recognized that there is a gap between our controlled conscious lives and the unconscious foundation which swirls beneath everyday behavior. This gap can only be glimpsed through the analysis of dreams, mistakes and slips of the tongue. Projective techniques, which try to circumvent rational thinking, were adopted by the Freudians as another means of channeling into the unconscious mind.

C. G. Jung (1875-1961) quarreled with the Freudians but also looked for understanding in the structure of mind (Jung, 1981). He bequeathed the idea that all humanity shares common structures of emotion represented by a set of archetypes, which transcend history and culture. These archetypes, such as the trickster, are encapsulated in our attraction to various celebrities, products or marketing communications (Cooper and Patterson, 1999).

Freud's thinking and that of his followers' also traced human development through a series of stages, in which people learn to acquire gratification and resolve frustration in different ways. The evolution of individual character is rooted in the bumps and grinds through the course of growing up across these stages, and leaves shadows on the workings of the mind. These drives that underlie character in different times and places ultimately have strong impacts on consumer preferences as well as all other social choices. Marketers often try to appeal to these drives through communications strategies. It can be argued, for example, that the tendency to collect Barbie™ dolls, Beanie Babies™ or corporate stocks is rooted in a propensity for hoarding based in the anal stage of development.

Symbolic interactionism

Herbert Blumer (1900-1987), originator of the term 'symbolic interactionism', was a devotee of the philosopher George Herbert Mead (1863-1931). The main impact of Blumer and his followers' school of thought focuses on the importance of meaning to individual behavior, the need for direct empirical observation as a methodology, and, following W. I. Thomas, the centrality of the 'definition of the situation' as the basis of social reality.

Mead's ideas about 'social behaviorism' saw the self growing out of social interaction in which the individual takes on the role of the 'other' and internalizes real or imagined attitudes. This concept makes us essentially a product of our social surroundings but in a very limited way. While human nature to Mead is connected to biology and evolution, language and symbolic communication allow human action to free itself from natural determinism.

Central to symbolic interactionism are three primary premises. First, that people act towards things on the basis of the meanings those things have for them, second that such meanings arise out of the interaction between an individual and others, and third, that an interpretive process is used by everyone throughout their lives as social beings. Thus, people are continuously selecting, formulating, checking, challenging and revising meanings in relation to everyday situations.

A theoretical implication of these beliefs is that behavior is less a result of unchangeable forces that predicate specific individual patterns than an ever-evolving string of sometimes rational and often irrational actions that we ourselves are challenged to understand fully.

For methodology, this means that the determination of problems, concepts, research techniques and theoretical schemes should begin with direct examination of the actual empirical social world rather than by slavishly following some grand theory about social behavior.

What qualitative research has learned from symbolic interactionism is the recognition that behavior in the marketplace sometimes arises less from social upbringing than from what commodities symbolize in terms of personal meanings. Thus, the hopes and aspirations that people imagine for themselves can incline them toward various category and brand choices. Symbolic interactionism has also placed direct interaction with consumers at the center of research practice.

Robert Park and the Chicago School

Robert Ezra Park (1864-1944) spent much of his life as a journalist and came to academia relatively late in his career. A student of John Dewey, Park worked for daily newspapers in Minnesota, Detroit, Denver, New York, and Chicago when America's urban areas were undergoing profound transformations as a consequence of the industrial revolution's maturation and the massive immigration wave occurring at that time. In the manner of fellow critics and reformers like Lincoln Steffens, Jane Addams and Jacob Riis, Park's reporting described the squalid conditions of the city's immigrant areas and the criminal world that was ensconced there. As a result, he came to view the city as a natural laboratory for the study of the new urban man whom industrial society had created.

Influenced by the classical anthropologists like Boas and Malinowski, Park advocated studying contemporary urban life and culture with the same painstaking meticulousness and attention to detail that was used when describing 'primitive' tribes.

Park's main impact was felt through his teaching and by his becoming the leader of what has become known collectively as the 'Chicago School'. His impressive roster of students included Everett C. Hughes, Herbert Blumer, Louis Wirth, E. Franklin Frazier, John Dollard, Robert Redfield, Harvey Zorbaugh and many other students who became leading social scientists. Many of these successors in time made their own theoretical and methodological contributions and produced novel insights through qualitative research. For example, Louis Wirth's study of Chicago's Jewish community, *The Ghetto*, (1956) demonstrated how traditional forms of organization and affiliation were undergoing change in response to the challenges and opportunities afforded by the urban environment. Harvey Warren Zorbaugh's classic study of the contrasts between rich and poor in Chicago's Near North Side, *The Gold Coast and the Slum*, (1976) made the then surprising observation that gang leaders in the slums were hardly mental defectives; instead, they were extremely intelligent youths who had become lawbreakers because no one had discovered or channeled their talent in other ways.

Erving Goffman

Although Goffman's (1922-1982) work is rooted in symbolic interactionism and the Chicago School, his main contribution to qualitative research is radical skepticism about human behavior (Goffman, 1959). His approach to social life revolves around the metaphor of the *theater* with its actors and audience, backstage, characters, roles and performances. The conduct of social life to him involves 'impression management', or making yourself believable to others through speech and gestures despite inner feelings of doubt, insincerity or cynicism. Playing your roles involves intense 'dramaturgical discipline' in making sure your face, voice and mannerisms do not represent discrepant emotions which may disrupt what he views as the thin veneer of conventional social life.

Despite his pessimism, Goffman's legacy is an appreciation of how we appear to others as we go about being managers, businesspeople and researchers. He has taught us to apply a studied skepticism when respondents claim to be or want something. Do they really have an interest or are they just enacting a role, trying to make us believe they are 'progressive', attempting to justify their cash incentive? Goffman's approach does not offer easy answers but he certainly directs us to the right questions.

Carl Rogers

Carl Rogers (1902-1987) founded client-centered psychotherapy and was a pioneer in developing ways to study therapeutic outcomes and processes. His impact upon qualitative research arose from both his humanistic perspective on behavior as well as his approaches to interviewing and interacting with patients.

Rogers promotes complete respect for the autonomy and integrity of the individual. His approach to interviewing, therapy and group dynamics integrates concepts and methods that aim to reveal people while appreciating their sometimes quirky and unique qualities. Like the phenomenologists, Rogers believes that direct experience is the fundamental basis of analysis. In *On Becoming a Person*, for example, Rogers teaches:

> Experience is, for me, the highest authority. The touchstone of validity is my own experience. No other person's ideas, and none of my own ideas, are as authoritative as my experience. It is to experience that I must return again and again, to discover a closer approximation to truth as it is in the process of becoming in me. Neither the Bible nor the prophets – neither Freud nor research – neither the revelations of God nor man – can take precedence over my own direct experience. My experience is not authoritative because it is infallible. It is the basis of authority because it can always be checked in new primary ways. In this way its frequent error or fallibility is always open to correction. (1961: 23-24)

Carl Rogers is associated with concepts such as 'empathy', 'reflection', 'unconditional positive regard', and 'self-actualization'. These are simple and optimistic ideas that are effective in exploring the basis of consumer behavior in the marketplace. He insisted that people take responsibility for themselves and believed that the experience of being understood and valued gives us freedom to grow. In contrast, pathology grows from attempting to earn others' positive regard rather than following one's own inner guidance.

Edward T. Hall

Through his popular works which include *The Silent Language* and *The Hidden Dimension*, Edward T. Hall (b. 1914) has elaborated on the concept of culture and provided insights into how this feature of the human experience is expressed in thought and behavior (1959, 1966). Challenging deterministic and doctrinaire approaches to culture, his work has offered a special focus on its irrational and non-apparent aspects and on how people can escape the grip of culturally-produced limitations. Culture hides more than it reveals, Hall recognizes, and this poses a particular challenge to qualitative researchers drawn to understanding, interpreting and predicting human behavior.

Hall's work provides important insights into the cultural basis of non-verbal behavior. His work draws attention to how culture establishes the parameters for how we experience the passage of time and the perception of territory and space. He even focuses our attention on the hidden meanings inherent in verbal communication, for example, how tonality and voice nuance can reveal more about our feelings than words.

Researchers conducting focus groups and research visits to respondents' homes and workplaces are continuously challenged to apply Hall's insights. As participants enter a conference room to hold a group session, for example, their placement at the table may immediately reveal their feelings about authority. In sitting opposite the moderator, they may be positioning themselves as a competitor during the discussion. At the moderator's right side, they may be betraying a desire to be a supportive ally.

The placement of objects and the arrangement of features in the home says a great deal about cultural values. The central position given to home electronics, such as televisions and computers, in worldwide households indicates the degree to which contemporary technology is wound up in feelings about status and propriety. In watching housewives enact routine daily chores, additionally, we can learn a great deal about their affect for a possession on the basis of how much time and attention they lavish upon its cleaning. Mementos and collectibles receive special care often and consumers commonly change the products they use to clean surfaces that they treasure.

1.3 Qualitative vs. Quantitative

Since qualitative research is commonly contrasted to quantitative research approaches, it would be useful to provide some definitive guidance here regarding the proper questions to address with each. Quantitative research in the parlance of marketing studies encompasses studies which emphasize precise numerical measurement of consumer behaviors – the 'how many' or 'how much'. In practical terms, quantitative research is generally implemented through some type of questionnaire survey – by telephone, by personal intercept in shopping malls or downtown streets, by post or over the Internet. Alternatively, a broad range of auditing strategies are also applied, for example, to measure the size of television audiences or to measure movement of products from manufacturers through sales channels and to ultimate consumers. Statistical sources collected include manufacturing data, measurement of warehouse shipping traffic and data from store checkout scanners.

Surveys lend themselves well to so-called 'panel' or 'syndicated' studies in which the same or similar consumer samples are subjected to identical batteries of questions over time yielding precise information on trends or patterns in the marketplace. 'Desk research' or secondary analysis of data collected for other purposes can also be interpreted and integrated with a company's own marketing information to produce instructive findings. Comparisons of the information produced by sources such as periodic governmental census of population, surveys of business and economic patterns and health and mortality data can be compared to the company's own sales statistics to demonstrate how well the company's targeted sales strategies are working.

Quantitative researchers generally distinguish between 'descriptive' statistics as listed above and 'analytic' statistics. The latter uses probabilistic methods in order to test hypotheses, analyze the strength of relationships, determine trends over time and make predictions for future marketplace behavior.

Using qualitative or quantitative approaches

Whether a qualitative as opposed to a quantitative research strategy is implemented generally depends on the kinds of questions addressed, the nature of the population being studied and the overall objective of the research. Most commonly, these two strategies are applied either as separate studies or as alternative approaches to the same subject matter within a research program. The most effective global marketers, including major producers of everyday household products, banks and media companies apply a dialectical approach or what is known as 'triangulation' by regularly using a multiplicity of methodological tools to constantly advance market knowledge and consumer insights. For example, a research unit at a major packaged goods company is likely to conduct several focus group studies each year and maybe a set of at-home observations of consumer practices along with a large 'attitude and usage' (A&U) survey and regular analysis of supermarket sales data for each of the brands that they monitor.

Within corporate research programs, qualitative research is used appropriately for both 'exploratory' and 'explanatory' types of research objectives. Several examples of each are reviewed here.

Exploratory

Qualitative approaches are called for when the information needs of the research include the following investigative objectives:

- *Discovery* when very little is known about a product, category or respondent group or when the researcher wishes to expand the current state of knowledge.
- *Consumer familiarization* to gain background information or details about purchase, usage, factors involved in satisfaction with products, actual consumer language and decision making criteria and anything else about specific usage behavior which helps to better understand consumers.
- *Hypothesis generation* to make educated guesses about the preferences and attitudes of buyers and users.
- *Positioning studies* to learn about how to describe or talk about a product in ways that distinguish it from its competitors and make it unique and meaningful to buyers.
- *Research program initiation* as a first step in research – to learn the right questions to ask and the most meaningful ways to pose questions in a larger survey.
- *Idea generation* to come up with creative new ideas for products, line extensions, advertising copy, etc.
- *Future plans/scenario generation* to learn more about consumer intentions, imminent goals, likely evolutions. For example, when a new technology, such as flat screen television, permits unheralded opportunities for placement of units within the home, qualitative studies help to diagnose likely patterns of consumer demand.
- *Process description* which analyzes the steps in a behavior – for example, how home makers clean their wood floors or how shoppers make decisions about buying a toothpaste.

Explanatory

Qualitative approaches also are called for when the information is expected to provide profound and provocative insights into market-related needs, behaviors and feelings, including:

- *Motivational analysis* Sometimes there is a need to stimulate an understanding of the grounds, meanings, reasons and conditions associated with an attitude or behavior. This analysis may include motivations consciously avowed as well as those likely to be subconsciously held.

- *Cultural analysis* Researchers want to understand group differentiation based on the impact of culture in product choice and usage. For example, patterns of personal hygiene vary across countries and continents – and even between cultural and regional subgroups in a single country – and these differences will have an impact on the personal care products that consumers demand.
- *Consumer differentiation and segmentation* For whatever reasons, consumers are subject to almost infinite patterns of variation in the marketplace. Some may be seeking the highest possible quality while others may be seeking the lowest price. Some users may be highly influenced by brand image while others choose to emphasize a product's sensory attributes such as flavor, color, smell. Depending on the product category, many users may be driven by convenience factors, such as easy-to-open packaging or portion control, while others may be influenced by health-associated factors such as total calories or the number of fat grams. For every product category, qualitative research is important to understanding the range and extent of consumer segmentation.
- *Interpretation* Qualitative tools often constitute an important final step in research programs. Large-scale surveys and audits often fail to clarify underlying reasons for a set of findings, while a qualitative study can yield further insights. Techniques sometimes used for achieving this objective can include re-interviewing some participants in the larger survey or by finding similar respondents. Interpretation through a theoretical perspective, such as Jungian archetypes or the concept of culture commonly adds an additional layer of understanding.
- *Additional probing* When earlier studies are confusing and inconclusive, commissioning a qualitative research study can provide depth and insight into the feelings and emotional meanings attached to brand or product usage statistics.
- *Comprehension analysis* This refers to written materials. Qualitative techniques are used as a screening tool in businesses to make certain that consumers understand directions, promotional copy or product claims.
- *'Disaster checks'* These make certain that copy and images are not offensive. (NOTE: These checks provide minimal assurance and should not be regarded as definitive.)

Quantitative

Quantitative research is called for when the objectives demand strict enumeration of the phenomena or when probabilistic projections are demanded. Using qualitative strategies in these circumstances would be inappropriate and the results would be highly suspect. Situations that require quantitative research include the following:

- *Quantification* is used when the researcher desires to learn about the overall size and segmentation of markets. While a qualitative first step is useful in determining the degree and character of consumer differentiation, further survey analysis is required for precision about the extent and degree of differences.

- *Audit or bookkeeping functions* are used to gain a precise breakdown of how many people hold a certain attitude or choose specific products.
- *Accurate projection of findings* might be required to demonstrate that the findings are representative of a defined target group.
- *Replication* is used to obtain consistent data about defined targeted groups. This includes monitoring comparable statistics at different points in time.
- *Analytic tools* use probabilistic statistical methodology as a discipline for discovering market segments (cluster analysis) or consumer choice processes (conjoint analysis).
- *Pricing and sales dynamics* estimate sales volume and optimize pricing for various packaging options.

1.4 Organizing Qualitative Research

The worldwide practice of qualitative marketing research has evolved its own complex social organization of work and productivity. These roles, structures and businesses translate information requirements into a set of practical activities designed to address those needs.

Qualitative research is considered a branch of market research, an industry responsible for gathering and delivering information about the consuming public to the manufacturers and marketers of goods and services.

Several indicators convincingly demonstrate the significance of marketing research to the global economy: According to the ESOMAR (European Society for Opinion and Marketing Research) *Annual Study on the Market Research Industry 1996*, over $11 billion (US) is spent on conducting market research world wide each year. Of this total just under half (46 per cent) is spent in Europe; just over a third (36 per cent) is spent in the United States; 10 per cent is spent in Japan and the remainder divided throughout the rest of the world.

This report further notes that in Europe approximately 10 per cent of the total expenditure is allocated to qualitative research of all types. Furthermore, the employment statistics associated with this research indicate that there are 35,500 full time employees of European full-service market research institutes and an additional 4,250 research consultants. The report speculates that a large proportion of qualitative research activities are organized by the consultant group.

In the United States, the *1997 Business Report on the Market Research Industry* prepared by Jack Honomichl indicates that the European research is likely to be underestimating the American market. Based on an analysis of the top 50 US research organizations plus 119 member companies of the Council of American Survey Research Organizations (CASRO), Honomichl reports that over $5.5 billion was spent on market research in the United States during 1996. This figure, too, fails to represent the full qualitative research market because it does not include the substantial number of small companies and independent consultants involved in qualitative research. Some estimates indicate that a full 22 per cent of market research expenditures or up to $836 million were spent on qualitative research in 1997 (Sabena, 1999a: 1).

The American Marketing Association (AMA), which numbers 38,518 members involved in various aspects of marketing, lists one-quarter (9,811) of its members as primarily or secondarily involved in marketing research. The AMA's Academic Council, additionally lists about 300 members in its special interest group representing professors of market research. This is only a fraction of the total number of instructors in the field and largely represents the elite and not necessarily the bulk of the discipline.

Subdivisions of the field

The vernacular of the field sometimes divides the universe of market researchers into employment-based subgroups, namely, consultants, suppliers, agencies and clients.

There is sometimes a good deal of career mobility between these components of the market research discipline, with professionals moving from agencies to suppliers to client companies and then back. Sometimes, market research managers gain sufficient background and skills within their companies to be eligible for promotion into critical marketing or management positions. (They sometimes even rise to the position of company president.) At a number of firms, a stint in market research is considered good preparation for upper-level management since it gives the aspiring career manager a close look at the firms' customers.

When a study is commissioned a wide network of resources are brought into play to guarantee the timely delivery of the information. Teams of various internal and external experts and stakeholders get involved in determining the priority, structure and budget for any given project.

Clients

The ultimate user of the research is the client. Heavily dependent upon marketing research data are the marketers of consumer products – packaged goods, including foods, personal care and household products and over-the-counter remedies purchased in drug stores and supermarkets – and media companies, including producers of printed media, broadcasters, cable and network television and web sites on the Internet. Research data also has a major impact upon marketers of financial services such as banks, insurance companies and credit card suppliers; marketers of computer technology and other consumer and home electronics; automotive products; pharmaceutical companies and health care organizations, such as HMOs; and large public utilities such as the telecommunications industry. Less well-established as market research users but increasingly dependent upon data are industries as diverse as retailing, professional services, political candidates and not-for-profit organizations.

Client companies typically sponsor research through a 'consumer insights' or 'marketing research services' group – the names are evolving as organizations renegotiate their structures or ways of encountering customers. These groups are sometimes allowed to play a consulting role with respect to senior management but increasingly their function is being relegated to procurement and processing of information services on behalf of other members of management.

For the most part, a 'research manager' is responsible for organizing all the aspects of the study, coordinating all of the internal and outside resources brought into play and, most importantly, channeling the participation and making reports to corporate management particularly as they relate to decision making and the implementation of research findings.

Clients initiate research by having a problem – a critical question whose answer can benefit from objective, empirical data. Those raising the questions may come from senior management, the internal marketing, corporate communications, advertising or technical product development departments or from various sales groups. Increasingly, corporate players responsible for a longer-term perspective within the corporation such as strategic planning, quality management or senior technology officers are taking charge of initiating research studies to address their own unique problems.

The range of questions commonly brought to the research group is enormous: Will the expansion of a brand into a new product line produce profitable sales? What types of new products will appeal to evolving publics, for example, to health-conscious consumers? What should be the name of a new product and how should it be positioned or advertised? What are the ways to enhance public perception of the company and its primary businesses?

Most clients' companies lack all of the internal resources required to answer these questions nor can they maintain the necessary degree of objectivity. Consequently, they call upon various outside supplier firms and consultants to support and carry out the research. Many clients expect that their consultants and support agencies will cooperate and even play a major role in initiating specific studies.

Consultants and support agencies

Qualitative research may also be offered or initiated on behalf of client companies on the agency side, such as companies that provide marketing and management counsel. The consulting role implies that whether information is collected by themselves or by an outside research supplier, the agency acts as ultimate interpreters of research data making recommendations for communications, new product initiatives, etc.

Advertising agencies and public relations firms such as J. Walter Thompson and Young & Rubicam are most likely to get involved in qualitative research in order to familiarize themselves with consumer characteristics, or to develop strategic marketing plans, including positioning and promotional copy. Agencies use research to identify the 'hooks' which will engage consumer interest and the 'reasons to believe' which can link consumer interest to the product's principal underlying benefits.[2]

The use of qualitative tools to pick winners among several creative ideas is very controversial and agency creative directors sometimes vocally complain that focus groups can kill good ideas and promote safe and banal ways of reaching out to consumers. This criticism is valid if the research does not probe for an understanding of consumer motivations and relies only upon a head count vote of group participants.

Qualitative research consultants have been increasingly challenged in recent years to understand the creative process better. Much of the antagonism provoked by research can dissipate, many suggest, if analysts have a better understanding of the needs and strengths that agency creative teams bring to the process (Spier, 1993a).

Account planning, a discipline begun in the United Kingdom which has proliferated wildly within modish worldwide advertising agencies, seeks to improve the linkage between the brand and consumers via creative communications. Agency account planners have revolutionized the application of qualitative research by favoring active confrontation with product users through ethnographies and various other forms of naturalistic research.

Management consultants, political and legal advisors, independent research and development labs and industrial or graphic design firms are increasingly utilizing qualitative research. Specialists within the firms and sometimes senior consultants may conduct focus groups or other studies as a component of the consulting engagement. For example, an effort to align the corporate cultures of companies going through a merger may rely upon an observational study plus a series of depth interviews to help develop a unification strategy. Alternatively, designers are increasingly eager to test the user interface of products they develop through focus groups or through at-home studies of consumer practices.

Suppliers

Suppliers are the ultimate providers of research data and sometimes offer related services to interpret and consult on the implications of the findings. These companies are often segmented by research specialty. By far the largest and most influential firms are the syndicated research services offering large-scale surveys which track product usage and media consumption or measure the recall and impact of advertising. Other firms specialize in tracking a specific industry; such as automobiles and computers. Some suppliers repackage census data in usable forms to marketers and others provide social monitoring studies which track attitudes and trends in society as a whole. Others offer weekly or monthly 'omnibus studies' – national surveys onto which particular marketers may add their own unique questions.

Many supplier firms claim to offer 'full-service' custom research studies, applying a wide range of approaches for various research problems. Commonly, in continental Europe and Asia, but less so in the United Kingdom and North America, full-service firms may comprise specialized qualitative units within their organizations. Alternatively, they may have relationships with independent consultants or smaller firms that offer such services.

'Field services' – organizations that provide qualitative research labs, studios and facilities as well as related services such as recruitment and taping – are situated in virtually every major worldwide metropolitan area. These companies specialize in data collection and usually can provide market researchers with local field interviewing, either in person or via telephone banks, test kitchens, etc. In the United States, field services tend to be independent businesses while elsewhere they are likely to be affiliated with full-service agencies or qualitative specialist firms.

Specialized qualitative research agencies are common in North America and the United Kingdom and are growing in importance throughout continental Europe. These companies commonly are smaller 'boutique' operations, with anywhere from 1-15 professional-level employees, typically organized as entrepreneurial business ventures. In order to distinguish themselves, some qualitative boutiques may offer specialized methodological skills, such as ethnography or semiotics. While most firms are generalists or maintain a range of specialties, others may focus upon particular vertical industry applications such as banking or pharmaceuticals. A few concentrate upon selected consulting skills, such as new product development; and yet others may emphasize their linkages to other small agencies including those with specialists in quantitative areas such as multivariate analysis and market modeling.

Many social scientists affiliated with institutions of higher education conduct qualitative research and sometimes offer services to outside clients; however, unless these are associated with an independent practice, they tend to focus upon studies for not-for-profit and community-based organizations or for purely academic research (Morgan, 1988; Stewart and Shamdasani, 1990).

The broad base of the field includes vast networks of independent consultants, freelancers and part timers who are employed on a project basis as the needs of larger firms expand. In many cases, these smaller practitioners represent new companies in early stages of development. They also include many individuals who are pursuing advanced degrees or who are staying out of the full time job market because of child rearing or other familial responsibilities. Periods of economic flux, full-employment economies and national employment tenure regulations can complicate the usage of part time and freelance resources.

Qualitative research services can be offered at several locations within this social organization. The full-service firms, field services, boutique firms and independent consultants can all provide qualitative research practitioners. There are important career consequences attached to each type of affiliation. Researchers attached to full-service firms are likely to conduct focus groups in conjunction with other quantitative projects for the particular clients they serve. Alternatively, several large firms employ full time qualitative research specialists who might handle projects for all of the company's clients. Employees of field services may also conduct focus groups consistently but they tend to have a less consultative relationship with the client.

Qualitative research as a career

Since the early 1980s, the practice of qualitative research has strived for enhanced professionalism and greater recognition of its unique role in business and public affairs. Worldwide, there are probably at least 2,000-3,000 professionals who make all or most of their annual income from the performance of qualitative research services. The Qualitative Research Consultants Association (QRCA) represents over 700 qualitative research practitioners.

The current methodology of choice among most moderators is the focus group interview. Approximately 70,000-130,000 focus groups are conducted in the United States each year and this figure is likely to represent about half of all those conducted worldwide.

Moderators are increasingly called upon to provide other types of methodologies, for example intensive individual depth interviews (known as IDIs) as an alternative to focus groups. Less commonly, qualitative researchers are sometimes asked to conduct web-based online focus groups and research studies which fit more squarely into the tradition of ethnography and participant observation.

There is also an increasing demand for cultural and linguistic skills among moderators driven by organizations that wish to sustain a more effective outreach to racial and other subcultural groups within their national borders. While this is currently monopolized by specialists in the Latino, African American and Asian communities, it is likely that this phenomenon will expand. For example, greeting card companies in North America are increasingly responding to social expressions beyond Bar Mitzvahs, Cinco de Mayo, and Kwanzaa to celebrations of Divali in the Hindu community and Ramadan among Muslims.

Responsibilities of the qualitative research consultant

Regardless of the specific techniques employed, the qualitative research supplier is generally expected to take responsibility for a wide range of tasks of both a research and operational nature (Qualitative Research Council, 1992).

- Consulting on the most feasible and meaningful methodological approaches, for example, the proper mix of focus groups and IDIs. Helping to determine the characteristics of subjects recruited for the study. Composing the recruitment screener.
- Recommending locations for the study – in particular selecting local field facilities and research sites. Several particularly busy operations have been professionalizing this role recently in the position of the outsourced 'field supervisor'.
- Managing and supervising local facilities as they recruit subjects in the study. Arranging for any special needs such as videotaping, and for the creature comforts of clients.
- Developing the interview guide (or the 'discussion guide') that will be operative during the focus group.
- Conducting the interviews, of course, and selecting additional moderators if there is a need for special skills such as Spanish language interviewing or simultaneous French translation in the viewing room.
- Composing careful transcriptions or field notes from the tapes of the group interviews.
- Developing the final report of findings which generally include marketing strategy recommendations based upon the study findings.
- Making presentations to marketing managers or to upper management on the findings and their implications.

While carrying out all of the tasks associated with the primary market research projects at hand, the consultant must also take responsibility for the business side of their enterprise. Subcontractors and subjects must be paid and these arrangements must be financed. Above all, qualitative research consultants sell their services in a highly competitive environment in which the research managers who commission projects must always respect limited corporate research budgets. Consultants are always hard-pressed to balance the demands of acquiring work at a competitive rate against the need to remain profitable and receive adequate compensation for their services.

Entering the field

Entry into the field of qualitative market research combines elements of two models of occupational attainment, the *craft* and the *profession*. The latter emphasizes formal training and the acquisition of credentials while the craft model focuses upon apprenticeship and learning on the job.

Correspondingly, within the field of qualitative market research there is no single model of career entry and most practitioners' histories contain elements of both occupational attainment models.

Analysis of career histories suggest that up to a fifth of moderators hold PhDs. Most of these are in psychology, however sociology and other social and behavioral sciences have a considerable representation as well. Others hold terminal degrees in another business or therapeutic field. MBAs are well represented as are quite a number of MSWs and MSs in counseling. It is not unusual for career changers to have come into the field after practicing an occupational specialty, for example publishing or dentistry, in which they now conduct market research. Some practitioners may have undergraduate training in fields as diverse as history, business and theater.

Regardless of the professional degree held or the amount of education, it is generally unlikely that the practitioner acquired qualitative practice skills in college or university. While some with sociological or anthropological backgrounds may have been exposed to ethnographic or participant observation methods, and the psychologists may have been exposed to group work or Rogerian methods, nearly none became qualitative research practitioners as a result of graduate or undergraduate training.

Since the early 1980s, efforts have been expanded to professionalize market research by offering graduate level degree programs in that specific discipline. The College of Business Administration of the University of Georgia began to offer the Masters of Market Research (MMR) in 1981. Since then, similar programs have become institutionalized at the University of Wisconsin-Madison, the University of Texas-Arlington and at the University of Arizona. None of these programs offer a specialization in qualitative research practice – all are organized to meet the wide methodological needs of corporate clients. On the other hand, all of the programs require coursework in qualitative research, so while graduates are not necessarily competent to practice the specialty upon graduation, they nevertheless have the insight to be effective managers and purchasers of qualitative research services.

In a similar vein, several colleges of business such as Rutgers and applied research programs such as the Graduate Social Research Program at Hunter College of the City University of New York have introduced coursework in qualitative research methods but these, too, fall short of providing integrated training for practitioners.

The training vacuum has led, over the years, to the establishment of several training institutes as entrepreneurial ventures on the part of research practitioners. Although these training institutes were originally formed to give research clients the background to become effective research users, their function has shifted gradually. By now, the training institutes, which typically run intensive one-week workshops, have many graduates who are employed as full time moderators.

The professional associations have also responded to the training vacuum by providing seminars and workshops for both beginners and advanced practitioners. The QRCA, ARF and ESOMAR have offered programs on nearly an annual basis since the early 1980s.

Regardless of their educational background, most practitioners enter the field through apprenticeship at the supplier, agency or client level. An initial appointment in qualitative research may involve field management or support on the analysis or presentation of results. As one's career progresses, however, responsibilities will expand into developing discussion guides, screeners and ultimately conducting focus groups. A mature moderator will eventually acquire critical consulting skills for client contact.

By mid-career or within ten years in practice, moderators typically have loyal client followings who can dependably direct projects to their firms. Although some moderators may position themselves as specialists in connection with a particular product category, such as computers, or with a demographic target, such as children, most moderators consider themselves generalists. Clients, in assigning projects, may demand experience in a particular area; however the transference of skills from one product category to another is widely accepted.

As moderators become attached to agencies, larger full-service firms or field operations acquire client loyalty, and considerable pressure is placed upon moderators to strike out on their own in an entrepreneurial fashion. At this point, opportunity costs and investments required for entry into the field are relatively low – office space, a personal computer, stationery and a fax machine. Nevertheless, sustaining the operation past an initial stage of enthusiasm requires persistent marketing efforts and the cultivation of broad networks of potential clients.

The professional affiliations of qualitative researchers

In terms of professional affiliation, a variety of organizations serve the market research industry by specialization or field of application.

ESOMAR has recently taken the lead in representing the wide range of specialties contained within this far-ranging profession. Through regular seminars, monographs, white papers and other activities, ESOMAR has tried to encompass the worldwide qualitative research profession.

The American Marketing Association (AMA) has a high level of representation by market researchers but also includes educators and other marketing disciplines within its ranks. The AMA has been active recently in promoting a program of certification for marketing practitioners, including market researchers. The Advertising Research Foundation (ARF) has also served the industry in a prominent way. Its annual spring conference in New York City offers the major trade show for market researchers where new advances in technology and techniques are exhibited. ARF has initiated efforts to unify the far-flung organizations in the field through the Research Industry Coalition (RIC) and its Industry Leaders Forum.

The Council of American Survey Research Organizations (CASRO) represents large and small companies engaged in survey research. Similarly, the American Association of Public Opinion Research (AAPOR) provides affiliation for academics and practitioners involved in that specialty. The Market Research Association (MRA) represents primarily field services and data collection organizations. And finally there are various industry-specific market research societies such as the Travel and Tourism Research Association

(TTRA), the Pharmaceutical Market Research Association (PMRA) and the Life Insurance Market Research Association (LIMRA).

In addition, most of the academic social science organizations have sections devoted to applied research which often provide affiliation for market researchers.

The Qualitative Research Consultants Association (QRCA) was founded in the early 1980s to provide affiliation for independent moderators and those affiliated with full-service research firms and field services, whose responsibilities primarily revolved around qualitative market research. A section of the ARF, the Qualitative Research Council, also represents the market research discipline, although its affiliates include professionals from the client and agency side who are primarily users and purchasers of qualitative research services and not exclusively practitioners.

Both of these organizations have sponsored seminars and conferences, published guides to practice, conducted internal research and have represented the legal and professional interests of the field.

The United Kingdom and the rest of Europe have particularly well-developed infrastructures. Practitioners in the United Kingdom are represented by an interest section within the Market Research Society (MRS) and also by the Association for Qualitative Research (AQR). While most details of practice are similar across boundaries, individual countries do have local traditions that pervade both analytic and consulting styles as well as the details of research execution. For example, while it is uncommon in the United States to serve alcoholic beverages in a focus group not discussing that topic, the British consider it wholly appropriate to recreate a congenial pub-like atmosphere while doing research. Many prefer a living room environment in the UK to the perceived sterility of an office-based viewing facility.

1.5 Qualitative Research Applications

Categories of studies commonly employing qualitative research in an appropriate way are described in this section. Different industries and product categories have their own terminology for some of these types of studies. Indeed, the very definition of researchable problems changes as one moves from goods purchased weekly to those bought once in a lifetime, or from those purchased by housewives to those procured by senior corporate officers. Nevertheless, these are some general issues that are normally addressed by qualitative approaches.

- Consumer familiarization and cultural assessments
- Idea generation
- New product development
- Positioning studies
- Branding studies
- Attitude and usage studies
- Naming and packaging refinement
- Advertising/copy and promotional development
- Usability testing

Consumer familiarization and cultural assessments

Consumer familiarization can take many different forms. Qualitative methods can be used to learn about unfamiliar market segments – for example, a product category that had previously targeted males now wants to target females. Alternatively a marketer may want to offer new products to a previously underserved subcultural group.

Examples

> **Condoms:** *A marketer of condoms that had previously targeted heterosexual males wished to expand its market to gays concerned about 'safe sex' practices. Initial reactions indicated that direct imagery and copy was ineffective because the men did not want to announce their sexual orientation at the drugstore. Further research discovered specific language and images that spoke subtly to gay males while not making itself obvious to those outside the target.*

> **Recreational vehicles:** *An industry association representing manufacturers of recreational vehicles (RVs) developed an advertising campaign to build awareness and encourage sales of the product. In order to conduct background research on the lifestyles, habits and preferences of the target population, members of the agency planning, research and creative teams rented a vehicle to visit several encampments. Naturalistic observations along with informal discussions with fellow campers yielded a series of insights into consumer motivations (Rydholm, 1997a).*

Consumer familiarization need not apply only to unfamiliar groups. Any group of people is a moving target continuously subject to the forces of change. Fads, trends and fashions may wax and wane; economic shifts may render one's customers more affluent or suddenly impoverished; new technologies may be seductive; proceeding through the life cycle may make young risk-takers surprisingly conservative. In other words, marketers can never remain complacent in the confident belief that they know their customer. The state of knowledge itself needs constant refreshment and refinement.

The cultural dimension of product usage and choice across the global marketplace also can be analyzed through qualitative research. Findings can provide direction for adjusting product characteristics, packaging, positioning, etc. according to the needs of people in different countries or for distinct ethnic communities within countries.

Example

> **Baking soda toothpaste in the UK:** *Even though 'baking soda' toothpaste was a success in the US market, there was little hope of transferring the product to the UK because consumers were not familiar with the term 'baking soda'. Research discovered however, that UK consumers understood the word 'bicarbonate' and associated it with the properties of cleaning and deodorizing. Further testing led to the successful introduction in the UK of products with bicarbonate as a central ingredient.*

Idea generation

Qualitative research techniques are useful in generating creative new ideas for products and communications as well as for testing concepts that emerge from ideation sessions.

Brainstorming methods that yield new ideas commonly rely upon intensive group discussion, open-ended exploration, imaginative exercises and games that are drawn from qualitative research techniques.

Alternatively, the intensive understanding of consumer needs, wishes, problems, dissatisfactions and work-arounds can suggest better ways of serving the customer. Results from focus groups of meal-preparation practices, for example, can suggest ways of simplifying the process or making it more satisfying. An observational study of consumer home cleaning practices can yield ideas for new tools and products that attack particular kinds of soiling and sanitize certain surfaces better.

Examples

> **Shower cleaners:** *Observational studies of shower cleaning practices demonstrated a high level of frustration with the soap, calcium, dirt and mildew buildups that shower stalls were subject to despite satisfaction with products meant to clean these soils. Consumer wishes for a product that would help protect their showers from problems in the first place led to the successful introductions of several shower maintenance products.*
>
> **Toilet tissue:** *Scott™ Paper Co. believed that it had a new product opportunity among toilet tissue users who were not satisfied with the results produced by current toilet papers. Qualitative research helped to develop and position several new entries in the Cottonelle™ brand – a hypo-allergenic bath tissue free of inks, dyes and fragrances, another infused with odor-neutralizing baking soda and moist personal wipes with aloe. Respondents helped to develop these products through brainstorming sessions and by reacting to various stimuli introduced by research and marketing personnel during the course of depth interviews (Rydholm, 1995b).*

Qualitative research also provides effective tools for creative problem solving in many contexts outside of marketing issues. Senior managers have used focus groups among employees, for example, to generate ideas for enhancing worker productivity. Legal researchers can also use creative brainstorming with mock juries to conceptualize alternative litigation strategies.

New product development studies

Qualitative methods are used to expose consumers to new product ideas, concepts or prototypes to get their reactions. Often in practice the concepts are exposed as storyboards or as concept statements; alternatively, some client companies invest in mock-ups or actual models. The objective here generally is to winnow down a large number of concepts into a few that are better suited for continued testing and refinement.

Examples

> **Flavored vodka:** *Finlandia™, competing in the increasingly crowded market for flavored vodkas, used individual depth interviews to test alternative formulations for its Arctic Cranberry™ variety. The surprising finding was that its market which tends to skew younger and female preferred a less alcoholic and more palatable richly-flavored formulation. This led to the*

introduction of a brand that set the pace for new entrants in the category (Rydholm, 1994).

Computer televisions: *A multinational consumer electronics manufacturer wished to obtain feedback on its concepts for merging video and PC technology into a single appliance. It created several attractive drawings of what these products might resemble and generated a list of specifications for features such as monitor size, color range, memory size and processing speed. Focus group participants examining these drawings were invited to assess how they might use these prototypes and describe the factors that may lead them to enjoy or dislike the product. These sessions led to many ideas for refining the technology.*

Games of chance: *The Missouri Lottery depends upon continuous refreshment of the products it offers customers of its instant games. Focus group testing has led to the development of many successful games, such as 'King's Ransom' and, 'Deal 'em Wild', through the screening of concepts submitted through various sources. Research has also been effective in understanding the factors that produce enthusiasm about new games such as extra scratch-off windows and action themes for men (QMRR staff, 1992).*

Multipurpose plastic: *Consumers wallets are filled with plastic and the supposition of marketers at Ameritech Corp. and Household International was that they might be interested in reducing the load by combining the benefits of two cards into one. Marketers subsequently used a series of focus groups and confirmatory research applying conjoint analysis to create a credit card that had all of the advantages of a telephone calling card. Their Complete MasterCard™ allows users to shop, pay bills, take trips and make phone calls (Tonneberger, 1992).*

When decisions to adapt or drop concepts are made on the basis of qualitative research, they should be based on the *reasons* given for acceptance/rejection rather than on an unsuitable head count or similar inappropriate measurement. Because qualitative research studies rely upon small samples that are not necessarily selected randomly, and as a consequence of excessive social influence within focus groups, making decisions based upon a poll of participants can yield highly unreliable and misleading results. Questions such as, 'Would you buy this?' or, 'Would you pay more than X for one?' are only useful for heuristic purposes and should not be taken as a reliable predictor of purchase dynamics.

Positioning studies

Qualitative research provides insights into the best ways to describe and communicate effectively about a product or brand. Positioning is critical in determining how consumers think about a product, a brand or a personality. Command over a positioning such as 'best for children' or 'the best value for the money' can guarantee unassailable strength with a major market segment. Thus, market positioning is fiercely guarded and highly competitive. In this connection, focus groups and other qualitative methods can provide a useful first step when the client wishes to establish or modify the positioning of its brands. Research studies are used in various ways through the positioning process. They can:

- Create a marketing strategy.
- Better differentiate a brand from its competition.
- Create or change a product or a brand image.
- Re-position a product after its market image has gone stale.
- Provide input into advertising or copy strategy.
- Link the brand to emotional benefits sought by consumers.

Examples

Mirror doors: Stanley™ Hardware realized that its Monarch™ mirror doors needed to be repositioned because customers were failing to see any value-added in the category and were making decisions only on the basis of lowest price. Qualitative research with customers (recent buyers as well as prospects) and professionals (distributors, contractors, builders) revealed that part of the problem was in the distribution system. Basic goods tended to be in stock, while top of the line items needed to be special-ordered. However, a larger problem was in the positioning – mirror doors were perceived as a 'hardware' item rather than as a 'decorative accessory'. By expanding its décor options and making them more accessible at point-of-sale the marketer was able to meet its sales goals (Haller and Benedict, 1994).

Glassware: It is difficult for marketers to impose personalities on prosaic everyday products such as glassware. Even though consumers had positive perceptions of the Libbey™ Glass brand, there were few ways to distinguish the product from competitors. Focus groups and a confirmatory mall-intercept survey suggested an effective approach – borrowing the image of famous personalities such as Vincent Price and Mary Lou Retton to suggest that certain entries in the line would be their 'favorite glasses'. Advertising emerging from these studies identified Price with a black-tinted product and Retton, of course, with a 'tumbler' (Rydholm, 1992b).

Branding studies

Marketing organizations have learned that an established and well-recognized brand is a valuable commodity. Brands provide a measure of value, also known as 'brand equity', and a point of reference, also known as 'brand image', for consumers. Brands have a history – evolving over time and entering consumers' lives at different points of a person's life cycle. Thus, their meanings can change with the passage of years. Because they are highly mutable, brands can become spoiled, old or disconnected from their users. The finely-polished mahogany RCA™ color television and hi-fi console that served as the centerpiece of affluent family life in the early 1960s can seem like a dated antique to the third millennium family more strongly drawn, perhaps, to a Sony Playstation™.

Qualitative research techniques are helpful in establishing an understanding of brand equity and brand image dynamics. Consequently they are frequently applied to studies which seek to modify a spoiled image, keep a product's brand equity vital, or subtly shift a product's equity to new product lines or changed product features that are more in tune with a changed consumer environment.

Examples

> **Paper towels:** *After their introduction a generation ago, Brawny™ paper towels seemed stale and dated. To reclaim vanishing market share, all aspects of branding, including, positioning, identity, packaging and advertising were subjected to scrutiny through focus groups. Some aspects of the research produced surprises, such as the enduring charm of the trademarked masculine symbol. Women who were asked to project what they might feel if they were stuck in an elevator for 20 minutes with the character did not find the prospect entirely unappealing. Subsequent modifications in the packaging, along with logo changes which included some adaptations to the character – he lost his lumberjack ax – and a new ad campaign emphasizing the brand's 'thirst pockets' served to update the image and produce higher awareness levels (Weber, 1994).*
>
> **Cosmetics:** *Helena Rubenstein™, a venerable European cosmetics name, needed to emerge from associations as grandmother's make-up. Even though the brand had died in the United States, women's mind maps revealed a stodgy, conservative and dowdy image. The same focus groups that diagnosed the problem revealed strategies for refreshing the brand. By identifying the brand with a master innovative colorist with great appeal to the younger demographic being courted, and by introducing the new line through a network of upscale spa boutiques, the brand was reincarnated in the American market (Sabena, 1999b).*

Attitude and usage studies/satisfaction studies

Attitude and usage (A&U) studies and customer satisfaction (CS) studies are generally conducted through large-scale market surveys. Product and brand management find it essential to keep tabs on consumer characteristics, usage and purchase patterns, comparisons to competitors, etc. Qualitative research, in this context, can be used to generate hypotheses about marketplace behavior or to test the research instruments, such as questionnaire items, that will be used in the larger survey in order to guarantee that all of the correct issues are being covered.

Qualitative techniques also yield a 'softer', more nuanced and textured approach to attitudes and usage and customer satisfaction. They are capable of discovering subtle factors involved in product satisfaction. An on-site ethnography conducted in connection with an A&U study of home cleaning, for example, can demonstrate subtle reactions to the smells and the effort involved in scouring various surfaces.

Examples

Airlines: An airline wanted to measure the overall satisfaction of its flying public. Listening to consumer communications, while important, tended to focus on complaints rather than measurement of overall service quality and gave little direction for improvement. Using a mix of focus groups, mini-groups and individual depths, the consultants developed an instrument that could not only measure the various service components, it could also assess how close service came to matching the ideal of customer 'delight' (Laflin and Hyatt, 1999).

Museum collections: The Mint Museum of Art in Charlotte, North Carolina serves a dynamic and rapidly changing population that is flocking to its area to take advantage of recent corporate and industrial expansion. Young professionals from other regions of the United States, Europe and Asia have challenged the museum's identity and outreach. In response, the Mint undertook an A&U study with 15 focus groups and a mailed survey of 10,000 Charlotte residents to identify the needs and expectations of its emerging user base. Analysis of the results have had impacts on the design of the museum building itself, its mix of exhibits and even several auxiliary services, such as the installation of a new restaurant (Straus, 1998).

Naming and packaging evaluations

Qualitative research is used for developing and screening product names, labeling and packaging. This can be helpful when the various packaging elements need to be assessed against strategic objectives such as their ability to communicate in a manner consistent with product positioning. Qualitative methods are particularly appropriate here because they are adept at capturing the symbolic element in communications. Such features as color, texture and shapes convey a level of meaning that is difficult to capture through any other approach. Packaging features that can be illuminated through qualitative methods include:

- *Size options* What is the price-value perception of different sizes and words used to communicate size, such as 'jumbo' or 'child-sized'?
- *Promotional tag lines* How motivational and meaningful are the words that are used on the package to describe the product or its effects?
- *Images and graphics* Are designs consistent with the overall message? Do they establish a positive brand identity? Are they appropriate for the targeted market?
- *Directions for use* Are they clear and do they promote satisfactory usage?
- *Secondary branding and endorsement* Does the use of an associated symbol or brand such as 'Intel™ inside', the 'kosher' symbol or approval by the American Dental Association or Cotton Council™ add value and enhance competitive market performance?

Example

Furniture: *The Ethan Allen™ chain of furniture stores had made tremendous progress at revamping its product mix to encompass both contemporary and traditional lines. Unfortunately, its logo was telling potential customers that the stores were steeped in dependable and functional American colonial-style furniture but not in step with current trends. A variety of bold new logo designs were developed by the design team and tested in a series of focus groups. Before the sessions, participants were invited to tour local stores in their areas to familiarize themselves with the current rather than the perceived product mix. The research findings impacted not just the logo design, moving to a blue rather than green color scheme, they also suggested the need for refreshing the chain's storefronts (Rydholm, 1992a).*

Advertising/copy and promotional development

There are both rational/conscious and emotional/subconscious components of any advertisement, representing the denotative and connotative constituents of communication. This means that there are several levels which must be considered in any promotion, including what is being said as well as what is likely being heard. Qualitative methods are effective in meeting the needs at both ends of the spectrum. By providing information about how and what consumers expect to learn about products and by providing tools for concept screening, qualitative research can support the development of effective communications and promotions. Additionally, through the use of projective tools, qualitative studies are effective at reaching beneath the surface to the emotional messages reaching the consumer. Examples of potential qualitative input in the development process include:

- Screening advertising concepts through the use of storyboards or positioning statements.
- Generating strategic concepts through ideation and creative problem solving.

- Assessing advertising copy and images to determine the degree of understanding and appreciation for various executions.
- Assessing the impact and emotional connection to spokespersons or background music.
- Discovering which media are most credible and motivational for particular types of messages.
- Understanding the value and meaning of various promotions. Qualitative evaluation, for example, can lend insight into whether cents-off coupons, free samples, or point-of-purchase displays convey sufficient value to stimulate trial and repurchase.

Examples

> **Oral care in Micronesia:** In introducing oral care products in Micronesia several years ago, marketers were faced with generating demand in a culture unfamiliar with Western standards of oral hygiene and with few channels for communicating with widely dispersed villagers. As an expedient, Colgate™ created, tested and implemented a 'play' whose performers traveled between villages and demonstrated product and usage features.
>
> **Sports car:** Pontiac™ needed input to develop advertising for its new Sunfire™ brand targeted to younger drivers who wanted a sporty car but couldn't quite afford one. Group sessions conducted with prospective purchasers relied upon creating a series of collages that focused on feelings and writing personal stories in relation to cars. Then photos of the new model were presented and participants were invited to react. Bringing the finished collages and responses to meetings of the creative team helped Pontiac™ position and prepare ads based on insights into customers' lifestyles and aspirations (Rydholm, 1995a).

Usability testing

Usability testing refers to evaluations of the ways in which people interact with and use technological products, such as computer software, cellular telephones and home appliances. As the functionality of technological tools has grown in sophistication and complexity, and as these tools have continued to multiply in a highly competitive marketplace, product designers and marketers are pressed to guarantee that usage is not hindered by any barriers and that consumer satisfaction is maximized. Consequently, usability studies based both in laboratories and in home or office environments have grown in frequency and importance.

Usability studies often take the form of having groups or individual users go through a usage scenario in which they are likely to encounter various challenges and opportunities. Dimensions of usability which are evaluated include such factors as comprehension, 'navigability' or the ability to move across various levels of functionality, and 'stickiness' or the degree to which the software or web site, for example, involves the user in extra levels of engaging and compelling interest. The latter is important because if users drift out of a site quickly, they are unlikely to revisit and explore advertising messages.

Example

> **Public utility:** *Power outages are a vexing problem for utilities customers and the crisis is made even more desperate when users have to interact with a voice recording to get service restored. Portland General Electric in Oregon determined that focus groups and a usability test could make its reporting system more user friendly. Problems identified in the usability test, such as various 'dead ends' in the automated answering system, were resolved for the focus group exploration. Further refinements of system characteristics were made based on the focus group findings, and guidelines for future adaptations were developed (Rydholm, 1997b).*

Other uses

As qualitative research methods such as focus groups have grown in popularity, new applications have multiplied. You may hear about these techniques used in non-marketing applications, such as:

- *Political communications* to tailor messages and craft speeches for various constituencies. The US president Bill Clinton used focus groups throughout his presidency to provide background for speeches to Congress and to finesse strategies during periods of political vulnerability. A rival to Stan Greenberg, Mr. Clinton's favorite moderator, once complained, 'The words he uses come right out of Stan Greenberg's focus groups. Greenberg literally pulls the words out of the mouths of ordinary Americans and puts them in the mouth of the president. The result is Bill Clinton speaks like real Americans speak' (Perry, 1994: A16).
- *Internal employee motivational studies* to support efforts at team-building, morale improvement, employee decision making and productivity enhancement.
- *Sales channel studies* to evaluate attitudes among intermediate decision makers such as importers or supermarket buyers.
- *Jury selection and litigation strategy studies* to better understand how to select prospective jurors, frame arguments in a case and create courtroom presentations that favor the position of plaintiffs or defendants. Simulated trials have also been used to help witnesses become comfortable with the jury setting or, craftily, to present information to the other side that may encourage settlement prior to the case's full presentation to a jury. Cases with high economic value that have used qualitative research include several involving issues such as product liability, lender liability, employment litigation, medical malpractice and libel actions (Odesky and Kerger, 1994).

- *Action research* to structure constituent input in the performance of public and community-based organizations. In this context, focus groups, participant observation and depth interviewing may be utilized to develop a university curriculum or to improve the outreach services of a health care agency (Masters, 1995).

1.6 Varieties of Qualitative Research

Until now, we have generalized about qualitative research as a 'family' of approaches, methods and techniques. In this section we will define the individual methods and techniques and briefly describe the pros and cons for using each of them. Later sections contain full details on implementing projects using each of these approaches.

Focus groups

Focus groups (also called 'focused groups' or 'group depth interviews') are the most commonly used qualitative research technique in applied settings (Goldman and McDonald, 1987; Greenbaum, 1993; Merton et al., 1990; Morgan, 1988; Stewart and Shamdasani, 1990). In North America, typical group interviews last about two hours and are conducted among 8-10 participants; the norm among European practitioners is for longer and smaller groups – 2-3 hours with 6-8 participants. Although these parameters hold true for the overwhelming majority of focus groups, project demands may sometimes require shortening the time frame to as little as an hour or extending it to as long as four or five hours.

As a general rule, focus group studies convene at least 4-6 separate group discussions, or more depending on the desired coverage of market segments. Studies with only one or two groups are generally undesirable because these are insufficient to understand the full range of responses. The interpersonal dynamics of focus groups are such that a single group may reflect situational elements that cannot be generalized.

Studies based upon twelve or more group sessions are uncommon. For many clients the cost of such a study can be prohibitive. Larger studies also produce such a high volume of data that thorough analysis becomes impossible within the study's allotted time frame.

The person that convenes a group or individual depth interview is called a *moderator*. This term reflects their role as both a collector and continuous analyst of the data.

There are several variations of the focus group technique.

Mini-groups

These groups generally convene from four to six respondents in the two-hour time frame. Situations that may necessitate a mini-group include:
- Scarcity or difficulty in recruiting particular respondents.

- A highly detailed and technical discussion guide which may require extensive discussion by participants.
- The expected depth of the discussion.
- The need to review a large number of concepts.
- The desire to maintain greater intimacy than is possible in a larger group.

Telephone focus groups

Telephone focus groups are conducted over a telephone conferencing system with the same number of participants as conventional focus groups but typically within a narrower time frame – no more than an hour. Telephone focus groups may not be necessary or cost-effective with average consumers, except in cases where follow-up with survey respondents is desired. Situations requiring use of telephone focus groups include:

- Access to widely dispersed groups of potential respondents in the same profession, such as studies involving leading business executives, experts or professors. For example, in a study of US history professors responsible for assigning textbooks to more than 500 students per year, a textbook publisher may use telephone focus groups so that they can reach faculty at highly dispersed major universities.
- Access to widely dispersed experts in a range of professions, including specialists – such as atomic scientists – or opinion leaders. For example, a public relations researcher eager to uncover ways to encourage improved opinions toward a regional 'hot spot' may convene telephone focus groups with leading academic experts, business executives with major investments in the region and journalists who cover the region for major news organizations.

As an alternative to telephone focus groups, if time allows, members of highly dispersed targeted audiences can be convened at national or international professional conferences. In-person focus groups can be arranged at the convention hotel or at nearby facilities.

Online (Internet) focus groups

Online groups are conducted at one of the special web sites that have been set up to facilitate the conduct of group sessions through personal computers. These may not be appropriate with average consumers at this time because the incidence of computer usage is still relatively modest; however, they can be very effective with groups that spend a great deal of time communicating electronically such as teenagers and young adults, computer programmers or corporate information technology decision makers.

Online focus groups are often essential when a computer-based application or an Internet web site is involved in the discussion. For example, a researcher evaluating the usability and positioning of a new computer game is likely to use online groups to refine game scenarios and advertising messages.

Online groups can be executed as either real time chats in which all participants are linked simultaneously or as bulletin boards in which conferees are invited to read and discuss each others' postings within a longer time frame, such as a full day. There is less moderator control over the latter type of session but it may be essential for international online discussions or among hard-to-reach participants.

When to use focus groups

Focus groups are appropriate for most qualitative research applications as listed in Section 1.5 of this text. They are relatively easy to arrange since there is a large professional infrastructure that supports the conduct of this type of research.

Benefits of focus groups

There are numerous benefits of holding focus groups. Some of them are listed below.

- Focus groups allow for group interaction among participants; thus, the researcher can learn about patterns of interpersonal influence regarding a specific product or communication. For example, if group participants who are positively disposed toward a new product concept turn negative as a result of the opinions of a single skeptic in the group, brand management may infer that this pattern may be replicated in the marketplace.
- Peer pressure in a focus group can support honest disclosure. Participants may be less likely to falsify their attitudes if they perceive themselves to be among similar types of people.
- The moderator can use group dynamics to support research objectives. For example, he or she may encourage conflict or competition to draw out opposing viewpoints.
- Focus groups are flexible. They can be conducted with just about any type of targeted audience or at any time of the year.
- Focus groups allow for spontaneous, unfiltered input by participants.
- Most of the time focus groups are observable by brand management, advertising creatives and others involved in product development and marketing support. This allows them to gain a direct impression of consumers' attitudes and feelings.

Problems associated with focus groups

Most internal problems with focus groups are a consequence of problematic group dynamics.

Peer pressure within the group can suppress unpopular attitudes. Some participants may feel reluctant to express an unpopular opinion and the moderator in this situation may lack the skills to facilitate diverse opinions.

Group opinions may seem to be swayed by dominating respondents. Passive or shy respondents may feel reluctant to challenge a forceful group member.

Individual depth interviews

Sometimes also called 'IDIs' or 'one-on-ones', in-depth interviews usually last from one-half to a full hour, but can go longer depending on project requirements. These sessions employ a focused interviewing strategy in which questions are open-ended and non-directive, allowing the discussion to follow the subjects' responses and issues. IDIs should not be confused with survey research interviewing in which a strictly defined sequence of closed format questions constitute the predominant format.

Anywhere from 5-50 or more respondents, interviewed one at a time, may be invited to participate in an IDI study. Interviews may be conducted at a central interviewing facility or they may take place at the respondent's home or office.

When to use IDIs

IDIs are the preferred methodology when the project demands intensive probing of respondents, or reactions to ideas without influence from peers. IDIs facilitate a high degree of psychological depth, that is, investigation of motivations, associations and explanations behind product preference.

Focus groups vs. IDIs

The decision about whether to select a group vs. individual depth interview approach is very subjective and without strict guidelines. The table below lists several considerations that might influence the decision.

Table 1 Considerations for focus groups vs. IDIs.

Considerations	Focus Groups	IDIs
Cost factors	Economical use of moderator and facility time.	Extensive use of moderator and facility time, making it more expensive per interviewee.
Time	Economical use of time for interviewing and analysis.	Extensive time required for interviewing and substantial volume of information is produced, thus analyzing the results also takes time.
Group interaction	Group interaction is present and may allow for exchange of ideas and interpersonal influence.	No group interaction. Subject largely reacts to the moderator.
Peer vs. authority pressures	Group pressures may produce spontaneous challenge. Peer accommodation may facilitate honest disclosures.	No peer pressures but subject may react to authority of the moderator.

Considerations	Focus Groups	IDIs
Influence	Peers may influence change of opinions. This may result in some level of contamination, however, it is often important to learn how 'shakable' respondents' ideas are.	With only one respondent, there is no potential for influence or contamination by other respondents.
Sensitive topics	Some respondents may find it embarrassing and inhibiting to deal with sensitive topics in a group. Others consider it liberating to interact with peers who share a problem or preference.	Some respondents find it easier to deal with sensitive issues in a one-on-one clinical setting.
Respondent access	Limited time to talk to each respondent. Competition to take center stage may produce highly disproportionate participation by individual respondents.	Each respondent gets equal time. Thorough in-depth probing of each respondent is possible.
Scheduling	May be difficult to coordinate schedules of hard-to-reach respondents for a single meeting.	Easier to schedule at central facilities, homes or offices.

Dyads and triads

Interviewing respondents simultaneously in twos or threes is a method that can provide some of the benefits of both group and individual approaches. There are naturally occurring dyads and triads such as couples or family groups, as well as those that are put together entirely for research purposes.

When to use

Dyads and triads are appropriate when the researcher wants to:
- Combine intensive individual interviewing with the checks offered by peer interaction.
- Expose respondents to a large number of test stimuli and also allow for peer interaction during discussion.
- Hear from individuals who share decision making or product usage. For example, couples may share decisions about dental care professionals or a mortgage provider for their home purchase.

Creativity sessions

Creativity sessions refer to group discussions that rely upon various tools and projective techniques for eliciting attitudes that are latent or unformed in the consumer's mind. They can facilitate reaching beyond conventional and expected responses to questions.

These techniques are usually implemented through games or exercises designed to stimulate unconventional responses. Examples include sentence completion, spontaneous drawing and collage making, word and picture sorting, personification and other tools that are detailed in a later section.

When to use

Creativity sessions employing projective techniques can be used in group (6-15 participants is standard) and individual interviews. These sessions are the primary resource for corporate innovation. Warner-Lambert, for one, reports having trained more than 500 of its internal managers in the Synectics approach to help develop new chewing gum products (Knoll, 1992). Clients may also use creativity sessions with internal and external audiences. For example, members of marketing, sales or customer service organizations may be recruited to generate ideas for new products targeted to a customer segment not now being reached; manufacturing employees may be studied for ways to improve efficiency; and customers may be gathered in a brainstorming session on how the client may improve point-of-purchase services. The benefits usually sought in using projective techniques include:

- Generating breakthrough ideas.
- Picking up latent or unformed attitudes.
- Tapping into deeply held imagery and emotional meanings.
- Gaining information about low involvement products.
- Going beyond the verbal abilities of respondents.
- Adding variety to group or individual depth interviews.

Additional details on techniques appropriate to specific research objectives are provided in later sections on probing and projective techniques.

Problems associated with creativity sessions

Creativity sessions require a high level of skill and experience on the part of the consultant. Successful sessions can be energizing and stimulating while less competent sessions can be boring and produce trite results. Conditions for success include obtaining the right mix of participants. For example, combining employees with widely disparate levels of responsibility in an organization can be intimidating for some of the junior people in the session. Internal productivity and efficiency studies can also raise suspicions if participants feel that future employment decisions may hinge on the sessions' outcomes.

Balancing the composition of consumer sessions is critical. Many practitioners employ a 'creativity screen' to guarantee that recruited respondents have a minimal level of confidence and articulateness. At the very least, this type of screening weeds out participants who may only follow a group leader or provide complacent responses.

Ethnographic and observational research

Ethnographic and observational research introduces the cultural dimension in market research by going directly to the location where consumers use or purchase products in their everyday lives (Arnould and Wallendorf, 1994; Douglas, 1970; Fetterman, 1989; Garfinkel, 1967; Glaser and Strauss, 1967; Hirschman, 1989; Lofland, 1976; Mariampolski, 1998, 1999; Shaffir, Stebbins and Turowetz, 1980; Spradley, 1979, 1980; Taylor and Bogdan, 1984; Van Maanen, 1983).

Observational research is carried out by watching consumers in a careful and structured way as they buy or use products. How long the researcher stays with the consumer is open to deliberation. An encounter can last as long as a single product usage cycle or it can evolve over a lengthier time period – several days or weeks, if budget and project objectives so demand. In conceptualizing a study, decisions must also be made about the degree of contact between researcher and user. Pure observation involves no contact or interaction with the subject, while its opposite, 'participant observation', involves continuous interaction between the observer and the subject over some period of time. Both types of research strategies can be practiced in a variety of settings such as laboratories or research facilities, and in more natural settings such as homes, offices, retail stores, leisure locations, public spaces, etc.

When to use

Ethnographic and observational research approaches (also called 'on-site' or 'at-home' studies) have the advantage of providing both behavioral and attitudinal data. These methods are necessary when research objectives call for any of the following situations:

- To study high intensity interactions, such as a sales encounter, meal preparation and service, or communication between persons holding different levels of authority.
- To conduct precise analyses of behavioral processes, for example, tooth brushing patterns, home computer purchasing decisions or home cleaning behaviors.
- To address situations where the respondent's memory or reflection would not be adequate. Observational methods can stand alone or can complement interviewing by serving as a memory jog.
- To work with respondents who are likely to be ashamed or reluctant to reveal actual practices to a group of peers. If they are diabetic, for example, respondents may be reluctant to reveal that they have a refrigerator full of sweet snacks – something that an ethnographic observer would be able to see without confronting the subject.

Problems associated with ethnographic observational studies

Because ethnographic studies take place in the 'real world', they are subject to a wide range of threats that are less likely in a rarefied laboratory study. For example, the logistics of getting researchers on a widespread basis to consumers' homes and workplaces can be complicated. The observational encounters may also become subjected to spontaneous and unexpected events, such as emergency phone calls from the respondents' family and friends. In formal organizations, such as an office or hospital, the approval of persons in authority, such as an owner/operator or supervising nurse is necessary for the conclusion of a site visit.

Ethnographic studies are also challenged to maintain 'naturalness' in the ways people buy or use products despite the fact of being observed. Later in this text, several strategies for preserving true and accurate behavioral patterns will be reviewed.

Life history

Life history is a mode of in-depth interviewing which focuses on the evolution of behaviors and attitudes over the life course. A single case may take anywhere from 3-5 hours of interviewing. During life history interviews, respondents are asked to dig deeply into their memories and experiences. They may be invited to recall:

- Childhood memories of a brand, product or category.
- How people significant in their upbringing, such as parents or teachers, talked about a product or category.
- How tastes and preferences have changed over time.
- How perceptions and preferences have been altered by various experiences.

Lois Steinberg, who refers to her life history approach as 'story analysis', reports an interesting case.

> One woman said in a focus group that she drank wine because she liked the taste. In the story analysis part of the in-depth interviews, we asked the respondents to recall their first experience of drinking alcohol beverages. In recounting her earlier experiences, the same woman recalled that her father advised her to drink wine because it was most 'ladylike' and socially acceptable to drink. She now feels uncomfortable drinking beer or hard liquor in mixed company. (1997: 40)

When to use

Life history interviewing is often useful in studies of brand imagery, in product positioning and in new product development.[3] Because it relies on highly intensive biographical probing, it is effective in diagnosing problems and developing strategies for revitalizing mature or 'damaged' brands or categories. This technique is useful when management believes that other techniques are delivering only top-of-mind responses.

Life history interviews with former users of beef who were now largely vegetarians or heavy users of chicken and fish revealed a wide range of sympathetic memories associated with beef – the Sunday stew at Grandma's house or the juicy steak grilled by Dad on the backyard barbecue.

Content or text analysis

Content or text analysis is a technique for deriving new meanings from written or printed texts and images. The method generally requires a systematic review of content on the basis of analytic or coding categories that are either fashioned beforehand or inductively developed following an initial review of the material. Materials for content analysis can be generated in a research exercise, such as the graphic results of collages drawn by respondents. Alternatively, materials can be drawn from archives or other publicly available sources. The types of resources that can be subjected to content analysis include:

- Personal documents, letters, diaries, etc.
- Advertisements, including both images and copy.
- Mass communications.
- Literature.

Sometimes, principles of a theoretical system are applied to this research. Semiotics, a discipline for analyzing texts through a search for inherent symbolism, has been popular in recent years as an approach to content analysis. Semiotics seeks to understand how signs perform or convey meaning in context.[4] It posits three areas of significance for analysis.

- The sign itself.
- The codes or symbol systems into which signs are organized.
- The culture in which the signs and codes acquire meaning.

Advertising, brands, tag lines and catch-phrases are all full of significance as signs and symbols. The purpose of semiotic analysis is to reveal the subtext, hidden meanings and messages that reach a subconscious level of understanding. For example, the manner in which characters in an ad position their bodies, their expressions and appearance, the manner in which they relate to others all contribute to the essential meaning that the images are communicating. The shape of a perfume bottle, for example, can signify seductive charm or classical beauty. The color, shape and brand of a piece of candy can yield multiple meanings about sweetness and flavor.

When to use

Content or text analysis is the preferred approach when analysis of written or printed texts and images is desired to complement or replace personal interviewing. This approach is particularly important in highly image-driven areas such as the analysis of beauty and fashion imagery, packaging design and in the evaluation of political campaign effectiveness.

1.7 Benefits of Qualitative Research

When clients commission a qualitative research study, they usually expect a number of substantive and practical advantages.

Deeper understanding through confrontation with the consumer

Qualitative research is a strategy for going beneath the surface. It yields a holistic overview of consumer behavior which provides insights into emotions and motivations. Most importantly, the achievement of understanding happens in real time through a personal confrontation with respondents. Insights are not channeled through graphs and statistical tables but evolve as researchers confront actual consumers.

Direct client involvement

By observing qualitative research studies, clients outside of research departments gain a degree of exposure to consumers and their attitudes not available in survey studies. For this reason, it has become very popular recently for senior executives and members of local sales forces to sit in the back room during focus group sessions. This is also useful in studies supporting advertising copy development where members of the creative team can observe direct consumer reactions to their materials and use an iterative process to refine them. An effective moderator is able to structure the interview to maximize involvement by observers.

Easy to organize

Qualitative research studies are usually easy to arrange and manage. A substantial infrastructure of research organizations is available to handle all project-related services, including recruitment of participants, group moderation, convening and taping of interviews, etc. The internal management responsibilities for the commissioning organization can thus be minimized and efforts can be focused on implementing the research findings.

Fast turnaround

Relative to other approaches, some qualitative studies can offer fast turnaround when low level decisions – such as narrowing down a series of advertising concepts through focus groups – need to be made. Most qualitative projects can be completed from approval to final report in 4-6 weeks or less if circumstances so require. Because of their complicated logistics, however, some ethnographic studies require a longer time frame.

Greater confidentiality

Group and depth interviewing can be conducted in a highly restricted number of markets and among a limited number of participants. This allows for enhanced security and less exposure of confidential business plans and compares favorably to market tests which require broadcasts or sales exposure of unfinished products.

Quality control

Qualitative research lends itself to close supervision and tight management of research providers. Since every step can be monitored, there is less likelihood that project objectives will not be respected.

Economical and cost-effective

Qualitative studies are relatively economical and cost-effective. That is not to say they are cheap! Considerable investment is involved in mobilizing the professional resources and consumer input that good qualitative research requires. Nevertheless, since samples are small and managerial time can be tightly focused, qualitative studies provide a cost-effective alternative to survey studies when either approach may be used to address research goals.

1.8 Reducing Bias and Error

Conclusions reached through qualitative data collection and analysis are likely to be denigrated as subjective, non-replicable and invalid unless the researcher takes steps to reduce errors and bias. All research methods aim toward achieving valid and reliable measures of social reality. For qualitative researchers, validity – defined as the ability to produce correct answers – and reliability, or the ability to produce the same answers repeatedly with reasonably similar measures, are related to the process of engagement between researcher and respondent.[5]

There are many who argue that the application of positivist concepts such as validity are inappropriate for qualitative research. Focus groups and other approaches tap into a dynamic and changeable reality that is distinct from that sought in survey studies.

Qualitative research aims toward a substantive validity – that is, the approach works in that it produces findings that are valuable in designing products, programs and communications. The assertion that findings are factual arises from the researcher's direct confrontation and insightful challenge to the evidence at hand. Thinking hard and not being satisfied by simple answers are part of the process. Whether qualitative findings represent the market or its segments as a whole may or may not be problematic. Determining how representative the findings are may require confirmatory research or may have to wait until experience and market performance have demonstrated their validity.

Since rules for random sampling are not followed in most qualitative studies, it is impossible to validate findings through probabilistic methods. Nevertheless, several types of controls and confirmation techniques can help to deliver the highest possible levels of validity – sufficient to help the client meet marketing objectives.

Listed below are several means of guaranteeing that conclusions reached through qualitative research can achieve a meaningful impact on brand marketing.

- *Don't promise more than can be delivered.* Qualitative research provides an important perspective on consumer behavior. However, conclusions need to be verified through other approaches if important decisions are to be based on them.
- *Select competent researchers.* Determine that the personnel conducting the research have strong methodological skills, political independence and sensitivity toward the brands, categories and respondent segments involved in the study.
- *Be objective.* No one should have a stake in any particular outcome. Management and researchers must take the risk that an idea, hypothesis or

concept may fail. An absence of partisanship must characterize relations between clients, suppliers and respondents.

- *Clarify your own assumptions and expectations.* Because researchers are fellow participants in social life and consumer behavior, they necessarily enter a study with knowledge and feelings about the category and brand. These must be set aside and not allowed to contaminate interactions with respondents. Qualitative researchers may personally dislike convenience foods, cigarettes or budget hotels but these attitudes should not distort findings about consumers of these products.

- *Use the critical eye.* Everything about a qualitative research project should be subjected to continuous critical scrutiny – respondent definition, data gathering strategies, interpretation and analysis procedures. Nothing should be taken for granted or completed without checking and rechecking, particularly if anyone has some reason to hide true feelings. The researcher should put herself through the same skepticism – how is her personality impacting the respondents; has she bonded with them; are her elicitation procedures clear; are her interpretive categories meaningful.

- *Interview enough respondents.* A sufficient number of respondents should be interviewed so that meaningful comparisons can be made between groups or individual respondents. It is difficult to determine the precise point at which 'enough' respondents are being interviewed. Approximations of the saturation point include when all variations within a segment have been considered or when the investigator has reached redundancy after hearing the same thing from repeated respondents.

- *Ensure proper screening.* Careful recruitment screening should guarantee a reasonably accurate representation of a product's targeted markets. If respondents are poorly selected, the research will not be based on real customers and conclusions based on the sample will have no value. Screening procedures should also guarantee that respondents have no prior relationships with each other, such as work associates or members of the same professional association, that may influence their roles within a focus group.

- *Hire multiple suppliers.* In highly sensitive or controversial situations, astute clients will sometimes assign parallel versions of the same project to several different research companies. If multiple unbiased investigators reach similar conclusions, the substantive validity of the findings has been strengthened.

- *Validate through interview procedures.* Because of intense involvement with respondents as both the collector and interpreter of the data, the moderator has an important role in validating the findings during the interview. Several validation techniques are listed below.

  - *Probing* involves repeated questioning and testing for the limits and conditions of a respondent's attitudes, beliefs or behaviors.

  - *Rejecting alternatives* is a type of probe, and is important to assure that alternative practices, motives or explanations are cast aside by respondents.

  - *Interpreting body language* is a way of guaranteeing that a respondent's verbal expressions are consistent with their non-verbal mannerisms. Unexpressed attitudes at variance with what people say may become apparent in averted eyes or defensive body posture.

- *Triangulation* involves asking questions in different ways at various points in the interview or seeking data through a variety of techniques – for example, direct questions and projective techniques – to validate a conclusion.

Above all, validity is supported when the data are not oversold. Inappropriate inferences such as estimates of market outcomes, and major marketing decisions such as the distribution of advertising media should not be based solely on evidence from qualitative research.

1.9 Inappropriate Uses

Several situations do not call for qualitative research approaches. Implementing studies under these circumstances can constitute an ethical lapse or an abuse.

Statistical projections

Qualitative research is not appropriate where market measurement and statistical projections are required. Some examples of these situations are listed below.

Estimates of market characteristics, including market size and segmentation

Studies of this type require a sufficiently large sample size to allow reliable estimates of population characteristics. These estimates also depend upon the assumption of random sampling so that respondent selection is excluded as a rival hypothesis for observed results. Qualitative approaches can provide insights into market segments by explaining the alternative grounds and meanings of product usage and choice. They can, for example, describe the differences between value shoppers and premium shoppers in a category.

Estimates of market acceptance, such as forecasts of product trial, market share or market penetration

Forecasting models also depend upon large sample size and random sampling. From a probability perspective small sample sizes in forecasts are highly unstable. Qualitative research, on the other hand, offers a necessary perspective on product purchase motivations and dynamics, without which most forecasts have little meaning.

Strategic pricing decisions

Pricing decisions depend upon an understanding of the interrelations between demand, price and the underlying costs of production. These relationships are best expressed through mathematical models. Qualitative research cannot deliver more than an understanding of consumers' perceptions of value – and even these can be highly unreliable due to small non-random samples. Furthermore, focus groups have a tendency to degrade into wishful thinking and unreasonable demands in discussions of pricing. Group thinking often yields the lowest possible price and highest level of promotion.

Cost/benefit trade-offs

As above, qualitative studies can provide insight into consumers' sense of value associated with alternative ingredients, packaging, components, etc. However, here, too, mathematical models accounting for incremental production costs should be considered.

Winners in the marketplace

Qualitative research provides a sense of how well consumers regard a new product or service or how effective a communications approach may be in speaking about the product. Unfortunately, the setting offers only a hermetically sealed environment for decision making. In the 'real world' marketplace, sales factors cannot be controlled. They are much more vulnerable to competitors' product and communications initiatives, to the vagaries of economic cycles and other factors which influence market outcomes.

Media weight and frequency decisions

Qualitative research can yield insights into how well certain types of messages may communicate via various types of media. It can help demonstrate how market segments use the media. However, frequency and weight decisions need more careful market modeling.

Decision making

The use of qualitative research in making business decisions is very controversial. Some would argue that any kind of information, even though it may be anecdotal and non-replicable, is better than making decisions without any consumer input, using only the managerial intuition. Others insist that decisions need to be made only on the basis of precise mathematical measurement with clear guidelines on the probabilistic parameters of various choice options.

Regardless of one's position between these two extremes, the right way to use qualitative information for decision making is an open question. Obviously, no source of information is infallible, thus, several considerations should be addressed before basing a decision on any type of research data.

- Is there enough information.
- Has it been collected and analyzed in a disciplined manner.
- How confident are you in the validity and reliability of the information.
- What risks are associated with the decision.

In this context, some commentators complain that qualitative research is often taken too seriously or not taken seriously enough. Here are examples of how qualitative research can impact decisions.

- Management may narrow down a large number of concepts to the most desirable ones because they understand the reasons, grounds and conditions behind consumer preferences.
- Packaging or product design may be modified because research-based observations of consumers interacting with the product demonstrates various problems. Qualitative research can consequently provide decision making guidelines for product refinement and improvement.
- An understanding of consumer lifestyles or culture based on qualitative research findings can lead to the design of products that are more satisfying and manifest a better fit with emerging consumer needs.

Pragmatics vs. substance

The primary consideration in selecting a methodology should be its appropriateness for the research issues to be addressed. Unfortunately, sometimes the fact that qualitative studies are less costly or faster to implement has too much bearing on the choice of method. Studies that need to be carried out in five or six countries before a reasonable decision can be made should not be trimmed to one or two without an appreciation of the extra risks being absorbed. Selecting the wrong research approach for the decision being made can have a destructive impact on marketing plans. Any organization's planning cycle should allow for sufficient time to design and implement a sufficient program of research.

SECTION 2

Managing Qualitative Research

- Understanding internal client needs
- Developing a useful project brief
- Determining clear project objectives
- Project planning
- Project budgeting
- Global fieldwork
- Locating, comparing and selecting research firms and moderators
- Locating and selecting field facilities
- Conducting research in homes and offices
- Other resources
- Recruitment issues and concerns
- Creating an effective and foolproof screener
- Quality management of screening

2.1 Understanding Internal Client Needs

Qualitative research projects usually are undertaken by a corporate service group charged with handling consumer research and market intelligence. Alternatively, projects may be managed by an advertising or consulting agency on behalf of the client company. The *research project manager* is the key individual charged with coordinating all aspects of project communication and implementation. He or she is responsible for being the link between the internal decision centers that are commissioning the project and the internal and external resources that are being mobilized to execute the project. The research project manager is also in charge of communicating the findings in usable form at the conclusion of the study.

The first step in managing a qualitative research project is to understand the information needs required by the internal clients that are raising questions and presumably funding the study. The research issues may be originating in a marketing or communications group, in operations or through senior management. The need for information may be arising at the corporate level, in a specific business unit or within an overseas subsidiary or affiliate. Regardless of which level is sponsoring the study, it is helpful to review several issues with the internal decision maker.

- What strategic or tactical goals are generating the need for the research.
- Precisely what type of information is the research expected to turn up.
- How will the information gained through the research be used. That is, what forward actions will be taken; which knowledge gaps are expected to be clarified. How will the information contribute to decision making.
- What methods have been used in the past to study these issues and what gaps have they left.
- What alternative research information is available to address the issues at hand, for example, through secondary analysis of existing information or available syndicated studies.
- What are the budget parameters.
- What time frame must be respected.
- In what reporting format will research information be most helpful.

The answers to these issues will influence several decisions that need to be made before the project is initiated. These same answers will also guide the development of a Market Research Request for Proposal and a *supplier brief* which, in turn, guides implementation of the research.

Questions preceding research execution

Answers to several important questions should be ascertained before research projects are initiated. Resolving these issues will lend direction and focus to the project once it is begun.

Should the research be conducted

If there are sources of information that can be reused, there is no need for a new custom study. Alternatively, if the available information is out-of-date or no longer relevant, a fresh study should be undertaken. The viable life of a research study, depending on the category, brand and targeted segment, is 1-5 years. Also, if there is insufficient time to act on findings or too meager a budget to support acquisition of the information as requested, internal clients should revisit their need for decision support.

Research should be conducted only if it will supply information that is necessary for product development and marketing decisions. This needed input may take several forms, including:

- Information about purchase and usage of a product that is needed for product development or reformulation.
- Information about consumers' expectations, emotions, etc. to guide strategic marketing and communications development.

What is the most appropriate methodology for conducting the research

Qualitative research is called for when the objectives are *exploratory* or *explanatory*. Some of the primary applications are to:

- Gain background information, such as information about actual consumer product usage situations.
- Understand motivations, contexts and conditions behind product usage.
- Explore the cultural dimensions of product usage including information about ethnic, regional and demographic differences.
- Generate hypotheses or learn the right questions to ask in a larger survey. Qualitative studies are useful for comprehension checks and to test for non-apparent sources of bias in the ways larger studies are conceptualized and executed.
- Gain further insights into survey findings.
- Generate new ideas.
- Learn about consumer intentions.
- Analyze behavioral processes.
- Discover feelings and emotional meanings regarding products.
- Learn consumer language.
- Test comprehension of written marketing materials.
- Conduct a 'disaster check' of copy and images.

In contrast, quantitative research is called for when results are desired that help researchers to:

- Learn about the overall size and segmentation of markets.
- Conduct precise measurement.
- Analyze findings which can be projected within specific confidence limits to a larger sampling frame.
- Receive consistent data from a large number of people.
- Create and project from statistical models of behavior.
- Estimate sales and optimize pricing.
- Monitor comparable statistics at different points in time.
- Make evaluative decisions or judgments.

What type of an in-house or outside research supplier would best handle research execution

There are a variety of reasons for managing the research in-house vs. assigning the project to an outside research company. Listed below are several considerations that might enter into a management decision. First are listed some reasons to conduct the project in-house.

Cost savings By leveraging internal human resources rather than retaining an outside supplier, the company can avoid incremental costs. On the other hand, consideration of cost should be evaluated in relation to the practical skills, time availability and objectivity of internal personnel. The final equation may not necessarily favor internal personnel as the most cost-effective method.

Efficient turnaround There are time savings associated with avoiding outside suppliers – the need to obtain comparative bids, briefing the moderator, coordinating schedules with an outside firm, etc. On the other hand, if necessary skills will need to be acquired by internal personnel before executing the project, the efficiency equation may actually favor an outside supplier.

Product expertise Internal staff can be expected to be 'up to speed' and more readily in connection with brands and categories that they handle on a day-to-day basis. On the other hand, professional qualitative researchers can be trusted to spend considerable time gaining product expertise through readings and briefings prior to project execution.

Confidentiality Some projects may be too risky to assign to an outside supplier even if they are under a confidentiality agreement. These may occur in highly competitive categories and in studies involving the introduction of new technologies.

Corporate culture Many organizations prefer to use inside researchers for certain types of small scale or early stage projects. In this case, management should pay careful attention to the possibility of 'groupthink' and destructive politics which can thwart needed innovation and creativity.

In general, it is preferable to contract the project with an outside vendor unless there are compelling reasons to restrict the execution in-house. The following are reasons for using an outside vendor.

Methodological expertise Outside vendors are skilled in determining the best methods and approaches for data collection. They tend to practice their methodological skills on a regular basis, thus bringing greater competence to a project. Because they usually handle a wide range of product categories and consumer types, professionals can bring insights from other areas to the specific problems at hand. On the other hand, a supplier with a limited repertoire of methodological talents may have a stake in selling his own tools to the exclusion of any others, whether or not the study requires them.

Professionalism Committed to research as a profession, outside vendors are generally more adept and subtle at executing qualitative research techniques. They also have wider experience, deeper commitment and leverage in selecting and managing fieldwork subcontractors. In tough situations, outside vendors have a broader base of knowledge and relationships to draw from.

Objectivity By hiring an outside firm, the client can take advantage of a third-party outside perspective. Internal managers can become so emotionally involved in a product development or marketing project that they lose their critical sense. Insiders may be restricted by political allegiances and social obligations in speaking the truth. An outside resource can help to restore balance.

Political independence Outsiders have more freedom to make recommendations regardless of internal pressures. This is not to say that outsiders are entirely neutral and free from political restraints. Indeed, continued client satisfaction and even maintaining a client relationship may force them to silence inhibitions and objections. Companies should pay close attention to whether internal political dynamics may be creating a culture of 'yes-men' for hire unable to speak their minds due to fear of political players who put their own egos and self-interest ahead of corporate goals.

Fast turnaround Internal managers normally have multiple projects and responsibilities which reduce the time they can devote to executing research. They tend to be more vulnerable to the organization's bureaucratic requirements, too, and have responsibilities for preparing budgets, managing staff and consulting to other corporate units. In such situations, outside suppliers can usually turn projects around more quickly and efficiently than in-house staff. Of course, this should also be balanced against the multiple project responsibilities that the preferred vendor may carry. Sometimes, popular qualitative researchers cannot devote sufficient time and attention to an extra complex project because they are beholden to other clients who are giving them more revenue or being more insistent in their demands.

2.2 Developing a Useful Project Brief

After the research manager is satisfied that internal client needs are understood and that the questions preceding research execution have been addressed, the next step is to lay out a *project brief*. Even though it does not need to be lengthy, an effective project brief is an important management tool. It creates a consistent set of expectations which research managers can use in obtaining competitive proposals from vendors. It also provides a set of guidelines to measure the progress and effectiveness of the research process. And it is a way of closing the feedback loop at the end of the study and evaluating the degree to which strategic information has been acquired or continues to be needed.

A project brief should contain several elements that are essential in conducting consistent discussions about the study. Listed below are the categories which should be included and the questions that should be answered in a project brief.

- *Situation analysis* What is the current status of the brand and the category. Which are the major competitors and how are they strategically positioned. How has the brand evolved over time. What factors are driving the need for change vs. stability in the brand.
- *Marketing objectives* How will the research impact the brand's strategic directions. Are findings and conclusions expected to drive new flavors or varieties, a shift in the targeted consumer, new communications directions, alternative media for reaching customers.
- *Project objectives* What are the specific information needs that the research is expected to resolve.
- *Methods* What approaches do you expect will be used, such as focus groups, IDIs, etc. The methods section should also discuss:
  - How many focus groups, IDIs, etc. should be convened.
  - Targeted respondents, or who should be recruited for participation. How will these characteristics be operationally defined. For example, brand users can be defined in different ways – those who have purchased within the past three months, consumed within the previous week, etc.
  - Preferred locations, including which countries and/or markets should receive attention.
  - Research issues, or what areas would you like to explore with consumers.
- *Timetable* What are the turnaround expectations for the project. What dates are driving the need for information, such as the deadline for an advertising plan, a presentation to senior management, etc.
- *Deliverables* In what form do you want the research information submitted – a full report, in-person presentation, etc. Who should receive the results and in what format.

- *Budget* What is the maximum investment that will be made for this project. You may or may not want to reveal this figure to your suppliers.

The next several sections will provide additional details on the thinking necessary for the preparation of useful project briefs. The Appendix at the end of this book contains a form for developing a project brief.

2.3 Determining Clear Project Objectives

Executing research is simplified if the manager establishes a clear set of research objectives at the outset. The statement of objectives represents ground zero – the starting point against which all other elements of planning and implementation must be measured. A useful set of objectives has a number of characteristics that shape all of the details, including the respondent screener and discussion guide. Here are some guidelines for developing a statement of objectives.

- *Express in terms of outcomes.* The results emerging from a study have a direct relationship to expectations at the start. The statement of objectives should aim to describe precisely the kind of information needed at the end of the process. Rather than seeking generalities such as, 'a better understanding of consumer needs', the goal should be concrete, for example, 'ideas for products that consumers would be willing to buy if they were available in the marketplace'.
- *Focus on information.* Be specific about the facts that will guide your decision making.
- *Prioritize.* Clarity about what *needs* to be known as opposed to what would be nice to know is helpful in guiding the analysis process. If reports and memos have to be prepared in a hurry, a clear understanding of priorities will economize the expenditure of scarce time.
- *Use it to impact decisions.* An ideal statement of objectives anticipates the expected use of the research in decision making. A consultant who knows how the analysis will be applied is better able to maintain focus and direction. For example, objectives should state if the research wants to discover alternative ways of describing a new dairy spread that will be further evaluated in a sample survey.

Cautions in framing objectives

In order to be prepared for contingencies, there are also some cautions to keep in mind while writing the statement of objectives.

- *Allow for surprises.* Statements of objectives should not be framed so narrowly that the research misses unanticipated findings. As Spier says, '...there are also things you don't even know you want to know. It can be magic when these findings emerge' (1993b: 14).
- *Avoid unwarranted assumptions.* Don't under- or overestimate the importance consumers attach to the brand or how involved they are in the decision process. Research investments are sometimes wasted when a segment believed to have a great deal of involvement in some purchase

decision ends up being minimally involved. On the other hand, this may be an important finding which saves marketing investments down the road.
- *Be sure your objectives are appropriate to the brand's marketing requirements.* Needless research investments are often made by managers who execute projects prematurely. For example, a positioning study commissioned before adequate competitive intelligence or market segmentation information is known can lead to spurious or incomplete results.
- *Make sure the objectives are appropriate to the study's scope.* By necessity, qualitative research studies are limited in scope and application. Research managers and consultants should understand that global and comprehensive research objectives, such as 'understanding American health care patterns', cannot be met by a few focus groups or depth interviews in a limited geographic range and covering a small sampling frame.

Common research objectives

Research objectives that are generally appropriate for qualitative studies include those that describe current or expected users in ways that will help the brand achieve its marketing goals, for example:
- Reasons for selecting brands or products.
- Benefits consumers expect.
- Who makes purchase decisions and the process by which that decision is negotiated.
- How products are actually used or consumed.
- How brands or products fit into consumers' daily lives.
- Emotional connections to brands or what brands *mean* to consumers.
- Factors that will promote changes in brand or product loyalties and preferences.
- Communication elements associated with positive affect toward the brand.
- Reactions to proposed new product concepts.

Several other details related to project objectives should be considered and shared with the consultant. These are reviewed below.

Situation analysis

Sharing the background behind a study is necessary to prepare both internal and external personnel. Here is a list of questions that should be treated in a situation analysis.
- What is the current status of the brand or proposed product.
- How is it competitively positioned.
- Who are its principal users. What demographic trends are influencing current users, for example, are they getting older; are tastes changing. In what ways is usage expected to grow.
- What have been its marketing and advertising strategies.

- What current social trends are influencing both usage and attitudes toward the brand and category.
- Who are the brand's principal competitors.
- What are the brand's and the competition's share and sales histories.
- What marketing strategies, such as positioning, advertising and communications, have been used by the brand and the competition.
- How mature is the brand or category in its product life cycle.
- What research information is currently available.
- What research is being planned in the future and where does this project fit into the overall research program.
- What are the importance of decisions or forward actions based upon the research.

Being aware of your current situation helps the research manager orient execution appropriately and plan for filling in information gaps.

Marketing goals

The most important question that must precede any research study is the strategic one: Where would management like to take the brand?

- *For an existing brand* What changes are anticipated for the brand. How and to what extent is it expected to grow. What marketplace dynamics are spurring change and continuity in the ways that the brand is marketed.
- *For a new product* How will the product fill a gap in the marketplace. Who are its expected users. For what purposes will the product be used. What is the compelling rationale – the 'unique selling proposition' for the brand.

In summary, establishing clear project objectives helps to guide all of the study's implementation details, which are described in the next several sections. Above all, managers should clarify what decisions will be impacted by the information and how the information will be used. If there are specific questions that managers want asked, this is the time to initiate precise formulation of the questionnaire. If there are particular details that managers will want covered in the final report, this is the time to specify them.

2.4 Project Planning

Project planning is accomplished interactively between research managers and suppliers after setting the objectives. The process can be made simpler and more efficient if the research manager starts with a tentative set of expectations and assumptions regarding the execution details. These can be discussed and elaborated in discussions with prospective or actual vendors. The areas that should be covered in these planning discussions are reviewed in this section.

Project management approach

There are several different approaches to managing the research project. Usually, the client contracts with an independent moderator or qualitative research company who subcontracts the field service and other suppliers. This is the most common approach to managing a qualitative research project. In international studies, the client usually contracts with a single lead company that will either obtain local suppliers within a known network or otherwise put together a group of local independent agencies to execute the project. Rather than using a lead agency, some clients prefer to contract the services of preferred suppliers in each of the individual countries that are being included in the study.

Alternatively, the client may wish to contract with field services and have them obtain moderators. Unless the field service is well-known for strong consulting skills or has ties to a set of good qualitative researchers, this can be a risky or self-defeating approach because the client has minimal control over the moderator who normally has the central role in developing the conclusions.

The client may contract the moderators and field services separately. Although there is some degree of added control in this situation, there is also a higher level of accountability and responsibility. Some qualitative researchers may be cheered by not having to maintain financial accountability for the field portion of the study; on the other hand, they may feel their work is compromised if the field services selected by the client do not match their own quality standards.

Preferred research methods and techniques

The client and the qualitative research firm should jointly determine what methods, tools and techniques will be applied. Different qualitative companies have varying experience with specific techniques, such as special skills in new product or brand consulting. The search for an appropriate supplier should focus on the company's competence at executing the techniques research managers believe will answer the research questions that the internal clients have presented. Most experienced moderators, however, have skills in a broad range of techniques. Thus, someone familiar with the product category or consumer segments can be sure to provide strong support regardless of techniques applied.

Research managers should be wary of research agencies that are so wedded to a single set of techniques that they advocate an approach that is inappropriate to the study's objectives.

Targeted respondents

Determining the targeted respondents in a study constitutes one of the most critical areas of project planning. Choosing appropriate respondents has implications for pricing as well as for the validity of the entire research since if the wrong respondents are selected, the ultimate findings have little meaning. People recruited for participation in the study should either reflect the expected consumers of the product or service, or they should be from a group who will be targeted in the media program. There are several ways to conceptualize consumer segments.

- Demographic targets defined by gender, age and household characteristics, such as women aged 18-39, mothers of children under 15, persons about to move into a new residence, etc.
- Core users of a brand or category, such as those who use the Internet for at least one hour and visit at least three different web sites each day, or persons who regularly use a stomach remedy such as Zantac™ or Tagamet™.
- Persons who favor particular sales channels for acquiring various goods and services, for example, people who purchase at least $200 worth of clothing through direct mail catalogs.
- Current non-users of goods, services or trade channels who are possibly being targeted for line extensions.
- Persons with specific lifestyle characteristics, such as those who work out of their homes or take family vacations using their own automobile.
- Attitudinal segments, for example, people who are environmentally concerned or who are seeking to improve their health through nutrition and exercise.
- People who think of themselves as 'creative' – an expectation often made for participants in studies requiring innovative thinking and problem solving.

Regardless of the types of segmentation applied to target respondents in a study, research managers and consultants should challenge themselves with several substantive issues which go to the heart of the study's purpose and objectives. These are reviewed below.

- *Are the right participants being targeted.* A common mistake is to define the target too narrowly or too broadly or to seek those without actual decision making authority. It is sometimes disappointing, for example, to complete a set of focus groups only to discover that the targeted segment was not involved in brand or category decisions.

- *Is the research targeting actionable for strategy.* Research becomes just an intellectual exercise if the findings cannot be translated to a marketing or media strategy.
- *Does segment differentiation allow a clear understanding of motivational differences.* When the definition of the targeted respondents is too complex, it is difficult to evaluate the major causal factors in a finding. For example, a recent focus group study of nutritional supplements required segments that were differentiated by an interaction of age, chronic disease status, employment status and health related attitudes. Although meaningful differences were uncovered, it was difficult to trace them to any particular one or all of these characteristics.
- *What is the optimal number of respondents in the group.* In the US, while ten participants have been the norm, evidence suggests that sessions are shrinking and increasingly conforming to the European standard. When a high level of technical information will be exchanged in the session, for example in a group with doctors, lawyers or engineers, it is helpful to reduce the size even more – possibly to five or six – and to consider lengthening the amount of time devoted to the interview.

Respondent differentiation

Determining how the focus groups or depth interviews should differ from each other is a critical decision that will have a strong bearing on findings and conclusions. Normally, previous knowledge or study hypotheses should lead research management to expect that some types of respondents would hold divergent views regarding the issues being discussed.

Structuring a high degree of homogeneity within focus groups allows differences among various consumer types to be highlighted. In studies based upon depth interviews or ethnographic site visits, diversity can be structured across the range of consumer types included in the study. Some of the types of differentiation used by focus groups and one-on-ones include:

- Age segments, such as 'younger' vs. 'older' categories, which may vary depending on the product category.
- Men vs. women.
- Product usage vs. non-usage, or 'customers' vs. 'prospects'.
- Regional segmentation, such as high volume vs. low volume markets, or rural vs. urban.
- Subcultural differences between different regions, such as Northern vs. Southern Italy, Central Spain vs. Catalunya or Galicia vs. Andalucia.
- Lifestyle and demographic segments, for example, working vs. non-working women, or households with children vs. households without children.
- Attitudinal segmentation, for example, brand loyalists vs. price shoppers, fashion conscious vs. non-fashion conscious.
- Channel usage, such as those who purchase from a web site vs. retail stores.
- Any other characteristic that management believes will make a critical difference in purchase or usage dynamics.

Dealing with divergent status

It is normally not a good idea to mix respondents with highly divergent verbal skills, levels of preparation or hierarchical social relations in the same session because it is difficult to avoid having these status indicators affect personal responses and group dynamics. For example, it is not helpful to mix employees and their bosses in a session because both may be inhibited about seeming intelligent and authoritative in a different context.

Mixing husbands and wives in the same focus group may also present complications unless they are involved in a joint purchase, for example a home or vacation destination, and the research objective is oriented toward learning about their negotiation and decision making process.

Preferred recruitment methods

As we will see in later sections, there are a variety of recruitment methods that can be applied in a qualitative study – telephone, face-to-face, by referrals, etc. Research managers often raise the question but allow their local suppliers to make the final decision about recruitment strategy. In the United States, for example, most recruitment is conducted by telephone from respondent databases; in Europe, recruitment is typically accomplished through face-to-face recruitment at busy public streets. Differences in local recruitment practices are important insofar as they may not allow exact replication of approach in multi-country studies. Consequently, this factor should be considered when coordinating projects internationally.

Geographic distribution

The interviews' locations also constitute a critical planning decision. The basic question to address is which markets are best suited for the research objectives. Some considerations that often guide the selection of research sites are listed here.

- *Convenience* How convenient is the location for observation by brand managers, ad agency or other interested observers. Sometimes companies prefer to hold interviews close to headquarters because of the belief that it will result in cost savings – since little or no travel is involved. Unfortunately, nearby cities may be unrepresentative of the marketplace as whole. Sometimes local respondents are overused or oversensitive to the brand name behind the study and consider it their civic duty not to criticize the home team.
- *Geographic differentiation* A project objective may be to evaluate differences in purchase dynamics in diverse geographic regions. Normally, however, qualitative research is an inefficient tool for getting a clear measurement of regional differences. Exploratory stage qualitative insights should be confirmed through disciplined survey research.

- *Resource availability* Travel to particular facilities may be necessary to gain access to special resources such as a 'living room' style interview room or special video equipment.
- *Targeted populations* Clients often prefer particular locations because they represent a high volume market or a competitor's best market. Some markets are selected for their high representation of various demographic or lifestyle targets, for example, South Florida or Arizona may be chosen for their representation of seniors and retirees; California for persons highly involved with the Internet; New York, London and Paris for fashion and trend-conscious consumers.
- *Seasonal contingencies* Weather patterns in different continents, regions and countries may create opportunities as well as risks that the project may not be executed conveniently. For example, the Northeast and Midwest United States may be subjected to snow emergencies during January and February; research in continental Europe during the summer months will be complicated by the lengthy vacation season.

Number of interviews

Determining how many depth interviews, site visits or focus groups are enough to achieve research objectives is another profound point of planning discussions. Most studies are effectively conducted with four, six or eight focus groups or 15-30 individual in-depth interviews (IDIs). In general, it is not recommended to conduct studies with only one or two focus groups or fewer than ten IDIs. Similarly, studies with more than ten focus groups or fifty IDIs tend to be unwieldy, difficult to analyze and not cost-effective.

Nevertheless, to test for adequacy it is appropriate to answer the questions of *comparability* and *comprehensiveness*, in other words:

- Are there enough participants and segments represented in the study so meaningful comparisons can educate the analysis of findings.
- Are all of the potential segments that are significant to project objectives being represented in the research.

Length of time

The norm in the US is to have sessions run two hours in length, the European standard is for somewhat longer sessions – three, even four or five hours. The advantages of brevity include increased efficiency, greater moderator and observer alertness and lesser costs associated with facility rental and respondent incentives.

The advantages of extended groups, on the other hand, include:

- More time for exploration of complex feelings.
- Extension of opportunities for cultivating rapport and stimulating group solidarity.
- More time for creative expression and completion of projective exercises.
- More time to review a large number of concepts.

One factor that should influence the decision about session length is group composition. Sessions longer than one hour, for example, are experienced as tiresome by children. Executives and professionals may have competing responsibilities that reduce willingness to cooperate beyond a certain length of time.

If a session is longer than two hours, it should provide for frequent bathroom and smoking breaks. The guide should also guarantee variety and diversion in the session's proceedings.

Pre-tasking

It is increasingly popular for studies to involve subjects in a sensitizing activity prior to the conduct of the sessions. The product of the preparatory task is typically discussed at some point in the session. If managed well, the pre-tasking exercise can add a level of depth and excitement to an interview session, and guarantees better oriented and more highly involved participants.

Studies involving pre-tasking always require extra preparation time and additional research consultant involvement throughout all stages – preparation, administration, follow-up, and analysis of the exercise. It also requires a substantially higher respondent incentive than studies without pre-tasking.

Several common forms of preparatory exercises include:

- *Product placements* Samples of a test product are placed with a consumer and they are expected to use it some number of times over the test period.
- *Diaries* Written and visual (photo) diaries are often used to get respondents to record the satisfactions and dissatisfactions involved in some aspect of product usage. For example, they may create a record of their experiences doing the laundry, preparing a meal or using the telephone. Researchers may request that they represent accustomed habits, or respondents may be presented with altogether novel tasks to complete. If diaries are employed, they need to be carefully structured. Respondents need highly specific instructions and it is helpful to make reminder calls to check for accurate record keeping at several points during the diary period.
- *Creation of stimuli* It may be effective to have respondents create and bring visual stimuli that will be used in exercises during the focus group. For example, have them bring photographs of family members, pets, an area of the home that they hate to clean or a particularly soiled item of clothing. The availability of inexpensive one-time-use cameras and one-hour processing has allowed researchers to let their imaginations run wild. Alternatively, they may be encouraged to bring an item from home representing a brand they use – a toothbrush, a bottle of vitamins, etc.
- *Media usage, store visits, etc.* Respondents may be encouraged to watch certain types of television commercials, read several fashion magazines or visit a store at which they do not normally shop in order to get prepared for the session.

Time of day

Decisions about scheduling the time of day for interviews should reflect the needs and convenience of targeted respondents. Most focus groups and one-on-one in-depth interviews are conducted in the evening – starting from 5:30 or 6:00 pm. This allows working people and those actively involved in child care to be relieved of their primary responsibilities and to undertake travel to the research location. Research managers should exercise caution in trying to schedule sessions that are not convenient to most respondents in the category because they may end up with an unrepresentative subset of subjects. For example, teachers and nurses are often available for late afternoon groups because their daily schedule allows this type of flexibility; nevertheless, relying upon only these respondents will result in subtle biases that may affect conclusions.

Depending on the targeted respondent, there may be opportunities to conduct research sessions at other times of the day, such as at breakfast or lunch time. Senior executives and business managers, for example, often favor an early morning session.

Time of day issues are critical in studies involving site visits to the respondent's home or place of work. Special attention should be paid to guaranteeing that the time of the visit coincides with the time of day that respondents are accustomed to using a particular product. For example, a recent study which targeted diabetes patients for a study of blood glucose measuring devices had to make sure that visits were conducted when respondents were actually using their equipment.

Research issues

Research managers should prepare a brief outline of the objectives and research issues to be covered in the study. Although qualitative consultants will be expected to prepare meaningful discussion guides or topic outlines for the sessions, outlining the issues that management would like to see addressed during the interviews helps to provide a framework for project planning discussions.

Timing

The project's timing should be driven by the internal client's information demands. However, research managers should plan realistically for executing each step of the process. Various steps of the process will require coordination with both internal staff and subcontractors – many of which will have competing demands for their attention. Rushing through a project can threaten research quality; on the other hand, the need for timely marketing information may require research managers to complete projects expeditiously. Project managers should discuss timing issues with their vendors prior to making commitments to internal clients. Business managers also should be educated about some of the logistical entanglements that may bedevil qualitative research assignments so as to help them temper expectations and demands.

The table below provides some guidelines for scheduling parameters.

Table 2 Project timing outline.

Task	Time required
Obtaining and evaluating proposals from research companies	1 – 2 weeks
Preparation and approval of recruitment screeners and discussion guides	1 week
Recruitment of participants	2 weeks
Conducting interviews in three markets	1 – 2 weeks
Preparation of toplines or summary reports	1 week
Preparation of full report	3 weeks
Total project	6 – 10 weeks

Deliverables

During the planning stage, research managers should develop clear expectations of the form in which they will want the final deliverables from the suppliers. A variety of conventional data recording and interpretation formats are generally available from qualitative research companies; however, these are often open to interpretation and negotiation. Some clients have strict policies about formats for final deliverables from suppliers; others leave this decision to the particular project or business manager.

There are advantages and disadvantages associated with the type of report that is expected from outside consultants. Minimal reporting is less costly and takes less time to complete. On the other hand, this places a greater onus on the research manager to deliver information in actionable form to internal clients. Extensive reports are expensive and time consuming; however, this permits the broadest scope for consultant insights. In the latter case, the research manager may still be responsible for preparing written briefs and memoranda for internal research users but he or she now has access to a richer body of detail.

Reports and presentations

Project deliverables generally take the form of reports and presentations, normally in one of the forms listed below.

Topline or executives summary Length: 2-5 pages. Content: a review of major findings and implications, recommendations for forward actions. Basis: top-of-mind recall of sessions' content; debrief of client observers; notes taken during session. Use of verbatims: usually has none or just a few.

Summary report Length: brief 15-20 page analysis. Content: attention to most significant and actionable findings emerging from the study, recommendations for forward actions with some explanation. Basis: recall, notes, debrief, limited review of interview tapes. Use of verbatims: select quotes to support key points.

Full report Length: 25 pages and up. Content: full coverage of session details, complete description of methodology, usually includes an executive summary outlining key findings and recommendations. Basis: detailed analysis of interview transcripts and exercises. Use of verbatims: comprehensive review of representative verbatims for all topic areas of the study.

Oral presentation Clients sometimes require their consultants to deliver an oral presentation of findings and conclusions to research, brand and/or senior management. The bullet-point style used by presentation software packages such as PowerPoint has become popular as both a talk-along resource during oral presentations and, in printed-out form, as a style for delivering summary reports. Supplier presentations allow for delivering firsthand findings to internal clients in a way that allows them to challenge and probe the conclusions.

Video presentation Video presentations have recently become a popular format for delivering qualitative research conclusions. This presentation format allows for a review of findings supported by scenes depicting consumer discussion during focus groups and/or material recorded during ethnographic site visits. The process of editing videotapes and producing a quality video presentation can take from two to four weeks, depending on the amount of raw videotaped footage that needs to be summarized.

Computer presentations As presentation software has grown more sophisticated, computer generated slide presentations are now readily available as are other alternative formats that utilize animation, and desktop video and audio.

Data collection

Most clients expect the consultant to deliver some primary data collection materials along with the final report. These are kept as an internal resource for further study and analysis or for presentation to internal audiences. The following types of materials are generally available as a courtesy or for an extra processing fee.

Audiotapes Facilities routinely audiotape all interviews. An extra set of tapes is generally made as a backup and is usually available to clients immediately.

Videotapes Facilities routinely provide for videotaping of interviews. There are two ways of doing the taping. Stationary video uses a fixed camera that photographs the entire conference room at once. Custom video provides a videographer who does close-ups of participants as they are speaking. The latter, as expected, is more costly since a skilled technician must be used to operate the recording equipment.

Transcripts and field notes It is sometimes helpful to have an exact transcript made during the interview or from the audiotapes after the interviews are completed. Alternatively, managers may find it helpful to order 'field notes' which, in contrast to an exact transcript, provide only important points and selected participant verbatims. These services are generally optional and will require additional fees.

Exercise materials Many research managers find it useful to keep on file copies of all notes, drawings, etc., that respondents complete as exercises conducted during the interviews. These can be repeatedly mined at later times for new ideas.

Internal distribution

Research managers at the planning stage should carefully consider how they will manage the distribution of the research results to the internal clients or to other interested parties such as the advertising or public relations agency. Some marketers require research staff to complete an internal brief or memorandum at the conclusion of a study; others expect that consultant reports will be passed along.

Storage requirements

This detail should be discussed during the planning phase. All suppliers should be expected to maintain complete project files for at least one year following the completion of the project. Maintenance of files beyond this limit should be discussed at the outset. It is appropriate for the consultant to charge a fee for files kept or retrieved beyond the one year window.

Project planning checklist

The table below provides a checklist that may be used in project planning. Before obtaining supplier proposals, research managers should have considered and prepared themselves to answer questions about each of the following issues.

Table 3 Project planning checklist.

Item	✓
Project objectives	
Project management approach	
Principal research issues	
Preferred research methods	
Targeted respondents	
Preferred recruitment methods	

Item	✓
Number of interviews	
Time of day for interviewing	
Respondent differentiation	
Geographic distribution of interviews	
Timing demands	
Expected deliverables	
Internal distribution needs	
Storage requirements	

2.5 Project Budgeting

This section reviews considerations that should be made regarding budgets for qualitative research studies. In budgeting for a project, the research manager should realistically consider all of the cost factors inherent in the research process. Understanding all of the costs that are generated in carrying out research will allow research managers to provide better feedback to their own internal clients about investments required for qualitative projects. Fully comprehending costs also provides research managers with a better understanding of vendor proposals and invoices as they are delivered.

Moderator's fee

Some qualitative research suppliers charge a flat fee for all of the services they provide, some charge on an hourly basis while still others charge separately for each service component. The project-related efforts for which moderators expect compensation include most or all of the following:
- Attending briefings and other meetings.
- Writing the recruitment screener.
- Developing questionnaires, the discussion guide or topic outline.
- Developing special research tools for the engagement, such as written exercises, picture sorts, etc.
- Conducting the focus groups, depth interviews, site visits, etc.
- Analyzing the interviews and exercise results.
- Writing the report of findings and recommendations.
- Delivering presentations.
- Managing and financing subcontractors conducting the fieldwork, videotaping, etc.

Besides these direct project expenses, generally moderators will also want compensation for:
- Overhead, including office, business services and staff expenses incurred in operating the business.
- Travel time.
- Special equipment, such as extra computers or display hardware.

Whenever research managers are considering a supplier's proposal or comparing bids from several companies, it is best to understand the basis on which they are charging their fees. Some moderators have a closed fee structure which sets a cap on charges; others have an open structure which charges for time allocations beyond a set number of hours. Be certain that you are making fair comparisons and that no hidden charges will appear at the end.

In contracting for a project, research managers should endeavor to make the moderator as much of a partner in the process as possible. A promise of confidentiality should be secured in writing. Background readings and other information, including previous research studies, will make the moderator as well-informed as possible about the entire context of the project. This will produce numerous benefits at the end of the study when the analysis and forward recommendations are delivered.

Field services

In continental Europe and Asia, qualitative research companies commonly run their own in-house field services to manage participant recruitment and provide viewing facilities for staging interviews. In the United States and United Kingdom, however, independent moderators and qualitative research consultants are generally responsible for selecting and managing external field services (sometimes known as recruiters or data collection companies). Even if the field service has an internal moderating staff or makes referrals to regularly used moderators, the service will still be utilized primarily by other independent companies. The services offered by field organizations, which should be reflected in project budgets, can be broken down into several categories.

- Manage facility rental, which may require a viewing room, conference table, test kitchen, etc.
- Oversee on-site services including audiotaping, hosting and reception, providing pencils and paper for participants and observers and supplying easel pads, which are usually included in the rental fee.
- Recruit participants according to written specifications.
- Pay incentive fees to participants.
- Provide meals and refreshments for participants and observers.
- Supply materials needed to conduct exercises within the session, such as crayons, marking pens, scissors, glue sticks, magazines for collages, etc.
- Procure special equipment such as extra lighting, presentation tools, extra computers, etc.
- Coordinate special services, which may be handled by either the facility or the moderator, including videography, transcription and translation services.
- Assist with on-site services including copying, duplicating extra tapes, providing telecommunications and secretarial support, and mailing and forwarding of research materials, which are generally not covered by the facility rental fee.

If the study is not being conducted at a professional field facility, moderators or internal personnel will have to manage these responsibilities on their own.

Travel

In budgeting for travel, the research manager should consider internal travel needs as well as funds required to transport moderators to the various research sites. The travel budget should account for all of the costs that will be incurred, including:

- Air or rail transport.
- Airport transfers.
- Local transportation.
- Parking, tolls, gas, auto service.
- Lodging.
- Meals.
- Gratuities and charges for baggage handling and special services.

Some travel-related issues generally arise that need to be negotiated between the research manager and the consultant, particularly if neither has a continuing policy on these matters. These include:

- *Class of service* Many senior consultants insist upon business class or premium air and rail service because they want their check-in and transfer procedures handled in the most expeditious manner, and they need the extra space provided for maintaining productivity and for relaxation while on the road. This matter is particularly important in hotels – most consultants and moderators will need a room which supplies adequate telephone lines, Internet linkages, etc. and will expect their hotel to provide off-hour meal service, meeting rooms and concierge services. Normally, only hotels classified as 'four-star' or 'five-star' will have the level of service needed.
- *Who pays* The research manager should expect that the client will be paying for any travel-related expenses incurred whenever project tasks are undertaken. For example, if briefings are conducted in a restaurant over lunch, it is the client's responsibility to handle the bill.

Contingency limits

Most research companies will express their bids as estimates bounded by contingency limits which are typically plus or minus 10 per cent of the total fee. This means that on the basis of the project specifications as *currently defined*, the final fee will not go over or under 10 per cent of the targeted cost. If project specifications change, for example, if respondent quotas are defined more rigidly or if additional tasks are set after the proposal is submitted, it is acceptable for the supplier to submit a revised estimate. It is generally wise for the research manager to use the upper end of the contingency limit to forecast project costs in case extra services may be needed or unexpected expenses incurred while executing a project.

Table 4 Project budget worksheet.

Budget item	Cost
Moderators' fee	
Attend briefings and other meetings	
Develop recruitment screener	
Develop questionnaires, discussion guide	
Develop special research tools	
Conduct the focus groups, IDIs, etc.	
Analyze and report findings	
Make presentations	
Oversee project management	
Allocate travel time	
Secure special equipment	
Field services	
Facility rental	
Recruitment of participants	
Incentive fees to participants	
Meals and refreshments for participants and observers	
Other on-site services	
Special services	
Special equipment	
Moderator travel	
Staff travel	
Airfare	
Airport transfer	
Local transportation	

Budget item	Cost
Parking, tolls, gas	
Lodging	
Meals	
Gratuities	
Contingency limit	
TOTAL	

2.6 Global Fieldwork

This section will review the issues that need to be considered during global qualitative research collaborations.[6] Working outside of ones' native country involves anticipating problems and meeting numerous challenges throughout the planning and execution of the research. These include selecting local sites and suppliers, project monitoring and communication, adapting project execution materials, arranging translations, producing reports and business arrangements etc. while respecting local situations and meeting mutual needs. All of these matters require extra care and consideration on the part of research managers.

Determining where to conduct the research

When clients decide to conduct a global qualitative research study, the primary question is generally where to locate the research. Normally this question will be addressed by either the multinational client's scope of product distribution or media coverage or by assessing regions of potential opportunity. All of the criteria raised earlier – convenience, resource availability, seasonal patterns, availability of targeted populations, etc. – also apply to cross-national studies. Multinational companies that wish to evaluate opportunities for a new laundry detergent format, a new 'super-premium' cognac or a television campaign for a line of soft drinks have to think hard about where research investments will have the greatest meaning. This is an issue that is highly complex and vulnerable to errors.

Some marketers will try to conduct studies in each of the countries in which they have marketing operations. While this is certainly preferable for the final stage of a research program, in conducting preliminary studies marketers will often seek to obtain a 'representative global sample'. Often this takes the form of a study conducted in a subset of markets representing North America, Europe, Asia and possibly Latin America. However, determining which local markets are most representative of their continents requires careful planning. The same problem is faced in conducting regional cross-country research, for example, what is a representative European, Asian or Middle Eastern sample? Some additional guidelines that clarify the research manager's options in these situations include answers to the issues listed here.

- *Are the targeted respondents representative of the country as a whole or do they constitute a unique segment.* In some countries, residents of the national capital or primary business centers are not representative of product users while in others, for example in some Eastern European countries, capital residents may be the only ones with access to major media and distribution outlets.

- *Is it easy to locate members of targeted segments in the market.* Studies that seek creative, Western-oriented or fashion forward consumers will need to gravitate to national capitals and business centers.
- *How much national diversity is necessary for a good understanding of a region.* Studies which focus on the Western European market, for example, will often seek to obtain input from Northern, Central and Southern Europe. The question then becomes whether findings from a German focus group can be generalized to France or from Spaniards to Italians.
- *Once the country has been chosen, how do you determine locations.* If a decision has been made to go outside the national capital, clients may want to address markets that are somewhat more 'traditional' or 'regional' in their orientation, for example, Sheffield in the UK or Barcelona in Spain, to obtain information that is more representative of the country as a whole.
- *How do you assess convenience vs. the most suitable location.* Saving money and time will always be easiest in the national business and population center. However, if this will bias the study toward non-representative consumers, it should be avoided.

Gaining local cultural familiarity and background

Prior to undertaking research in a different country or region, research managers should make certain that they understand local patterns of product and category usage. The emotions and practices associated, for example, with a laundry detergent will be different as one shifts from North America to continental Europe to the Middle East because of different laundry technology and cleaning habits. There may also be unexpected differences in the brand's image and the decision making structure associated with a category. For example, premium sneakers may be worn during athletic contests in the US and Western Europe, but in Eastern Europe and Asia may serve as only a fashion statement to be replaced by less trendy sneakers during play. Faulty assumptions based upon one's own country may thus introduce biases or fundamental invalidity.

In addition to basic category knowledge, researchers should familiarize themselves with local cultural values and traditions that may impact the conduct and outcomes of the research. Practices associated with major racial or cultural minorities in a market should receive the same standard of consideration as the predominant culture. Needless to say, local holidays, feasts, weekend customs, etc. must be respected, otherwise the researcher risks having no one show up for a focus group.

Generally the advice of local research partners should be solicited and followed when scheduling and adapting research execution details to local requirements. Most will readily provide information on local conditions affecting research quality. However, value-added market information on local brands, market share, competition, distribution channels, etc. may not always be readily provided without charge before the engagement. Research managers should not place an unfair burden on local suppliers in unfamiliar markets by expecting them to provide a high level of market information.

Locating local suppliers

Picking and managing the best local suppliers is a problem faced by all international research managers. Relying only on the largest established international networks is an expedient solution for many inexperienced managers but may not offer the level of expertise, attention or pricing required by everyone. Otherwise, managers must use their own resources to create a network of reliable local researchers. This requires planning time and considerable focus.

International directories and other published or interpersonal resources may be helpful in building this network. Nevertheless, thoughtful evaluation of all personnel specifics should be made in light of study requirements.

In evaluating the credentials of local suppliers, attention should be paid to the agency's overall experience and skills. Additionally, the specific staff who will be responsible for the engagement should receive thorough scrutiny. Academic credentials, experience in the category or with the targeted consumers, technical or language skills may be relevant to determining the suitability of a research company.

Local and individual agency approaches to qualitative research may differ across national boundaries. This may affect the manner in which interviews are ordered and questions are asked, as well as the expectations researchers may have for participants. For example, the four and five hour group discussions that are common in France are considered highly unusual in the United States where the norm for discussion length is two hours. Research managers should be able to either accommodate to local norms, in some cases, or to contract with local suppliers who are willing to accept what they may view as unconventional practices in their own markets.

Who pays

If a newly developed, proprietary or unfamiliar methodology or set of techniques are being applied in a project, training and orientation will be required. Coordinating agencies should expect that local companies will not bear the cost of the training – in fact, local companies may sometimes merit compensation if a high level of staff allocation is necessary. Local research agencies need to make a decision about the relative value of the skills they are receiving vs. the time and attention required to learn new techniques.

Establishing equivalence of project execution details

A major problem faced by all international coordinators is the need to establish equivalence in the project execution details. Even though local practices may need to diverge for cultural or methodological reasons, without reasonably tight controls it will be impossible to make meaningful comparisons during the analysis. There are trade-offs between flexibility and creativity on the one hand, and control and comparability on the other. It is valuable to mobilize the local practices, special skills and talents of local agencies in matching project requirements. However, the coordinating manager must continue to tie these variations back to the central project objectives. As Pearson and McCullough insist:

> It is important to realize that while the core methodology will remain basically the same from country to country, even within the same study, what works in one country will likely need to be modified for the next. By balancing adaptability and adherence to research objectives, you can generate the desired output that is comparable from country to country. (1997: 38)

Targeted segments

Study details where local variations are commonly necessary include respondent segmentation and targeted market definition. People's family roles, occupations, interests and self images are in a continuous state of dynamic change throughout the world. There is a high range of variability across markets, for example, in emerging women's roles. Thus, targeting a 'traditional home maker' segment in the United States and Western Europe may be very difficult. The same is true in targeting 'retirees'. In the US, many seniors continue to practice their trades or professions after they have officially retired – in contrast to Western Europe where social programs create disincentives to continuing employment.

The recruitment approach

Recruitment often will have to be modified as one crosses borders. Face-to-face recruitment in busy public streets is relatively uncommon in the United States – the only place this may be practiced is at suburban shopping malls. Alternatively, the bulk of recruitment is conducted by telephone from established respondent databases, which are just starting to be utilized in continental Europe. Thus, German research managers expecting face-to-face recruitment in the US are going to confront the prospect of an unusual and expensive recruit.

Recruitment screeners

Screeners must also be adapted as one crosses national boundaries because the types of questions, the manner of asking questions and the response categories will change across national borders. Americans, for example, are relatively uninhibited about answering income questions – something that would outrage respondents just about anywhere else – and these are normally used as an indicator of social grade in the United States. On the other hand, indicators of social grade in the UK may not apply in many other locations. In various markets measurement of social grade may also be influenced by factors such as military credentials or family ties, and may be unrelated to income.

Discussion guides

Guides for discussion will normally need to be adapted in the same manner as screeners, as they need to accommodate local interview styles and terminology. It is also important for the coordinating manager and local moderators to reach a common understanding about structured vs. unstructured approaches in the interviews. US firms sometimes have an awful reputation in Europe and Asia for demanding highly structured interviews, but this is not always the case.

Exercises and techniques applied during interviews may not work across national borders and may need to be adapted in selected markets. This is because the objectives for a task may not be well understood or because the fantasy state required by the projective exercise causes some unanticipated discomfort or embarrassment. In Asia, for example, writing 'obituaries' for a product – an exercise which produces interesting insights into emotional bonds to brands in the West – makes respondents uncomfortable because they believe the task is unlucky.

Incentives

Cash or gifts may be appropriate as incentives for different social classes across diverse markets. In the US, research participation is considered as a form of employment and respondents expect cash compensation, roughly in relation to their social status or occupation at any level in the social scale. This is in contrast to practices in Europe, the Middle East and Asia where research participation is sometimes perceived as a social event or for the public good and participants at both the lower end of the scale and senior corporate executives are happy to be compensated with a gift instead of cash, which they in fact may find somewhat insulting.

Facilities

It is important to remember the research infrastructure in various markets may not match expectations based on the experience of one's own country. The professional fully-equipped viewing room with two-way mirror, video setups, etc., may not be available everywhere or the technical specifications may not match the norms at home. Similarly, community or home-based interview sessions are less common in the United States; thus a British research manager expecting to conduct a focus group in a participant's living room may face unanticipated roadblocks.

Translations/adaptations

Translations become an extra problem in multi-country studies. Execution materials need adaptation, including screeners, interview guides, exercises, concept statements and terms employed. This translation need applies even when different dialects of the same language are spoken by coordinating and local companies, such as the Portuguese spoken in Brazil vs. that spoken in

Portugal or the English usage of the United States as compared to the United Kingdom. Research managers should not assume that a British moderator would suffice in the United States or that one from Portugal would do fine in Brazil because there are many contextual and cultural issues that may be missed by a non-native speaker. Similarly, they should not expect that a discussion guide produced in Germany or Spain by a non-native English speaker will need no translation to eliminate the 'accent' that can pervade written communication and that can create misunderstandings when used without correction.

Some words may shift meaning as they cross national borders, and consequently create misunderstandings. The English word 'scheme', for example, carries no pejorative sense in the UK and may be used as a substitute for 'plan' in describing promotional tools. In the US, however, 'scheme' connotes something sneaky and conspiratorial and is never used in connection with marketing plans.

Translating and adapting research materials are important skills carried out by persons with great sensitivity to the linguistic, cultural and business issues involved. Research managers should expect that all of these services require adequate compensation of both company-based personnel and outside consultants that may often be necessary for this task.

Since English is rapidly becoming the lingua franca of international communication, it is not surprising that it is used in professional situations where neither party speaks English as a native language. Agreements over English vs. American spellings and usage often need to be accommodated. Professionals who have acquired language skills in an English-speaking country are usually preferable to those who have not worked in an English environment.

Regardless of the common language used between professionals, backroom translations may be necessary to help non-native observers understand the interviews. Career translators with some background in marketing, who can understand nuance and context as well as the words, are usually preferable to translators of convenience.

Even though local company principals and research managers may have a good foundation in English, it is necessary to guarantee that the actual moderator is speaking a language he or she is confident in using, in order to convey precise information during the sessions.

Notes and reports based on the research will have to be produced throughout the study and research managers need to come to some agreement with local agencies about the language used for reporting. In completing reports, agencies should ascertain that the vocabulary is adequate for high level professional communications in the target language.

Logistics, supervision and control

The supervision of logistics in multi-country studies requires a great deal of attention and sensitivity. Strict expectations should be tempered by consideration for the problems and complications that are inherent in moving materials, traveling and communicating across national boundaries and time zones.

On-site vs. off-site

Some research managers are content with managing their local contractors from their home base. In contrast, others expect to exercise a high level of on-site project supervision. Managers need to come to an understanding about the level of control that will be exercised during the project and should clarify the responsibilities associated with local logistics. Most local suppliers should be expected to provide recommendations for business class accommodations and directions to local service providers. Local suppliers should not be expected to take on financial responsibilities, act as booking agents or serve as local tourist guides.

Transparency and standardization

Standardization is important between the coordinating agency and the client, on the one hand, and particularly important between the agency and local companies, on the other. The primary research manager is responsible for guaranteeing that the 'look and feel' of the study are maintained across national boundaries and that any deviations from a central plan are understood and accepted. This issue can be particularly sensitive if local agency representatives are the same nationality as the client or if the client and the local agency maintain a separate ongoing relationship. The client and local agency, in this case, should make sure that all communications are cleared with the coordinating research manager and that no deviations from the central plan are made without authorization.

Time differences

Different time zones present complicating factors in coordinating and managing projects. Although an American research manager can conveniently keep tabs on focus groups being conducted on a weekday evening in Madrid, the reverse is complicated by inconvenient time differences. Inexperienced European project managers often forget that the United States crosses four time zones and that scheduling of research activities needs to respect time differences. Thus, assigning one set of group interviews in Los Angeles on Monday, Chicago on Tuesday and Miami on Wednesday can create scheduling complications that American moderators normally avoid.

Travel timing and scheduling, visas and documents

International project coordinators also need to respect the delays and roadblocks that are often set by nations outside of the European Union. In some areas, for example, business travelers may require special visas and authorization or may otherwise come under local government regulations. These issues can be particularly distressing when it involves the delivery, storage and transportation of stimuli, concept boards or product samples. In many areas, particularly in Asia, time will have to be set aside for customs clearance and approvals.

Developing countries present their own problems regarding communications, dependability of the electrical grid and access to local services. Research managers should discuss these issues sensitively with their local partners.

Analysis and reporting

A multi-country study has little value if the results cannot be compared meaningfully across markets. Most clients and research managers take steps to ensure that coordination of local suppliers is accomplished efficiently.

Debrief

Many companies believe it is valuable to unite all of the local agencies participating in a study to a 'debrief conference' at the conclusion of data collection. This is indeed a valuable exercise provided it is carefully managed according to a strict debrief agenda and that it comprises all of the research agencies involved in a project and not only the ones that can be flown in conveniently.

Guidelines

Maintaining consistency and comparability in reporting is also assisted by preparation of clear guidelines for the final deliverables. The guidelines should interpret the interview guide in a manner that provides meaningful analytic categories that local research agencies may follow. This tool is effective as long as it respects the unique findings and deviations from the norm that may have been discovered during the research.

Local styles of reporting may differ from those commonly delivered in one's own country. Theoretical analysis, for example, is common in continental Europe and is almost never applied in the United States. Some agencies and countries prefer detailed discursive writing styles while in others brief 'bullet points' are favored. The principal management issue here is to clarify all expectations at the beginning of the assignment so that the entire effort can work together to a common conclusion. It is a mistake to defer reporting issues to the completion of the data collection phase because it may be too late at that point to make adjustments.

Business matters

Business issues involved in multi-country studies may be subject to controversy and misunderstanding because of distinctive local norms for handling various charges or interpreting services in different markets. All parties should handle business matters with courtesy and consideration for the sensitive cultural issues that may pervade economic transactions. Listed below are several areas that might provoke problems if they are not discussed when the engagement is initiated.

Proposals

Since detailed and complex proposals require considerable staff time and background research, they should not be solicited unless the assignment is likely to proceed. If local market information or research design assistance is required, the coordinating party should expect to compensate some local agencies even if they do not receive the assignment.

Terms of payment

The scheduling of payments and whether late fees are charged for remissions that exceed specified terms should be discussed prior to the engagement. In the United States and many other countries, a prepayment of some portion of the project fee is normally expected before research tasks are initiated. Clients and research managers should understand that local research companies often have to provide prepayments to field services in order to keep the study on track and cannot provide project financing without charge.

Currency

The currency in which service providers expect to be paid and currency transfer issues also need to be clarified at the start of a project. Currencies may become problematic if they are subject to high foreign exchange fees and lengthy delays in the receiving country or if there are currency exchange rate fluctuations between the sending and receiving countries. The introduction of the Euro in 1999 has provided one basis for a common currency formulation. Otherwise suppliers may quote and expect to receive payments in a major international currency such as Swiss francs, British pounds or US dollars. The remitting party should expect to bear any charges associated with currency transfers and exchanges. Some companies may expect payment via electronic funds transfer (EFT) in order to reduce the delays and fees associated with foreign exchange. In situations of currency fluctuations, the matter may need to be subjected to negotiation since rates may change considerably between the date of project assignment and the final invoice.

Handling problems and legal disputes

Contracts between parties to a multi-country study should specify the legal authority that will have jurisdiction in the event of contractual disagreements. If problems arise, research managers should seek the advice of legal counsel. Several professional associations, including ESOMAR, provide resources for arbitration and negotiation of business disputes and these should be consulted before legal systems become involved.

2.7 Locating, Comparing and Selecting Research Firms and Moderators

There are several thousand companies that offer qualitative research services worldwide and the research manager's job is to make judicious selections among them. This section discusses factors that can help guide these choices.

The selection of a research company ideally should take place after the research manager and/or others in the marketing, planning or consumer insights groups have personally interviewed the people that will be doing the work, in addition to company principals. Agency presentation materials as well as any articles, sample reports or company policy statements turned in by the researchers should be thoroughly reviewed so that the manager can become familiar with the basic orientation, values and skills of the prospective supplier and determine how well they match the needs of the sponsoring client.

References and credentials supplied by qualitative research consultants should be checked and verified. Recognizing that other research and marketing executives lead busy and overscheduled lives, no unfair negative inferences should be made if a reference is slow in responding to an information request.

Proposals submitted by at least two companies or moderators should be compared before a project is assigned. It is generally unfair and unprofessional, however, to solicit proposals from agencies that are unlikely to be assigned the project or to use a competitor's proposal to manipulate a favored supplier into changing their fees or terms.

Proposals

Research managers should prepare a detailed 'Request for Quotation' or 'Request for Proposal' (RFQ, RFP) that follows the project brief as outlined earlier in this book. Prospective research partners should respond with proposals in writing within a reasonable amount of time – at least 3-5 days should be allowed. Rushing the quotation process can be risky. Verbal or 'ballpark' estimates of project costs that are based upon a verbal outline of study requirements can be highly vulnerable to unexpected modifications as project specifications become clarified.

Proposals should demonstrate that the moderator understands the conceptual and marketing issues that underlie a project. They should also establish clear plans for project execution. Listed below are the details which may be expected in proposals.

- A review of project objectives which demonstrates that the conceptual, methodological and marketing issues involved are clearly understood by the researcher.

- A project implementation plan, specifying the specific research activities, for example, the number of focus groups or site visits, where they will be conducted, how long each is expected to take, how participants will be recruited, what the screening requirements will include, etc.
- The names and qualifications of company principals and associates who will be handling major project responsibilities such as moderation or report writing.
- The names and locations of other companies and subcontractors that will be handling major fieldwork responsibilities.
- The project fee and clear explanation of cost factors. In this area, some research managers expect a simple sum of project fees while others expect a detailed cost accounting of the entire expected budget. The estimate of fees normally has an applicable life span of three months unless the consultant specifies another length of time. Costs may have to be revised if the project scheduling moves beyond this point.
- Description of the deliverables, that is, the form and length of topline summaries, full reports or presentations. If the contracting client wishes to have the findings delivered in a particular form, such as a PowerPoint™ presentation, this should be clarified in the proposal.
- Schedule for project execution.
- Expectations for client tasks, accountability and responsibilities.
- Expected terms of payment. The research manager should expect that issues such as currency, due dates and late fees will be discussed in detail.
- Clear guidelines for what could trigger added or unanticipated costs. In particular, the research manager should expect that changes in project execution details between the submission of the proposal and the start of the project, such as changes or further precision in respondent specifications, extensions of the number or length of interviews and imposition of respondent quotas will generate revised charges.
- If a confidentiality agreement has not yet been signed by the vendor, the proposal should contain assurance of confidentiality.

As noted earlier, contingency limits around cost estimates equal to plus or minus five or ten per cent should be expected and accounted in the internal budget.

If the research manager is unfamiliar with the research companies' policies about contingencies, these should be reviewed – particularly if there is some uncertainty and indeterminacy in the execution details. For example, handling of weather emergencies should be discussed if the project is headed to a wintry or stormy climate, and responsibility for recruitment failures should be discussed in the case of rare, low-incidence or sensitive targeted respondents.

Is the proposal a contract? This matter should be reviewed with legal counsel. However, for the most part, the proposal outlines a set of mutually accepted responsibilities and terms for a business engagement and should be treated as a binding agreement.

Unethical proposal practices

Research managers should understand that some practices in relation to proposals constitute a breach of professionalism, courtesy and ethics. Examples of common faults include:

- *Expecting the research company to provide value-added consulting services prior to winning the assignment.* These may include project design, developing research instruments and special exercises and providing customized local market information. The research company may wish to supply some of these services to place themselves in a better competitive position; however, it is wrong to make this an expectation.
- *Disclosing details of one research company's proposal to another.* This might be done in order to place the second company in a better competitive position. The research company's approach, company information and pricing structure should be treated as proprietary and confidential.
- *Seeking 'comparison bids' without charge.* Research managers should not use another company as a lever or check on a regular supplier.

Evaluating proposals

Once several proposals have been submitted, the research manager typically must review them with senior research, brand and marketing management. The process of vendor selection can sometimes become derailed by individual egos and political dynamics which are harmful to successful study execution and should be avoided.

The primary criteria that should be applied in the selection process are the fit between the project's substantive requirements and the personal qualities, skills and professional capabilities offered by the research company. Some guidelines for making a judicious choice in these areas are reviewed below.

Cost should be a secondary consideration and only applied if two or more research companies are deemed completely equivalent in all other respects, which is rarely the case. If costs are to be compared, the research manager should be certain that the proposals offered are equivalent in all respects, particularly in terms of specifications and possible hidden costs not apparent in the quotation. Cost alone should not stop a research manager from assigning a study to a desirable agency. If budgetary requirements present limitations, the manager should consider adjusting project specifications and assumptions – provided, of course, that these do not imperil research quality.

Depth of relationship

Selection of a research company should be grounded, first, in the manager's judgment of how intense the relationship between coordinator and contractor needs to be. Some problems or studies require a great deal of direction and guidance from the moderator; others require a less intensive collaboration. In selecting a qualitative research firm or moderator, the manager should consider the depth of the expected relationship. There are two main types of relationships representing overlapping 'ideal types', that are separated here for primarily heuristic purposes.

- *Consultant* Provides value-added services in project planning and execution; is expected to offer broader guidance and strategic insights; gains more thorough grounding in the client's marketing issues.
- *Vendor* Executes project responsibilities such as group moderation in a manner planned by internal management; operates with little autonomy and independence.

Reviewing a presentation by Dr. Alfred Goldman, Pierre Belisle asserts:

> Moderators design studies, collect data, evaluate data and make recommendations based on that data. Consultants may encompass the moderator's role but also advise clients on product tactics and overall marketing strategy, realms that go well beyond the results of one study. (1993: 34)

Any relationship with a moderator will reflect elements of both models. Nevertheless, the degree of guidance expected will have some impact on the type of company that should be chosen. Greater technical expertise, background and interpersonal skills are usually demanded from a consultant. As Zanes suggests:

> ...the professional qualitative researcher has the ability to combine unique marketing instincts with an intimate understanding of human behavior and motivation. The professional qualitative researcher delivers perspectives of the marketplace that allow managers to see new possibilities for the services and products they manage. They deliver insights into the motivations and needs of the marketplace that allow advertising creatives to develop strategy and executions that are inspired and on-target. (1992: 24)

It should be added here that the research company normally prefers to develop a consulting relationship with the client because most believe that their best work is performed in a relationship of full confidence and trust.

Personal traits

The research manager should connect with qualitative research consultants who are self-confident, warm and outgoing as people. Some other questions about researchers' personal characteristics should be evaluated by research decision makers, including:

- Are they able to establish rapport with others quickly.
- Are they good, active listeners.
- Does their body language demonstrate sensitivity and caring.
- Do they show poise and professionalism.
- Are they quick thinkers and problem solvers.
- Are they enthusiastic.
- Are they dedicated to the profession and up-to-date on new techniques and ideas.

- Do they have the intellectual skills necessary for making independent judgments.
- Are they detail oriented.

Qualifications/experience

Moderators and other research suppliers come from a wide range of backgrounds and experience trajectories. There is no single source for certifying qualitative research consultants and this issue itself is quite controversial within the field. Before selecting someone for an assignment, the manager must carefully consider that a consultant's skills are consistent with study needs. However, this process is complicated by an absence of clear guidelines for qualifications. Listed below are several areas that may be considered in determining whether a candidate is appropriate.

- *Industry experience* Many qualitative research consultants have held previous positions in research or marketing management on the 'client side'. Others may have a client following and consulting experience in a wide or a narrow range of categories. The degree of industry experience that the project requires is a matter of judgment. It depends on how much confidence the manager has in the moderator's ability to gain background in the category under examination and how much valuable 'carry-over' that person can bring from other industries if he or she has not yet worked in that business. For example, moderators with wide experience in health care and pharmaceuticals may bring valuable experience to a consumer project in the oral health care category.
- *Methodological skills* Many qualitative research consultants profess skills and experience with particular methodologies or tools, such as ethnography, creative problem solving, laddering, etc. These skills may have been acquired through apprenticeship with a master technician or through special seminars and training programs.
- *Skills with the targeted respondent category* Many qualitative research consultants have acquired expertise with a targeted segment. For example, some moderators who have had training and experience in early childhood education turn this background into a specialty of focus among children. Others with medical training conduct research with physicians and still others who come from a particular ethnic background, such as African Americans and Latinos, end up consulting on marketing issues involving those sub-communities.
- *Training/special credentials* Some moderators have advanced training in social science and/or business disciplines with degrees such as the PhD, MBA or MSW. This is important if the study is looking for a specific intellectual orientation, such as skills in psychologically oriented depth interviewing.
- *Professional affiliations* Many moderators demonstrate their professionalism and commitment by holding leadership positions in various research and marketing organizations or educational institutions. A moderator with prestigious professional affiliations may be helpful in controversial or high visibility situations.

Where to find suppliers

An involved research manager should keep an active file of qualified qualitative research companies. Information about potential suppliers may be obtained from various sources.

Personal referrals

Colleagues in brand or research management may have previously worked with firms that they consider worthy of recommendation. Other experienced research managers may also have worked with or heard about various top quality research vendors. According to the Advertising Research Foundation, 'The predominant source of information used to obtain moderators is referrals from professional colleagues' (Baldinger et al., 1992: 83).

Directories

A wide variety of electronic and paper directories facilitate locating qualitative research companies throughout the world. The most popular directories provide information on company expertise and qualifications, in addition to the names and numbers of principals.

- American Marketing Association/New York Chapter, *GreenBook, Worldwide Directory of Marketing Research Companies and Services,* updated annually. Contact: GreenBook, New York AMA, Lakewood Business Park, Suite E-11, 4301 32nd Street West, Bradenton, FL 34205, USA. Tel: 1-800-792-9202; Fax: 1-800-879-3751; e-mail: ccrifasi@nyama.org; web site: http://www.greenbook.org
- American Marketing Association/New York Chapter, *The Focus Group Directory, Worldwide Directory of Focus Group Companies and Services,* updated annually. Contact information same as for *GreenBook.*
- European Society for Opinion and Marketing Research (ESOMAR), *Directory of Research Organizations,* available in both paper and CD-ROM versions, updated annually. Contact: ESOMAR, Vondelstraat 172, NL-1054 GV Amsterdam, Netherlands. Tel: +31-20-664.21.41; Fax: +31-20-664.29.22; e-mail: e-mail@esomar.nl; web site: http://www.esomar.nl
- *Impulse Survey of Focus Facilities,* includes both company-submitted information and the results of a researcher survey which provides 'Quality Ratings' of most of the listed companies. Contact: Impulse research Corp. 8829 National Blvd., Suite 1006, Culver City, CA 90232-2317, USA. Tel: 1-310-559-6892; Fax: 1-310-839-9770; e-mail: infor@ImpulseSurvey.com; web site: http://www.ImpulseSurvey.com
- *The Markets Directory,* updated annually. Contact: The Markets Directory, Ground Floor, 131 E. 39th Street, New York, NY 10016, USA Tel: 1-888-304-9454; Fax: 1-212-490-1221; e-mail: service@marketsdirectory.com
- Marketing Research Association, *Blue Book Research Services Directory,* updated annually. Contact: Marketing Research Association, 1344 Silas

Deane Highway, Suite 306, Rocky Hill, CT 06067-0230, USA. Tel: 1-860-257-4008; Fax: 1-860-257-3990; e-mail: e-mail@mra-net.org; web site: http://www.mra-net.org

- mrweb is a British Internet-based service for worldwide market researchers. In addition to contact information for employment listings and suppliers, the web site provides links to other international marketing research organizations. Web site: http://www.mrweb.com
- *Quirk's Marketing Research Review Researcher SourceBook,* the worldwide directory of research providers, updated annually; available in both paper and online formats. Contact: Quirk Enterprises Inc., 8030 Cedra Ave., Ste. 229, Bloomington, MN 55423, USA. Tel: 1-612-854-5101; Fax: 1-612-854-8191; e-mail: Quirk19@mail.idt.net; web site: http://www.quirks.com
- *Qualitative Research Consultants Association (QRCA) Facilities & Services Directory,* updated annually. There is also an online resource available at the web site called 'Find A Consultant' which facilitates links to moderators. Contact: Qualitative Research Consultants Association, Inc., P.O. Box 2396, Gaithersburg, MD 20886-2396, USA. Tel. toll-free in North America: (888) ORG-QRCA, (888) 674-7722; Elsewhere: 1-301-391-6644; Fax: 1-301-391-6281; e-mail: qrca@qrca.org; web site: http://www.qrca.org

Other directories are published by national market research organizations. Market research managers should become active in their local associations and take advantage of the available conferences, meetings and resources.

Publications

Several journals and magazines publish articles about qualitative research written by leading practitioners. Published articles give authors an opportunity to display their skills and expertise in an authoritative context. Marketing research publications often contain advertising and specialized directories which are helpful in locating particular skills. Professional publications regularly introduce managers to new techniques, ideas and approaches. Listed below are several publications that are available in North America.

- *Quirk's Marketing Research Review*
- *Marketing News*
- *Marketing Review*
- *Marketing Research: A Magazine of Management and Applications*
- *Journal of Marketing Research*
- *Journal of Advertising Research*
- *Public Opinion Quarterly*

Conferences/professional associations

Most marketing and research organizations offer regular conferences, meetings and courses which showcase leading research companies and methods that they use.

- American Marketing Association annual research conference
- Advertising Research Foundation annual conference and exhibit
- Market Research Association
- Market Research Society (UK)
- Qualitative Research Consultants Association
- Association of Qualitative Research Practitioners (UK)
- South African Market Research Association
- Market Research Society of Australia

Direct solicitation

Many research practitioners have marketing programs of their own and research managers may receive electronic, telephone and postal solicitations from research company principals. Commonly, these will include requests to visit the manager's office for in-person presentations or other forms of familiarizing the research buyers with services offered by vendors. Research managers should remain open to a regular program of visits by research companies since these may help to familiarize personnel with new available techniques.

2.8 Locating and Selecting Field Facilities

Evaluating field services is an important part of the research manager's role. In most cases, the qualitative research firm or moderator will make all necessary field arrangements and manage these suppliers. However, the manager should be concerned with quality standards for field facilities in order to make certain that projects will be implemented without flaws. Internal clients may also bring special needs to projects, such as the wish to bring along a large number of staff. Research managers may also recommend that qualitative research consultants use particular facilities if previous experience with them has been positive.

This section reviews concerns and best practices associated with field facilities.

Recruitment methods

Field facilities differ according to the methods they use to recruit research subjects. The best organizations in developed countries have created huge proprietary computerized databases which can sort potential respondents according to recruitment specifications. Others rely upon referrals from other respondents, professional groups and clubs or upon publicly available business or telephone directories. Field services also sometimes rely upon lists supplied by survey sampling companies or mailing list brokers. Recruitment costs generally increase if specialized lists must be purchased.

Independent vs. in-house recruiters

Although many field facilities hire regular internal staff to manage recruitment, others rely upon independent recruiters who work on a project basis. Many researchers believe that a company with its own recruiting staff can produce higher quality work and deliver a more consistent service (Harris, 1996). Sometimes, even companies with internal recruitment capabilities rely on outside recruiters to handle a rush assignment or special needs. Research managers and moderators may prefer to work with a particular independent recruiter or they may rely on the field service to make the choice in a transparent manner.

Client supplied lists

It is sometimes necessary to supply the facility with a special list of targeted respondents. This may occur if the project requires recruitment of the client company's customers or specific prospects. In this case, recruitment costs may be higher than if the facility uses its own resources because of the extra time and effort required to approach particular respondents. Clients who supply prospective names should be careful that their lists are current and provide telephone numbers, otherwise there may be incremental charges for directory look-ups.

Managers must also try to supply at least 7-10 names for each recruited respondent needed in the study because one cannot count on the availability for research participation of targeted respondents. For example, if the client is an airline seeking to study its frequent first-class passengers, it should be expected that most of these will be traveling on business when a recruitment call comes or at the time of the scheduled interview. If this ratio of names per respondents cannot be matched, the list may be insufficient to complete the recruitment. Without other costly options, such as offering high cash incentives to attract qualified respondents, or rearranging project execution strategies, such as on-site visits instead of a focus group interview, research with some targets may not be feasible. High cash incentives, while sometimes essential to get the job done, may jeopardize respondents' objectivity and truthfulness.

Intercept recruitment

As an alternative to list-based recruitment, many research companies are skilled at recruiting participants by intercepting them at major shopping thoroughfares, shopping malls, conference sites and other venues. These methods can get expensive if the targeted respondent is rare. On the other hand, if some behavioral criterion must be met, for example, purchase of a particular soap brand or usage of a specific bank's ATM terminal, this recruitment method can guarantee a match because individuals can be intercepted after they have actually purchased or used the product.

In Europe, intercept recruitment along major pedestrian thoroughfares is fairly common. It is less practiced in the United States where intercept recruitment, if conducted, is likely to take place in enclosed shopping malls with the cooperation of the center's management.

Physical plant

Field facilities and viewing rooms around the world vary widely according to how they are set up and designed. Listed below are several considerations that are important in guaranteeing that the project's objectives are matched by the facility's physical plant.

Location

Facilities may be located in urban centers, suburban neighborhoods and small towns. Correspondingly, they may be located in large or small office buildings, industrial parks or residential buildings. In picking a facility, the manager should make sure it is appropriate and convenient for the respondents he wishes to recruit. For example, it might be impossible to bring suburban home makers to a downtown facility in the evening because they may be reticent about late-night travel at the session's conclusion. Facilities should have good access to public transportation and/or major highway arteries, depending on how respondents are likely to arrive. If participants are likely to arrive by car, facilities should have access to well-lighted and convenient parking.

The living room

In many areas, particularly in the UK and continental Europe, interviews are likely to be conducted in the recruiter's home. Alternatively, some projects require use of a community-based facility, such as a conference room at a public library, a church basement, meeting rooms at unions or fraternal organizations. When considering one of these options, the manager should consider the matters of accessibility as well as the user-friendliness of the entryway. Convenience to public transport and car parking are necessities. A well-lighted doorway with welcoming signs directing respondents to the research site are also essential.

The office suite

Office suites with separate viewing rooms that follow the American model are becoming increasingly popular throughout the world. These facilities are organized in fairly standard ways. They have a reception area, waiting lounges, conference rooms where interviews are conducted, observation rooms, equipment rooms which hold tape and video recorders, offices, work areas. Research managers should ascertain that there is sufficient isolation of all of these areas from each other. For example, if waiting lounges are too close to the conference rooms, the chatter of waiting respondents may disrupt ongoing interviews or, similarly, waiting respondents may overhear interviews and be exposed to contaminating opinions. It is also best to have waiting rooms that are away from the entrances to observation rooms in case clients are overheard.

Conference room characteristics

A well-equipped conference room should have sound isolation, including protection from ambient environmental noise and sounds from mechanical systems (heating, ventilation, air conditioning, plumbing). It should also provide the following amenities:
- Comfortable cushioned seating with arm rests for 10-12 participants.
- A conference table which allows for good interaction among participants. Some facilities provide U-shaped or triangular tables which are convenient for observers but often do not allow for easy interaction among respondents.
- Equipment for playing both three-quarter inch and half inch (NTSC, Beta, VHS) videotapes or any other formats (PAL, Secam) which are common in the country where the research is located.
- Wall surfaces that allow for easy tacking or taping of visual materials.

- A shelf or ledge for displaying concept or story boards.
- Easels, flip charts and fresh marker pens.
- Space for serving food and beverages. NOTE: Coffee, tea, water, snacks and soft drinks should be available throughout each session. In many countries, it is common to serve beer or other alcoholic beverages at the interviews. Research managers must defer to local custom in terms of what is served at the interviews as well as whether smoking is permitted. In most locations in the US, smoking is not permitted and may in fact be unlawful in both interview and viewing rooms.
- An ample supply of note pads and pencils.
- Materials for creative exercise and collages, such as old magazines, crayons, marking pens, scissors, glue sticks.
- A thermostat for easily modulating temperature during the session. If it gets too warm, respondents will tire quickly. A chilly room will also ruin a lively discussion.
- Electrical hook-ups for conveniently connecting appliances or computers that will be demonstrated during a session. Increasingly, sophisticated research facilities are providing Internet access at each of the seats in the room.[7]

IDI or mini-groups rooms

Some research centers supply smaller rooms for sessions involving between one and three participants. The rental charge is lower than for standard rooms. If researchers are offered a smaller one-on-one or mini-group room, they should first make sure that the observation room is not also scaled down because long periods in a small space can be very uncomfortable to observers. If the observation room is average size or only one or two observers will be viewing from a small scaled room, the IDI room is an attractive option.

Living room formats

Some office-based interview rooms are designed like a living room with couches and coffee tables in lieu of a conference table to add a 'homey' touch. These rooms are very comfortable for targeted populations such as children that may react negatively to the more formal conference table.

Test kitchens

Many facilities also contain observable test kitchens so that product usage in selected categories, such as scrubbing a sink or preparing a recipe, can be watched. Other projects may require last-minute kitchen preparation by the research team before a product sample is tested by participants. Before commissioning a test kitchen, the research manager should make sure that a facility's test kitchen is sufficiently large and contains the equipment the project needs, for example, a commercial-sized refrigerator in case perishables need to be stored or a high capacity microwave for quick heating.

Observation (viewing) room characteristics

A well-equipped observation room should also have good sound insulation, from both the conference room and from the outside world, and offer the following amenities:

- Comfortable seating for at least 8-10 observers. The trend is to send more and more observers to the research sessions so that they can observe consumer interactions, thus newer facilities contain space for fifteen or more guests. Even smaller groups of observers will benefit from the extra space in the viewing room. Many facilities provide both sofas and chairs in the observation room. The best facilities have observation suites with separate rooms next to the observation room that provide sofas, work space with electronic hook-ups and phones and a wet bar along with a video feed of the interviews.
- A two-way mirror that reflects like a mirror in the conference room and is clear like a window in the observation room provides for unobtrusive watching of the sessions. The mirror should be large enough so that everyone in the conference room can be observed without strain. The best mirrors are floor or table length and cover most of the wall surface. NOTE: The research manager should be sure to advise observers in advance to avoid white shirts and bright jewelry in the viewing room because these are most likely to be visible through the mirror into the conference room or can cause reflections on the glass that will appear on the videotape.
- Writing surfaces for note taking.
- Lighting control. A dimmer switch allows enough light for note taking without leaking into the conference room.
- Temperature control. A hot viewing room is uncomfortable and makes observers tire quickly.
- Sound control for adjusting the loudness of the interview.
- Equipment for audio and video recording. The processing of the audio and video feeds should be located away from the observation in a private area of the facility.
- Sufficient electrical outlets so that several laptop computers, as well as video equipment in use, can be connected.
- A place for storing and serving food and beverages. Virtually all facilities provide coffee and other drinks and snacks during the session to keep observers alert and focused.
- Easy access to the wash room. Placing a toilet inside the viewing room can be rather disconcerting to some observers. However, if someone needs to use the wash room during the observation period, being sent to a hallway several floors away from the viewing room can also be annoying.
- A supply of note pads and pencils.
- Materials for recreation and diversion during waits, such as current magazines and daily newspapers. Some facilities even provide exercise bikes.

- Some facilities provide space where executives may conduct routine office tasks such as making phone calls or using a computer during breaks in the interviewing.
- It is acceptable for the facility to discreetly place promotional brochures and business cards in the viewing room.

Facility etiquette

Facilities always provide the services of a host or hostess who should be everyone's primary contact for service coordination while working at a research facility. Hosts should be contacted for routine matters such as obtaining extra note pads or making car service reservations. They also manage the tasks of signing in respondents, administering a re-screener if necessary and providing each person with a name tag. Most facilities expect the hostess to pay the incentive fee at the end of the session; if some other arrangement is preferred that should be mentioned.

Arrangements should be made with the host for the timing and substance of any meal service while the research team is working at the facility.

It is considered inappropriate to make excessive last-minute demands upon the hostess, such as requiring a high volume of copying or meals from restaurants outside of the facility's immediate neighborhood without prior arrangements. The privacy of the field facility and its other clients must be respected. Visiting researchers must not walk into back office work areas or other non-public areas in the facility.

Security issues

Field facilities with multiple suites offer services to many companies simultaneously and some may be the client's competitors. Security-conscious facilities provide for sufficient isolation of each project team so that encounters are unlikely. Good facilities generally do not knowingly rent to competing organizations at the same time, but it is difficult to be certain that the facility will be aware of who the client's competitors are. Consequently, several security procedures for protecting project confidentiality should be routinely followed.

- Don't refer to the company name or its brands or to study results in public places at the facility, including restrooms and elevators. It is best to refer to the project by a code name or by the name of the moderator's research company.
- When observers arrive at the facility, they should identify themselves by name only. The project manager should inform the moderator of observers' names and have them leave a list at the reception desk for check-in. In the absence of a list, some facilities require business identification at check-in.
- Do not wear company insignia items, such as jackets, shirts or totes at the facility.
- Don't leave materials such as screeners or respondents' work sheets at the facility overnight. If you must, be sure they are under lock and key.

- Don't throw research materials, such as extra discussion guides or concept statements, into the garbage at the facility.
- Be sure that the moderator runs a security check in both the observation and conference rooms and removes all notes and flip charts written during the session.

Facility services

Well-equipped facilities offer a variety of special services that may be needed for the project, including:
- Information about local amenities, such as late-night restaurants.
- Copying machines for use on a charge-for-service basis.
- Technology support, including someone knowledgeable about computer connections, video hook-ups, etc.
- Access to needed special services, such as note-takers, translators or suppliers of special equipment.

A good facility anticipates client needs and handles all the details of service in a cooperative and affirmative 'can-do' way.

Working outside of office-suite field services

There are several circumstances that may require work outside of an office-suite type of field facility. Some of these situations might include:
- A preference for a home or community-based setting. This may be to accommodate the wishes of a European client accustomed to this type of location or to oblige the sensitivities of a targeted population, such as recent immigrants and lower-income consumers, who may be intimidated by a trip to a downtown office suite or professional research lab.
- The study requires on-site observations at a store or in the consumer's home or place of business.
- There is no viewing facility in a market being studied. This might be the case when the targeted community is agricultural or military.
- There is no facility in a section of the metropolitan area under study. This may be the case when members of a racial or cultural minority or low income individuals are targeted.
- The study targets market segments who may find it difficult to come to an office-suite facility, such as teenagers, the elderly or disabled persons.

In situations that compel work outside of a professional facility, alternative venues that might be secured include:
- Hotels and restaurants which make meeting rooms available to the public for a fee.
- Community organizations such as clubs, unions and lodges.

- Schools, libraries and clinics which may have public meeting rooms. Some educational institutions and hospitals may even have viewing facilities for their own training and therapeutic purposes.

Some research facilities or recruiters will provide all the necessary services – hosting, tape recording, meal and snack service, etc. – outside of their primary business place. Otherwise, the research manager will have to improvise and rely upon the moderator to make these arrangements.

Client observation in locations that do not provide a two-way mirror is somewhat complicated. If observers are present, they should be discouraged from sitting in back of or too close to the moderator because their reactions or body language may influence respondents. Unlike a mirrored facility, the viewing area should be opposite the moderator. No more than three to four observers should be permitted to take part and it is best for them to be seated against a back wall so that during the interviews participants' attention is directed to each other and to the moderator instead of to the observers.

Client observers in this situation have a special responsibility to avoid asking their own questions, making visual or verbal gestures or otherwise compromising the moderator's leadership of the group.

Sources of information

Information about field services may be found in most of the previously reviewed guides and directories that list research companies and information about moderators, as well as some other sources, including:

- *Personal referrals* Colleagues may recommend facilities they have found useful. However, this may not work well since moderators are commonly the primary point of contact. Thus referrals from moderators may be more authoritative and timely.
- *Directories* The most popular paper, electronic and web-based directories provide listings of research facilities. The *Marketing Research Association Blue Book* is generally regarded as the most authoritative resource for fieldwork. The *Impulse Guide* offers user ratings based on the experiences of research companies as well as client research managers. Members of the Qualitative Research Consultants Association can take advantage of the 'Cities List', a personal networking resource identifying other members who have recently worked in a particular market.
- *Publications* Magazines, such as *Quirk's Marketing Research Review* and *Marketing News*, often publish articles, advertising and specialized directories describing research facilities.
- *Conferences/professional associations* Marketing and research organizations offer regular conferences, meetings and courses which showcase research facilities. Meetings of the Advertising Research Foundation and the American Marketing Association have large exhibit areas which include many vendors of field services.
- *Direct solicitation* Many research companies with marketing programs of their own distribute attractive brochures through the mail or make calls from sales officers directly to corporate research managers.

Table 5 Worksheet for selecting research firms.

Source of information	Notes
Personal contacts for referrals	
Directories	
Marketing research organizations	
Marketing research conferences	

Favorite research suppliers		
Name	Company	Phone e-mail
Specialty		
Name	Company	Phone e-mail
Specialty		
Name	Company	Phone e-mail
Specialty		
Name	Company	Phone e-mail
Specialty		
Name	Company	Phone e-mail
Specialty		

2.9 Conducting Research in Homes and Offices

In ethnographic and observational research studies, which often rely upon research encounters at consumers' homes, places of business or at a leisure location, there are several additional considerations that must be accommodated. Plans must be made for the extra time and logistics required. It has been suggested that the researcher must also respect the different etiquette demanded while conducting his business in public or in someone else's private space.[8]

- *Briefing* Be certain that participants are thoroughly briefed about how the research will be implemented, specifically, how many interviewers will be in attendance, how interviews will be recorded, etc. Provide necessary background information without tipping off respondents to such a degree that they lose spontaneity during the visits.
- *Permission* Provide information and gain permission from the various intermediaries that may have a role in the setting. For example, before an on-site observation at a place of business, make sure that approvals have been received from the respondent's employer or supervisor. If conducting an 'accompanied shop' with a consumer at a pharmacy, be sure that the proprietor or manager is informed if there will be any visible intrusions, such as photography.
- *Allow time* Be sure to leave enough time to study the phenomenon or the interaction of interest. Ideally, the entire 'life cycle' of a process should be covered from beginning to end. In studying a shopping experience, for example, attention should be paid to how it is planned, as well as details such as how the consumer orients herself to the store environment and how she navigates the store. As Dickie adds:

> To get clues about a whole activity, look at how people enter the activity you're trying to observe, and how they exit. What's going on just before and just afterward? How do they get to the point you're interested in? What and who do they bring with them? What mental state are they in? How do they leave? What do they take with them and what do they leave behind? (1997: 63)

Logistical planning should also recognize that site observers will have to coordinate travel and arrival, which may sometimes occur at peak commuting times. Travel time may add several hours to an already over-scheduled day.

Get natural

Researchers must preserve the most ordinary aspects of the behavior in question – the regular time it is conducted, the time allotted to the behavior, the normal clothes worn when engaging in the behavior and so on. The research participant should not be expected to adapt his customary behaviors or schedules to the needs of the observers. On the contrary, researchers must conform to the consumers' usual patterns particularly if they fall outside of regular business hours, even if that requires waking up early on a weekend morning to watch someone launder his clothes.

Don't be intrusive

Try hard not to let the fact of observation induce respondents to change their behaviors. Restrict the number of interviewer/observers invited to co-participate in a study to no more than two or three. Internal clients, to their credit, are often eager to observe home visits with consumers; however, going beyond a small number of observers threatens the validity of findings.

Remember the details about the real world

Ethnography takes place in the real world – a context outside of the researcher's control. Things will happen that you have not planned. Be sure that the research company carries insurance sufficient to cover any accidental breakage or other liabilities that might occur. Reviewing the details of external research activities with the company's own legal department may also be necessary to learn how to reduce liabilities.

Respect

Respect the privacy and property of participants. During home visits, research subjects may have other household roles and responsibilities that need attention, such as answering phone calls from friends or caring for children and pets. Visiting observers should handle these occasions for privacy with sensitivity and consideration.

2.10 Other Resources

Additional resources, including personal and professional services as well as technology, may often be necessary in completing assignments. This section reviews why and how these resources might be used and provides guidelines for gaining access to high quality suppliers.

Reasons to use videography

Videography improves the quality of deliverables and the analysis of creative expression. High quality custom videotaping is necessary if the output will be edited or used in presentations to senior management, the sales organization or outside the company. Additionally, some researchers prefer to review videotapes during the analysis because it more clearly records body language, nuance and interaction between participants, and it also conveys who said what during the sessions.

Locating sources

Videographers' services are generally arranged by field services or by moderators. The research manager should make sure that the videographer has considerable experience in taping research discussions because a sensitivity to interview dynamics is required if each will be recorded meaningfully. Additionally, the office-suite research facility setting presents several technical challenges – lighting, sound isolation – which experienced videographers can handle.

Videographers with strong documentary skills are helpful in studies conducted outside of an office suite. In this case they need to receive some orientation about the differences between standard documentary styles and on-site research taping.

The video format – such as VHS, Beta, High-8 – used in taping is an important consideration with implications for cost and production quality. Experienced personnel can offer counsel for the formats most appropriate for various uses (Wright and Fitkin, 1997).

With the growing proliferation of reasonably priced and miniaturized digital video (DV) cameras, there is a growing temptation to have non-professional personnel such as an intern or assistant in the research department do the videography. This may produce short-term cost savings if the intended use is only data capture; however, if the raw footage is intended for internal review and editing, the results may be disappointing.

Some researchers are now using these cheap DV cameras in creative ways, for example, having respondents record their own household behaviors or having them discuss products with other family members in their own private space outside of the researcher's supervision. Experiments such as these suggest that video technology has a promising future in qualitative research.

Reasons to use transcription services

In some situations, such as a highly technical research project or an ideation and brainstorming session, an accurate detailed transcription will help to preserve the integrity of the record. Viewing room transcriptions organized on a laptop computer while the interview is in session are helpful when the analysis needs to be rushed and a review of the tapes in real time will not serve client needs.

Locating sources

A transcription service with considerable research expertise is important. Companies primarily involved in legal or general business transcription are sometimes not sensitive to the demands and terminology of the research industry. The classified advertising sections of several research periodicals and the directories reviewed earlier often have listings or display ads from transcribers.

Systems for automating transcription through voice recognition (VR) software are rapidly being perfected and will become a major factor in qualitative research in the near future.

Reasons to use telephone conferencing systems

Conferencing systems are necessary for conducting telephone focus groups. These are necessary when respondents are highly dispersed or otherwise cannot be conveniently coordinated to be at the same place at once. Some examples include academic specialists and researchers, high level government officials or corporate managers and disabled consumers.

Locating sources

General facility and moderator directories have listings of telephone conferencing facilities. Although the conferencing systems offered by major telephone companies are temptingly priced and may suffice for an impromptu discussion, the extra services and training offered by the best research teleconference suppliers are worth the small incremental investment.

Reasons to use video conferencing systems

The desire to reduce travel costs, logistical complications and turnaround time have led several field service organizations to arrange for video conferencing systems to clients. The major suppliers of video conferencing technology have organized networks of research facilities using the same system.

Video conferencing allows the scheduling of focus groups or IDIs in different markets close together in time, thus relieving the lag required by movement between cities. Research managers and internal clients can observe the research sessions through a hook-up at the office or at a local research facility. In addition, a single moderator can be dispatched to each of the cities in rapid sequence or several different local moderators can work simultaneously in their own markets.

The majority of systems now in use rely upon dedicated hardware, and arrangements need to be made for acquisition and support of inventory. However, it is likely that this business will gravitate to the Internet, thus allowing anyone with web access and the proper bandwidth and software for video streaming to take advantage of linking to videoconference focus groups. Indeed, as secure community web sites, desktop video and inexpensive PC cameras grow in popularity, it will not be long before most research companies will be able to create 'virtual focus groups' linked visually through their computers.

Locating sources

Video conferencing systems have been heavily promoted by direct mail, at research conferences and in the pages of research periodicals.

Reasons to use Internet broadcasting (web-casting)

Just like video conferencing systems, web-casting responds to the desire for reduced travel costs and shortened turnaround; however, this technology offers the added advantage of accessibility at the desktops of up to twenty viewers. The production essentially involves uploading a video feed of an interview to a secure web site which authorized viewers can access with a pre-arranged password. The only thing needed at the viewer end is a computer that accesses the Internet at sufficient processing speed and the streaming software needed to run the video output.

Product enhancements allow the viewer to index specific clips and to integrate images of interview documents, respondent profiles, concept boards or consumers' exercises into the video feed. Chat capabilities among viewers are also integrated into the system. At the end, the output can be transcribed or copied to a CD-ROM.

At the moment, a limited number of viewing facilities are integrated into the system but setup is relatively simple for adding new rooms.

Locating sources

Web-casting systems have received attention at research conferences and in research periodicals. The sites can be reached through the standard Internet search engines.

Reasons to use online interviewing

The increasing acceptance of the Internet for interpersonal communication, access to information and for commerce in goods and services has created numerous opportunities for qualitative research. These include studying the Internet as a new type of media and distribution channel through qualitative research methods as well as using the Internet as a communications channel for reaching research subjects about any meaningful category. Although at the moment Internet proliferation through the mass market is inconsistent, within certain categories and demographic targets, including young, technologically sophisticated and professional consumers and even across national boundaries, web-based focus groups are a viable option.

Online focus groups can be scheduled as moderated 'chats' in real time or as asynchronous discussion groups (bulletin boards) lasting several days. They are recruited in the same manner as live groups and provide for focused interactive discussion when led by an experienced moderator. They offer the additional advantage of being convenient, requiring no travel expense and providing an instant transcription which clearly identifies the source of each expression of opinion.

On the other hand, critics point to several deficiencies of online focus groups, such as security and identification issues, and the inability to capture non-verbal cues such as eye contact, body language, speech and voice nuances.[9] Since computer keyboarding is required to express opinions, leadership and domination may go to respondents possessing superior typing skills. Attention management and distractions may be problematic when respondents are not in physical proximity. Additionally, online groups are limited in their ability to facilitate group interaction and creative exercises. The moderator's role can also become quite limited when face-to-face interaction is removed.

Locating sources

This field is currently emerging and rapidly evolving. Several organizations, identified in directories and magazines, currently supply resources to moderators who wish to recruit subjects and provide web-based resources for online groups. Although, this segment is likely to grow, it will not replace live face-to face research for most applications.

Reasons to use technology evaluation (usability labs)

Usability testing can be applied to both computer-based products or services – including hardware, software and web sites – as well as to any other form of electronic appliance, including television monitors, home appliances, cell phones and ATMs – many of which are gaining enhancements through computer technology. Usability labs offer systems which – through multiple video and data feeds – allow the client observer to simultaneously monitor the subject's interface with items such as computer screens or keyboards while watching and recording verbal and non-verbal reactions. The objectives of usability research typically include evaluating ease-of-use, common navigation patterns and how 'sticky', that is, capable of capturing attention, a resource can be.

Usability tests normally require a highly sophisticated level of interaction with respondents because pure observations of how consumers are managing do not reveal intention, expectations and affect. Active listening, probing and non-judgmental questioning strategies are necessary to resolve whether interaction with the technology is satisfying, difficult, prone to error or confusing (Tamler, 1998).

Many researchers involved in technology evaluation prefer a 'contextual research' approach which applies ethnographic methods to this area. In other words, in place of laboratory testing, the researcher goes a further step by evaluating the technology in the context of the home or workplace where it is normally used. In a recent study, for example, the objective was to observe how computer purchasers used a combination of paper and electronic resources to make decisions about new acquisitions and upgrades.

Locating sources

The emerging field of usability testing is also evolving very quickly. Only a small number of research facilities currently have capabilities for usability testing and recording through multiple video feeds. This specialty is expected to grow rapidly.

Reasons for needing language translation

Simultaneous translation and translated transcripts are needed if the research is being conducted in languages other than the predominant native language or if the project requires research in countries whose native languages are not understood by observers. It is always best to interview consumers in their native languages or dialects.

Locating sources

The most sophisticated translation transmission systems permit separate or even individual audio feeds into the viewing room so that the observers have the option of listening to both the actual discussion and the translation or to the translation alone. Portable systems can be rented if the facility does not own the proper equipment. Firms with special translation services indicate such in the directories.

Some consideration should also be given to whether one or both language feeds will be recorded and to which one will be imprinted on the videotape. If the video transcript will be subjected to editing and presentation, consideration should be given to employing multiple translators to represent diverse voices in the discussion.

Professionals with strong simultaneous translation skills and experience in business translations (rather than only diplomatic and legal) in major international languages can be located in national capitals, business centers and large metropolitan markets.

Reasons for needing qualitative data analysis packages

Qualitative analysis software is helpful when a large body of data needs to be compiled. Various programs are also able to integrate text, images, sound and video as resources for conclusions. After the information is coded, it can be retrieved in a manner that simplifies asking questions of the data – for example, determining whether men and women speak differently about their vitamin usage – and creating linkages between various components.

Locating sources

A later chapter on analysis provides additional details.

Reasons for needing hand-held opinion modulators

Opinion modulators, known through various trade names, allow focus group participants or subjects assembled in a theater-style setting to register their degree of interest in a stimulus on a hand-held device in real time using either dials or buttons to indicate points on a scale. The devices are often used with advertising executions – political ads being a particularly favored application – and television programming to determine which elements of a production have the strongest appeal or to pick winners when several are being compared. The output provided offers an averaging of the individual reactions fed into a central processor.

Although proponents of these devices tout their objectivity and standardized measurement, many consultants question their validity and authenticity as qualitative research. Practitioners counter the latter objection by claiming that they use the measurements as a springboard for discussion and probing following exposure of the results to the participants, thereby gaining insights into meanings and motivations.

Locating sources

Portable hand-held devices are available for outside rental on a per-usage basis or they may be installed as fixtures at a select number of research facilities and used on-site.

2.11 Recruitment Issues and Concerns

Participant recruitment in any qualitative research project is an important responsibility. Since respondents are expected to represent the targeted segments, failure to recruit the proper subjects will jeopardize the validity of the research. This section will discuss several issues that should be addressed during recruitment.

Who is doing the recruitment

Generally, responsibilities for recruitment are turned over to the principal research company or independent moderator who will secure the services of independent recruiters or field services. The research manager should make sure that the recruiters are experienced at handling any special needs or targeted populations that the study may demand, for example, recruitment of medical specialists or 'creative' individuals.

How is the recruitment being done

Recruitment methods should be consistent with project objectives; however, it is sensible to be flexible because the norms in local markets or the experience of different recruiters may suggest alternative approaches. Here are several common methods of recruiting research subjects.

- *Recruitment from internal databases* Experienced independent recruiters and field services often have large databases which can be mined for participants in most studies. These databases have largely replaced the 'little black books' that were the source of respondents a generation ago. Computer automation has speeded up the process of sorting by brand and category usage or demographic characteristics. In selecting qualified respondents, consequently, recruiters tend to prefer their own sources.

  Respondents on internal databases are generally eager to participate in studies and consequently can be recruited quickly and inexpensively. On the other hand, they can become overused – a problem that should be guarded against – particularly if several recruiters in a market share the same database. Additionally, it is sometimes necessary to question the source of names in the database. Sometimes, recruiters acquire lists from clubs and professional associations which may create validity problems if, for example, nurses are over-represented in a list that will be used in recruiting for a cold remedy.

- *Recruitment from lists* Survey sampling companies and direct mail suppliers sell targeted lists, such as subscribers to particular magazines or owners of specific types of computers or appliances. Lists can also be assembled from print or electronic editions of major business and professional directories, such as the *Thomas Register*. Working from outside lists tends to increase recruitment costs because individuals are not normally eager to participate and might be hard to locate if they are highly preoccupied or mobile during the day, such as physicians, sales representatives and repair workers.

- *Random recruitment* If a high degree of randomness is required in respondent recruitment, publicly available databases, such as telephone directories, or even better, random digit dialing lists may be employed. This approach is also costly, however, because reaching prospects and securing compliance may be difficult. The common use of phone answering machines further complicates going directly to the general public.

- *Referral or 'snowball' recruitment* Having respondents recruited early in the process recommend acquaintances with similar characteristics is often a pragmatic response to a difficult situation. People who share an unusual occupation like French language instructors, or an uncommon affliction such as lupus, are very likely to be aware of fellow travelers. Endorsement of the project from a credible source who is also participating has a positive impact on recruitment success. Nevertheless, this practice should be carefully guarded and used very seldom because it can be vulnerable to abuse and invalid results.

- *Intercept recruitment* Often subjects may be recruited after being intercepted in a public place such as a street, shopping mall or conference center. This method is common and widely accepted in Europe and elsewhere but may be difficult in the United States where norms of privacy in public space are somewhat more restrictive. Recruitment through intercepts are appropriate if the manager is reasonably sure that the type of person sought is likely to pass through the intercept point. In some types of recruitment efforts for low incidence and special respondents, this approach may be essential. For example, it may be used to recruit fashionable and 'trendy' consumers who spend their evenings in clubs, persons who shop at specific perfume counters or who purchase particular magazines at the newsstand. If recruitment will take place in public places, permissions from store owners or managers should be acquired if their customers will be solicited.

Strict adherence to specifications and screener

Recruiters should be given a descriptive list of respondent specifications as well as a screener based upon the list. Their first task upon receiving these materials should be to check the consistency of the two items and report back if anything needs to be changed to make the screening questionnaire consistent with specifications or to facilitate its administration. If final specifications vary from those described in the original proposal, this is the time to discuss any implications for costs and final budget.

The standard requirement is that the screener will be administered as written. However, if there is any flexibility, this may be discussed. Unprofessional recruiters may not always adhere strictly to the screener. They may prompt respondents beforehand about key screening requirements, warn them about responses that will cause them to be dropped from consideration or pay too much attention to the cash incentive in a manner that subtly encourages dishonesty. Quality control demands attention to how carefully the screening is being completed and measures should be taken against recruiters that deviate from expectations.

Setting the respondent incentive

The respondent incentive (sometimes called the 'co-op fee') is generally offered at the end of the screening interview. Incentive costs have risen dramatically over the last several years as consumers have become better aware of the value that marketing research delivers to companies. Since consumers feel there is an element of distributive justice operating in their favor, the scale for consumer incentives in the United States and Western Europe now ranges from approximately $50 to $100 (US) and more. Business and professional respondents require a minimum of $150 ranging upwards to $500 for senior executives or rare medical specialists.

The optimal incentive is usually determined by the considerations listed below.

- *Rarity* Cost is usually associated with rarity of the targeted respondent. High incidence respondents such as middle income home makers receive incentives on the low end of the scale; low incidence respondents, such as psychiatrists or construction engineers, receive incentives at the upper end. Sometimes even a high incidence target can be turned into a low incidence one if numerous screening requirements, such as specific product usage and lifestyle characteristics, are added.
- *Local norms* The 'going rate' in the countries, regions and markets being studied should be respected. Local research companies and recruiters are the best guides for these questions and it is unfair to expect the prevailing standard in one area to be applied equally in another. Fees that are too high for local expectations are vulnerable to attracting respondents who will be overly compliant. Fees that are set too low are bound to complicate recruitment and compliance with project tasks.
- *Pre-interview preparation* Costs are generally higher if some degree of respondent preparation is required prior to attending the session. For example, completing diaries, sampling the product, tracking usage behavior or taking photos within the home all require a comparatively higher incentive.
- *The offer* The incentive should never be positioned as 'payment for opinions' since that subtly tends to bias participants to views which are favorable to the client. Rather, the incentive should be described as

compensating for the 'time and trouble' of participating regardless of the views expressed.

- *Location* If the research is being conducted in respondent's homes or workplaces, they are entitled to a higher than standard incentive. Similarly, if they must travel long distances, assume high transportation or parking fees, or arrive at an inconvenient location, respondents merit higher fees.
- *Cash vs. gifts* In some regions or among some demographic and occupational targets, respondents expect to receive gifts instead of cash incentives. If gifts are being given their cash value should be roughly proportionate to scale for that category of respondent and they should be something desirable rather than an item of convenience. In the United States, the incentive is nearly always paid in cash at the end of the session – this is always preferable to providing items of value or goods.
- *Sampling* Promising samples of products in the category as an incentive may bias respondents and may also reveal the research sponsor. It is almost never appropriate to use product samples as the only incentive. Some clients enjoy offering samples or coupons at the *end* of the session, in addition to cash, as an expression of appreciation and when it will not influence responses.

'Money isn't everything', says Alice Rodgers (1992: 32) who in cooperation with the QRCA undertook a study of respondents' motivations for participating in qualitative marketing research.[10] Even though there were variations by topic and degree of experience with participation, the distribution of reasons to participate are instructive.

Gratuity	78%
Interest in subject	63%
Curiosity	48%
Want to participate in research	47%
Enjoyed previous research	34%

Some of this study's respondent verbatims shed further light on motivations for research participation:

> It was worth my time and effort. I enjoyed seeing the new product ideas.
> I enjoyed the session but it takes time out of your schedule and you have expense in getting here.
> I would not participate if there were no gratuity, because even though I was curious and the session was interesting, I had to take time off from work and drive for a half hour.

These findings suggest that even though incentives are important they should be played down as a sole reason to attend the session. Recruitment should emphasize the psychic benefits and rewards of research participation to prospective respondents – an opportunity to participate in a social event with like-minded peers, an activity on behalf of improving products for consumers everywhere – rather than just the money to be earned.

Over-recruitment

Since there is a natural attrition of participants between the recruitment screening and the time of the actual interview, field services generally over-recruit subjects. Reasons for the shortfall may vary – changes of plans, insufficient incentives, loss of interest in the topic, family or personal emergencies, illness – yet attrition should be anticipated in planning the focus groups or depth interviews.

The likelihood of attrition varies with the respondent category. The standard practice is to recruit 12-13 for 8-10 to show up for a focus group. For some respondent categories, such as seniors, teens or low-income consumers, even higher over-recruitment ratios are required.

In-depth interviews commonly use 'floaters' to cover for no-shows. Floaters are individuals willing to make themselves available for an entire morning or afternoon in case another recruited subject fails to arrive. Floaters merit a higher incentive payment as compensation for the incremental time commitment.

Since extra respondents will be recruited, decisions need to be made if too many potential participants show up. Some moderators like to interview everyone that arrives, regardless of the number, particularly if they are professionals or from sensitive respondent targets not accustomed to standard research practices. Others prefer to whittle down the number of respondents used. While some facilities can comfortably seat twelve or more respondents in a focus group, others cannot accommodate more than ten. In many situations where creative exercises will be conducted, even eight participants are adequate. Furthermore, a high number of respondents can make the sessions unwieldy and uncontrollable for some types of discussions.

The standard practice is to 'pay and send' extra respondents. This can be handled sensitively by the hostess with an explanation that usually involves a comparison to airline over-booking and a promise to consider the respondent for another upcoming study. Some recruits react to this joyously for being paid without further time commitment; others can be disappointed or hostile, as one young man who exploded when turned away from a group on sexually transmitted diseases, when he mistakenly believed that he would be deprived of information on his troublesome health condition.

Regardless, decisions need to be made about which individuals to eliminate. Usually, 'first come, first served' is the rule that prevails. Otherwise, it may be desirable to eliminate 'duplicates' – individuals that are closely matched in screening requirements. The best practice is to hold everyone who arrives until the re-screening procedure can verify that everyone is qualified. Then, the moderator and research manager need to make judicious decisions about respondents who are redundant.

This situation should not be regarded as wrong or wasteful since it is a tool used to guarantee the proper composition of study respondents. Clients should expect to pay for respondents dismissed without prejudice. On the other hand, there are sometimes reasons to capture the opinions of extra participants and some qualitative research consultants and research managers usually have them fill out a questionnaire or complete an exercise before dismissal.

Minimum shows

Decisions also have to be made about the minimum number of acceptable 'shows' – or respondents present – for the focus group to take place. The 'show rate' may be affected by normal attrition factors as well as external factors such as severe weather or traffic emergencies. Low turnouts should not be automatically blamed on poor recruitment practices. If a recruitment manager expects a problem in the show rate, even as late as during the final confirmation calls, this should be reported to the moderator and research manager immediately. Nevertheless, many low show situations cannot be anticipated and are encountered only at the final moment.

Most clients insist upon at least five or six participants to consider a group adequately recruited. If the minimum figure has not been met, a decision should be made about the disposition of the group. This decision must be met without rancor and hostility because it is in no one's interest if there is a low show rate. Everyone should show flexibility and cooperation and place the emphasis upon completing the study in a way that best addresses the objectives. Nearly all moderators and recruiters are willing to make accommodations to have an engagement turn out successfully. By the same token, as the commissioning party it is the research manager's responsibility to handle the financial consequences of the failure and compensatory steps. It is unfair to expect either the moderator or the recruiter to carry full accountability for the situation.

Here are several options in case of a shortfall.

- Hold the session anyway with as many participants as possible and fill in at another time. This is the least problematic reaction and does not waste the commitment of the participants who have arrived. At the end of the group, the research manager and moderator can assess deficiencies, if any, and plan appropriate steps to compensate. The range of possible additional steps should include the option of conducting one or several individual interviews if research management feels they have missed participation of a particular segment.
- Postpone the session. This is somewhat more problematic. It may be feasible to recruit additional respondents for another session, but it may not be possible for the people who have already shown up to return. In weather emergencies, it is often very likely that recruited no-shows can be induced to return at a later date. In any case, the research manager should expect to pay for the costs associated with extra recruiting, re-scheduled facility rental and incentive payments to the respondents that arrived and were sent home.
- Cancel the session. This alternative generally is problematic because moderators or field services have cancellation policies and fees which will be activated if the session is cancelled. Thus, payments will have to be made despite leaving the facility with no useful information. This alternative tends to harm interpersonal relations and is unfair to professionals who have been working responsibly.

The best practice is to proceed with what you have and then make decisions about how the study should be enlarged or changed in consideration of the problems that have arisen.

Quality management of recruitment suppliers

Quality control at every stage of the recruitment process is necessary if problems are to be averted. Here are some guidelines for maintaining the highest level of recruitment standards.

- *Establish strict expectations.* If there are areas of flexibility in respondent specifications or recruitment approach, these may be stated; if not, let the facility manager know that.
- *Put everything in writing.* Thus, if problems arise, handling the situation will be easier. Verbally engaging any subcontractors on an assignment should be followed up in writing with a clear implementation plan and statement of respondent specifications. Any changes that are made in project scope or specifications should be communicated in writing. If incremental charges are incurred as a result of a change, these should be confirmed.
- *Get regular updates.* Insist upon regular updates of recruitment progress from the moderator. Problems can be corrected early in the process if research managers are aware of difficulties being experienced. If there is an issue, for example, difficulty in meeting a particular quota or finding a particular segment, act quickly to solve the problem. Blaming and recriminations against the recruiter are unwarranted if the respondent definition was imprecise or unachievable – a situation the recruiter may not have anticipated at the time of bidding.
- *Provide enough time to do a good job.* As Fuller points out, time is essential 'to assimilate the screening information and to ask questions, clear up areas of confusion, plus foresee potential problems' (1995a: 16). Rush assignments always produce their share of complications. At least two or three weeks are often necessary to conduct a high quality recruitment. Make sure that the recruiter is giving the assignment priority and not delaying because it is regarded as easy or because another client's demands are more strident.
- *Avoid changes in specifications after recruitment has begun.* Client imposed screener revisions once recruitment has been started can be costly and threaten recruitment success. Charges may be incurred for respondents already recruited according to the original understandings; resubmission of the project may incur research company costs.
- *Do not use a facility or recruiter without a site inspection and/or referrals from at least three previous customers.* If an initial phone contact is unpleasant, move on to another supplier.
- *Do not use the lowest cost supplier.* Maintaining a superior professional service requires investments in staff and infrastructure that are repaid by loyal repeat customers who are willing to pay a premium for high quality.
- *Be flexible about recruitment requirements, if necessary.* Redefining participant criteria may be required if an unexpected incidence problem arises. This is not a *recruitment* problem; rather it represents an underlying fallacy in the definition of the target.
- *Avoid recruiting individuals who know each other as friends, neighbors or relatives.* It is disconcerting to discover halfway into the session, for example, that half the respondents visit the same health club each evening

and bring their outside roles into the focus group. Sometimes it is useful to screen for occupations in order to guarantee that half the group is not composed of students, nurses or teachers – groups which often seem over-represented in the pool of potential respondents.

- *Collect sign-in sheets from the facility.* Make sure that they specify the incentive paid to each participant.
- *Adhere to relevant professional standards of procedure.* In some countries, professional associations such as the MRS in the United Kingdom maintain national standards for administering questionnaires. Interviewers, under threat of penalty, must certify that they have followed codes in conducting the interview. The research manager should have a familiarity with and require adherence to these standards.

2.12 Creating an Effective and Foolproof Screener

Good recruitment depends upon the screener – the questionnaire used to ascertain that potential respondents match the definition of the targeted consumer. Writing an effective screener requires a combination of rationality and creativity. Here are several guidelines to create an instrument that achieves every project's objectives.

Respondent specifications

An effective screener starts with an explicit list of respondent specifications. The 'spec' list should reflect the targeted market in a general way. Workable specifications are clearly communicated, operationally defined and measurable in an objective manner. This means that nearly any trained interviewer can pick up the questionnaire and quickly learn to distinguish between acceptable and unacceptable categories. Several examples of clear respondent specifications are:

- Females, aged 21-49. Mix of ages.
- Household income, $20,000 if single, $30,000 if married. Mix to $100,000+.
- Primary purchaser of household cleaning products.
- Primary household cleaner.
- Looks for high quality when shopping for household cleaners.

Here are several examples of unclear specifications. All have been actually transmitted in client communications.

- Buys only popular brands.
  (*Problem:* Which brands are popular?)
- Middle or upper-middle class.
  (*Problem:* How do you define that?)
- Fashionable and trendy.
  (*Problem:* How is that defined – according to whose standards?)
- Upwardly mobile yuppie.
  (*Problem:* How is that measured?)

The list of specifications is generally provided at the top of the screener or on an accompanying memo. Although some field services will generate a screener from a list of specifications, for quality control it is a good idea to send the recruiter both a spec list and a screener derived from it.

Screener components

Screeners normally consist of several components and types of questions as long as they are relevant to identifying targeted respondents for a particular study. These are reviewed below.

- *Heading* Provides space for respondent name, address, day and evening phone numbers, project name, date of interviews and other elements that will help to track the productivity of employees.
- *Introduction* Describes the purpose of the study in a motivational way – making it interesting without divulging too much about the objectives. Entirely 'blind' screeners do not motivate respondents. This section should also immediately reassure the listener that this is not a sales call.
- *Security questions* Designed to eliminate respondents with potential conflicts such as working in the industry or for a competitor and consequently having a knowledge base or interests inconsistent with objectives. The occupations and company affiliations of spouses should also be solicited in case these disqualify on the basis of conflicts. Security questions are also used to exclude overused respondents, including those who have attended too many research interviews, have participated too recently or have already completed an interview on the category or topic being studied.
- *Demographic (fact) questions* Specifies the age, gender, income, household composition, geographic and ethnic parameters of the targeted respondents. Questions on race and ethnicity are not intended to be exclusionary – in fact, exclusionary questions are a violation of most researcher codes of ethics. In contrast, ethnicity questions should be included to guarantee that a range of patterns in a given market are reflected in the research study. Sometimes, however, when a specific culture is targeted in a study, screening questions should carefully and sensitively formulate clear criteria for inclusion or exclusion. For example, in a project on Spanish language media, specific self representation features, for example, 'identifies self as "Hispanic or Latino"', and behavioral standards, such as 'watches Spanish language television at least five hours each week' or, 'speaks primarily Spanish in the home', should be established. One should resist the temptation to rely only upon 'Spanish surname' or 'born in a Spanish-speaking country' because these are ambiguous conditions.
- *Product usage questions* Aims at establishing category or brand usage patterns of targeted respondents, such as frequent users, light users or users of competing brands. Be careful to establish clear operational definitions of product usage through behavioral criteria, for example, instead of saying 'Marlboro™ smoker', say 'purchases at least two packs of Marlboro™ per week'. Be clear about terminology and jargon in establishing usage. For example, a bank may specify respondents on the basis of 'transactions' but the consumer and recruiter may not know if that refers to a buy, sell, deposit, withdrawal, or opening or closing an account.[11] Also, recognize that if high usage categories are based upon national tracking studies, individuals may be difficult and expensive to locate in particular markets.
- *Lifestyle questions* Seeks to establish the respondent in a category based on daily life experiences, such as 'dual income, no kids (DINK)' or

'fashionable'. These can only be determined through a multidimensional set of behavioral criteria which must be specified. For example, recruiting DINKs involves guaranteeing that partners are either married or cohabiting, are both employed and that there are no custodial children in the household. Being 'fashionable' implies shopping within a certain subset of stores (Saks 5th Avenue™, Bonwit Teller™, for example), wearing the clothes of selected designers of the moment (Versace™, Calvin Klein™) regularly reading one of several fashion magazines (*Harper's Bazaar, Vogue, Mademoiselle, Glamour*) and so forth.

- *Attitudinal (opinion) questions* Seeks to establish the respondents' mindset in connection with the brand or category, such as receptivity toward new products or brand loyalty. Alternatively, attitudinal screening sometimes seeks to uncover a respondent's broad approach to life, such as concern about environmental issues, or category-defined segments such as 'transitionals' or 'alienated'.

  There has been a recent tendency to attempt recruitment of attitudinal segments through the use of a battery of questions that are then analyzed through a formula or algorithm into various 'types'. These scales are generally derived from multivariate analytic tools used in large-scale survey-based segmentation studies. Unfortunately, this method presents severe problems to qualitative research recruiters who cannot quickly duplicate the analysis. It also results in a substantial proportion of terminations because the probabilistic criteria used to establish the categories cannot be matched on a smaller scale.

- *Articulation and creativity questions* Seeks to establish that the respondent is capable of forming opinions and expressing them confidently in a group. These questions are *optional* and must be constructed very carefully to be valid. They may include a battery of projected self-image questions, such as 'My close friends think of me as shy' (or outgoing, intelligent, bossy, persuasive). Alternatively, they may set behavioral criteria, such as 'educational attainment of at least college graduation' or 'attends symphonic concerts, legitimate theater or the opera at least twice each year'.

  Sometimes, problem-solution questions are used to test for creativity or articulation but these often create ambiguities and other difficulties. Respondents often experience them as 'trick questions' and try to outwit the recruiter. These questions take the form of asking respondents to confront a challenge such as, 'Which historical figures would you most like to invite for a dinner party?', 'If you could travel anywhere in time and take a picture, whom and what would you take a picture of?', 'How do you feel about the death penalty?' or 'List five things that can be done with a paper clip'. Unfortunately, these can only be regarded as a test of willingness to answer the question. Recruitment interviewers cannot independently interpret the degree of creativity or articulation associated with any particular answer.

- *Offer/closing* The recruiter thanks the respondent for finishing the screening questionnaire, invites her to the interview if screening requirements have been passed, offers the incentive, and describes follow-up procedures. If a termination is necessary, the interviewer handles this positively, in a sensitive and non-blaming manner. The respondent's future cooperation and regard should be assured.

Screening requirements and quotas

Responses to screening questions can be classified on the basis of how they are used, defining and establishing acceptability to the range of targeted respondents required by the study. The types of questions can be listed as follows:

- *Screening requirements* These specify conditions that must be met in order to participate. Those who fall outside these parameters are terminated from continued screening and excluded from the study. For example, screening requirements may demand that the minimum age in a set of focus groups on cigarette smoking be 21 in order to conform to legal standards. Alternatively, those who eat dinner at a fast food restaurant less than one time each week may be considered poor prospects for a new menu item and thus not a target of interest in evaluating new product feasibility.

- *Quotas* These specify the desirable range within respondent categories that need to be represented in the group. For example, in recruiting for a study of personal care products targeted at women between twenty and fifty years of age, it is useful to establish quotas by decade (one third each in their twenties, thirties and forties) to guarantee the participation of women whose ages may be associated with distinctive demands or reactions to promotional imagery. Quotas may be set very strictly or loosely – indicated by the request to 'obtain a mix' within the range of a category. Otherwise acceptable candidates can be dropped from participation because their quota-defined classifications are filled. Thus, if quotas are defined very strictly, it can add to the length of time and effort required to complete recruitment.

- *Information questions* These are questions that require no action following a response and are for advice and intelligence only. Since these are not critical to the screening process, they should be minimized. Fuller and Pampalone go even further and insist that recruiters 'avoid asking questions that are not directly related to the screening criteria, as this can tire respondents and discourage them from completing the screening process' (1995: 40). Most information issues, consequently, should be handled during the interviewing process.

Past participation and security screening

Security questions are designed to screen out prospective participants who may have conflicts, too much background knowledge or are otherwise not representative of the 'typical' consumer. Persons working with competing companies, in the trade channels of the product category under study or with any marketing, advertising or research firms fall under these limitations.

Past participation limits are also set in order to shun respondents who are sufficiently over-educated about the research process or the category under examination that they also cease to be typical of average consumers. No moderator wants a respondent in a focus group to discuss consumer segmentation and targeted media as though they were a marketing consultant. Reliable research requires real consumers. Thus, the cutoff date for any prior research participation is commonly set at three months, six months or a year at the client's discretion. Persons who have previously participated in the category are usually dismissed and a maximum number, generally 5-10, is set for the total number of qualitative research participation events over a lifetime.

Security and past participation limits can impact the cost of a study and add an extra complication in low incidence recruits. This is particularly true if the study demands so-called 'virgin' respondents who have never participated in a qualitative research study.

Many clients and qualitative research consultants have recently challenged these norms, and many wonder about their worth in preventing market research participation. In many professional and executive studies, characteristically, participation limits are simply not feasible. Only a small proportion of physicians in general practice or any other medical discipline are willing to participate in marketing research studies and they are likely already to have completed studies on antibiotics or the most prescribed therapy for their specialty. Similarly, Directors of Information Technology (IT) at major corporations willing to participate are highly likely to have already completed studies on behalf of software package marketers. Thus, strict limits in these types of studies are not likely to be accepted by responsible recruiters.

Even among consumer studies, the desirability of inexperienced respondents has been challenged as illogical and impractical (Thompson et al., 1999). Perhaps, some commentators argue, it would be better to rely upon respondent teams who have acquired skills and are even better able to represent consumer culture.

Guidelines for screener development

Writing the screener in a way that accurately reflects targeted respondent characteristics, is easily administered and efficiently produces a desirable consumer mix, is a complex and difficult task. The exhortations listed below will speed the way to this achievement.

- *Be realistic.* Do not over-define the targeted respondent with too many interacting demographic, product usage and attitudinal characteristics. This will make them both difficult to find and unconnected from the real world.
- *Keep the screener as brief as possible.* Ask no more than 12-15 questions that establish basic participation requirements. Avoid asking questions not directly related to screening criteria as this adds to phone time and produces little information of value to study conclusions. Lengthy questionnaires can bore and exhaust respondents and produce disincentives to group participation.
- *Ask for only one variable per question.* This reduces and simplifies response categories making it easier to fit consumers into their proper 'box'. For example, in household composition questions, separate questions about marital status and number of children are desirable.

- *Ask questions directly using active verbs.* For example, 'use', 'prefer' or 'buy'. Ambiguous questions such as, 'How often are you at the store for breakfast cereal?' are harder to answer and may produce inappropriate respondents.
- *Do not frame questions in a leading way.* Also avoid asking questions in a manner that tips off the respondent to critical requirements. Leading questions often provide too much information, for example, 'We're looking for people who drink at least three cups of coffee per day. Is that your practice?'
- *Use plain consumer language.* Use language that can be understood by everyone without a college education. Avoid trade terminology or marketing jargon – even terms that have crept into everyday speech. Thus, call it a 'cell phone that can access e-mail and the Internet' and not a 'WAP-enabled device.'
- *Group related questions together on the screener.* Fuller and Pampalone (1995) suggest this method because 'random ordering of questions is disorienting for respondents'.
- *Place major disqualifying items – questions that could terminate a respondent from consideration if not answered acceptably – at the beginning of the screener.* This way time does not need to be wasted administering additional questions to someone unusable.
- *Advise recruitment facilities before the start of recruitment if contacts and terminations need to be tallied.* It is very difficult to reconstruct this information at a later date.
- *Save sensitive questions for last.* For example, questions dealing with income and ethnic characteristics should be covered later or toward the end of the screener after the interviewer has had a chance to develop rapport with the subject.
- *Be specific on screening and quota requirements within the body of the questionnaire text.* This is necessary so that the interviewer does not have to refer back to a memo or set of instructions while administering the screener.
- *Type instructions to interviewers in bold or upper case.* This is recommended so instructions can be easily differentiated when the screener is being read. Use a consistent print style and format leaving a reasonable amount of blank space between questions and response categories.
- *Test questionnaire items and the format.* It is advisable to ensure ease of use before sending out the screener.

Sample questions

Here are examples of the specifications listed at the beginning of this section that have been turned into screening questions.

- *Females, aged 21-49.*

This should be expanded to two questions. The gender question is usually not asked explicitly but simply recorded by the interviewer.

(DO NOT ASK UNLESS UNCERTAIN – SUBJECT IS:)
    [ ] Male   (TERMINATE)
    [ ] Female

What is your age: (FILL IN HERE _____ AND CHECK CATEGORY BELOW)

    [ ] Under 21   (TERMINATE)
    [ ] 21-29   (QUOTA - ONE THIRD)
    [ ] 30-39   (QUOTA - ONE THIRD)
    [ ] 40-49   (QUOTA - ONE THIRD)
    [ ] 50 or more   (TERMINATE)

- *Household income – $20,000 if single, $30,000 if married. Mix to $100,000+.*

This question should come relatively late in the interview. It is best to phrase the income question in terms of 'categories', rather than asking it directly, since specific income is not needed and may be a more sensitive issue than the range. The question phrasing above assumes that a marital status question has been asked earlier in the screening. Here is a more accurate way to discover the needed information.

Which category below represents your household income? Please stop me when I have reached your category.

    [ ] A. Under $20,000   (TERMINATE)
    [ ] B. $20,000 - 29,000 (TERMINATE IF MARRIED, CONTINUE IF SINGLE)
    [ ] C. $30,000 - 49,000
    [ ] D. $50,000 - 99,000 (OBTAIN A MIX)
    [ ] E. $100,000 and over

- *Primary purchaser of household cleaning products.*

This is a fairly straightforward question. Here is a good way to represent it.

Who in your household usually buys the cleaning products, such as soaps and cleansers, used in your home:

    [ ] I do
    [ ] I share the decision equally with someone else
    [ ] Someone else does   (TERMINATE)

- *Primary household cleaner.*

Who mainly does the house cleaning in your home:

    [ ] I do
    [ ] I do it equally with someone else

[ ] Someone else does   (TERMINATE)

- *Looks for high quality when shopping for household cleaners.*

This is an attitudinal question, and can be expressed in the following way.

What do you look for when shopping for a household cleaner: (READ LIST AND CHECK ALL THAT APPLY)

[ ] Lowest price
[ ] Whatever is on sale or discounted
[ ] Whatever I have coupons for
[ ] High quality   (TERMINATE IF NOT CHECKED)
[ ] A brand name
[ ] A product that has been recommended to me
[ ] Other
(SPECIFY)_____

Fool-proofing screeners

Cynical consumers known as 'cheaters and repeaters' who have made participation in market research almost a career, will lie and falsify their personal or product usage behavior in order to get accepted into research activities. Many of these have learned to listen for cues in the screener that may indicate termination conditions. The strategies listed here for fool-proofing a screener as much as possible will help to thwart respondents who are bent on misrepresentation.

- Avoid yes/no questions as much as possible.
- Be careful that the way questions are phrased does not prompt responses.
- Do not always use the first or last response category as the terminating conditions. Experienced research subjects often are able to figure out that the first and last categories ought to be avoided.
- As often as possible, make the respondent do the talking rather than having her simply react to categories. Phrase questions in an open-ended manner and use the categories only to code responses.
- Make the termination conditions as clear as possible. Do not leave it up to the recruiters because they have a stake in admitting respondents as quickly as possible. For example, if an articulation question is being asked, do not have the interviewer make a judgment about who is articulate or not.
- If a product or brand variant is required, do not rely upon the respondent to recall all of the fine points. It may sometimes be necessary to get them to reach for an actual product so that they can read information off the label or registration tag.
- Have respondents bring the actual medications or prescriptions in their names to the interviews.
- Check photo identification at the door.

Follow-up

The key to a good 'show rate' after recruitment is consistent follow-up. Here are several steps that should be followed to guarantee that respondents will keep their promise to appear for research participation.

- Inform respondents with the details of how the follow-up will be handled. Solicit good times and alternative numbers for call backs.
- Leave each respondent with a contact name and number. Instruct them to call the facility or recruiter if they are no longer available as scheduled so that a replacement can be found. Discourage respondents from sending a replacement on their own.
- Reinforce the critical importance of actual participation. It is affirming for respondents to know that someone with their specific characteristics is needed to complete the balance required for the study.
- Be culturally sensitive in handling the follow-up. Some participants may find repeated reminder calls disruptive or badgering.
- Send a follow-up letter with detailed travel directions. Describe how parking will be handled and if necessary (usually in downtown facilities) include a parking supplement in the incentive.
- Provide extra considerations for special populations. For example, mothers in low-income communities may need on-site child care at the facility. Elderly or disabled participants may need special pick-up service and/or information about building access.
- Instruct participants to arrive at least 15-20 minutes before the start of the session for check-in. Describe what the check-in procedures will be if identification will be checked or respondents will be re-screened.
- Remind respondents if a meal service will be provided.
- Call respondents at least twice to confirm. The last confirmation call should take place within 24 hours before the interview. If inclement weather is threatening, obtain alternative numbers in case of postponement or cancellation.

2.13 Quality Management of Screening

Screening quality is critical to the validity of study results and essential to client satisfaction. No one will believe research conclusions if they feel the study has talked to the 'wrong people'. The process can be optimized if everyone understands mutually interdependent roles and takes a problem solving approach. By following a number of strategies to monitor progress and manage issues as they arise, difficulties and strain can be minimized.

Responsibilities of the research manager

The research manager takes full charge of the project plan while delegating implementation details to responsible third party suppliers. The manager is friendly and trusting in supervision while demanding high standards and frequent communication. Associated responsibilities include the following:

- Does not launch a project before receiving thorough approval of all details and specifications from internal clients.
- Provides timely feedback about implementation tools designed by the research company, such as the screener or discussion guide.
- Avoids unnecessary changes and complications after implementation has been launched.
- Shows flexibility and consideration if difficulties and unanticipated crises occur.

Responsibilities of the consultant

The qualitative research consultant is the key contact and intermediary in screening and takes primary responsibility for quality control. Related functions include:

- Develops the specifications statement and screener, subject to client approval.
- Monitors progress on a daily basis and reports back to the client research manager as successes, questions or problems occur.
- Creates a 'paper trail' (which may, of course, be in electronic form) of any modifications in the original plan that have occurred.
- Handles contacts with the facility before and at the time of the interviews.
- Audits all screeners and other evidence of recruiter productivity.

Responsibilities of the facility, field service, recruiter

If a recruitment facility accepts an assignment, they should exhibit a proactive, positive, 'can-do' attitude in completing the project. Complaining, delays in returning calls and repeated questioning about matters that are explicit in instructions serve to complicate the success of the experience. Other requirements for the field service include:

- Provides the services of a single project manager who is continuously knowledgeable about progress and is responsible for communicating with the research company.
- Implements recruitment according to instructions. Does not deviate from protocol without explicit directions. Provides no information about the study to participants other than what the client has authorized.
- Provides updates of screening progress within the time frame required by the client. Produces regular written spreadsheets that identify and monitor respondent characteristics.
- Handles the follow-up procedures in a manner that guarantees the highest show rate possible.
- Provides filled out screeners to the research manager and moderator before the interviews so that they can be checked for errors.
- Provides reception and hosting, including sign-in of respondents.
- Handles all on-site needs of respondents and clients, including meal/snack service, comfortable environment for productivity, high quality recordings, orientation to local services and any other amenities as contracted.
- Manages re-screening as requested.
- Handles mistakes responsibly. That is, if someone has been incorrectly recruited and does not match specifications, that person is eliminated sensitively and without cost to the client.

Sign-in sheets

Sign-in sheets should list the names of attendees and acknowledge receipt of the cash incentive. These should be audited by the research company to guarantee that appropriate payments have been disbursed.

Re-screening

The field service normally takes responsibility for re-screening any or all respondents who arrive for the study. Some carry out this responsibility as a matter of routine, others only if it is explicitly requested. Moderators may prefer to conduct the re-screening themselves if the topic is sensitive, for projects involving creative respondents or when children or other problematic respondent categories are being researched.

It is uncommon for the entire screener to be administered again; rather only several key questions are asked of arriving participants. If there are special information questions that are needed prior to the interview, participants are sometimes asked to fill out a brief questionnaire.

Dealing with liars, cheaters, repeaters and other professional respondents

Sadly, many individuals seeking respondent incentives as an income source misrepresent their product usage patterns, previous participation and personal information. It is very difficult to ferret out cheaters because they may operate under different names, work with several different recruiters and be very knowledgeable about tactics to facilitate their inclusion. Vigilance during screening and check-in should be a matter of policy. Here are several suggestions for dealing with this problem.

- Sigma Validation, a US based research company offers a respondent tracking service in North America that will match the phone numbers of participants in a study against their proprietary database of research participation. Several professional associations have endorsed this service. The modest additional cost is worthwhile.
- Instead of or in addition to using an outside service, facility recruiters may also validate respondents by comparing phone numbers against their own databases.
- If a cheater is discovered during check-in, re-screening, or during an interview, that person should be discontinued immediately. He should receive a formal communication which sternly discusses the lack of ethics and morality involved in this practice. Many practicing cheaters consider this a game and do not realize how seriously disruptive this behavior can be.
- Recruitment interviewers should be carefully supervised and those exhibiting evidence of conspiring with prospective respondents to falsify specifications should be dismissed immediately.
- Some facilities and moderators are experimenting with the use of a signed affirmation in which, under penalty of fraud, participants are required to certify that they have not falsified their personal descriptions in order to gain admission to the session. This approach should be discussed with competent legal counsel and current experiments should be watched.
- The names of cheaters and repeaters should be reported to other facilities in one's area so that they are eliminated from other respondent databases.

Above all, research managers should refrain from the kinds of practices that set temptations for cheating in motion – limited time for recruitment, confusing and ambiguous specifications, a lack of explicit directions and the use of unprofessional suppliers.

Table 6 Project management checklist.

Item	✓
Set study objectives	
Determine appropriate methods	
Determine implementation tactics	
Develop a project brief	
Establish a project budget	
Solicit moderator proposals	
Select the moderator	
Select field services	
Obtain additional services	
Develop respondent screener	
Recruit respondents	
Develop discussion guide, interview	
Conduct research	
Receive reports	
Arrange presentations	
Manage internal distribution of information	
Arrange for payment to research firms	

SECTION 3

Group Moderation and Interviewing Techniques

- Preparing for an interview
- The qualitative researcher's frame of mind
- What are we looking for
- Thinking creatively
- Creating and using discussion and observation guides
- Guidelines for observing research sessions
- The stages of a research interview
- Playing the moderator role
- Understanding respondent motivations
- Using group dynamics effectively
- Asking questions fairly; avoiding leading questions
- Probing
- Interpreting body language
- Exercises in the focus group
- Projective and elicitation techniques
- Problem participants and how to manage them
- Keeping the discussion focused
- Managing interview contingencies
- Closing the interview effectively
- Maximizing the usefulness of creative brainstorming sessions
- Maximizing the effectiveness of observational research
- Maximizing effectiveness of research with special populations

3.1 Preparing for an Interview

This section describes steps to be taken in implementing qualitative research interviews, site visits and discussion sessions. For the most part, we assume that a research company, acting as suppliers or consultants to marketers or product developers, will be handling all or most of the details. A professional qualitative researcher is adept at coordinating project details, conducting the interviews and developing the analysis and final deliverables. Consequently, this section's guidelines are oriented to helping the research manager structure and evaluate outstanding service delivery. This section also contains information to help moderators conduct research interviews. Thus, the emphasis shifts from a strict focus on the organization of research to examining effective research practice.

Research managers without extensive training and experience in research techniques, group dynamics and strategic marketing should not handle group moderation by themselves. As we will see, even though leading group sessions may seem 'easy' it is based upon systematic considerations for producing the highest level of valid and productive consumer information possible.

Background knowledge and preparation

Conducting a successful qualitative research project requires a good deal of advanced moderator preparation.

- *Study objectives* The moderator should be well briefed about the objectives of the study, including details on what the internal clients need to know, how the research results will be used, and what decisions will be affected by the research findings.
- *Brand and category background* Research consultants should also be given detailed background information on the brand and category. Sharing recent research reports detailing competitive market dynamics, market share, brand history and traditions, etc. will help moderators gain perspective on the issues being treated in the current project. Reading publicly available industry studies and trade publications are another essential feature of moderator preparation. If there are any prevailing hunches, hypotheses or opinions which will be affected by the research, the moderator should know about them.

Sometimes it is helpful for moderators to conduct several 'guerilla' interviews or observations in the real world outside of the research industry to become better informed about consumer language and consumption styles, particularly if they have never worked in the category or used the products. For example, observing how particular brands are bought in the supermarket or a discount store and discussing decision making with the shoppers involved helps the moderator get ready for the research project.

- *Respondents* The moderator should become familiar with any special respondent characteristics or unusual discussion requirements. For example, if something technical will be discussed, be sure that the moderator has enough background to speak knowledgeably about that subject. If respondents represent a particular regional or ethnic group or if they represent a particular health status, be sure the moderator is familiar enough with those issues so as not to speak in an ignorant or insensitive way.

Fieldwork

The research company is generally responsible for managing the fieldwork aspects of the project. If they do not have the resources available within their own companies, as is likely, they must make arrangements with other partners. Selecting and managing the right recruiters, facilities and other needed resources is the hallmark of an experienced and competent qualitative research consultant. Previous sections have already described at length how selecting and recruiting the correct targeted respondents are essential for the success of a project because it is crucial to interview consumers that reflect the project objectives.

Most of the time desirable participants are defined in terms of demographics (age, sex, education, income), product usage, brand usage, usage frequency and other attitudinal characteristics. At times, additional requirements are imposed, for example, self-perception as 'creative'.

After respondent specifications are determined, individuals matching those characteristics must be recruited. The essential tool for recruitment is a *screener* – a questionnaire for determining whether a prospective respondent meets specifications.

Screening has a number of additional requirements. It must be objective. Participants who may have a stake in specific research outcomes should not be recruited. Individuals from potentially competing businesses should be screened out. Try to avoid recruiting 'cheaters and repeaters' or professional respondents who are not likely to offer valid data.

The respondent mix

At the time of recruitment, the researcher must decide which categories of respondents to mix or to separate in the various interviews. Since qualitative data analysis relies heavily upon making comparisons among different respondent types, selecting the right mix is essential. The moderator is usually a good guide since she is able to base this decision on previous experience.

Depending on the objectives of the project, it may be necessary to combine or separate satisfied from dissatisfied users, the brand's own customers from a competitor's customers, men from women, first time users from experienced users and so on. Alternatively, conflict and confrontation in group discussion may introduce instructive dynamics. In some cases, for example, the influences of group members can negatively affect opinions; in other cases, non-users can be persuaded by satisfied customers. These types of influence models should be watched carefully because they are clues to patterns in the marketplace.

If a specific mix is desired, it is often necessary to impose quotas within each focus group for certain kinds of respondents. For example, it may be desirable to mix heavy and light users in a group. However, so that one segment does not outweigh the other, it may be necessary to impose a quota of 50 per cent for each group.

How to look and dress – professional demeanor

Deciding how to look and dress during a face-to-face interview or site visit is an important part of researcher preparation. The moderator should focus her demeanor on the research participants and not on the client observers.

The moderator's appearance should match the expectations of the targeted group and reduce social distance while reinforcing authority. As a rule of thumb, if anything about the moderator's clothing, jewelry or appearance might prevent rapport with respondents, or if it is too ostentatious or culturally inappropriate, it should not be worn. By the same token, the moderator should avoid 'dressing down' if that is likely to weaken one's authority during the interview.[12]

With the increasing fashion of casual business attire in the United States, suits and ties nowadays seem stiff and formal for both men and women unless they are trying to portray a highly authoritative or clinical role in interviews with, for example, physicians or business executives. European norms for business attire, on the other hand, continue to favor highly stylish suits.

An attractive, distinctive and tasteful tie, scarf or sweater can focus attention on the moderator and command respect. On the other hand, flashy designer labels may produce impressions that the moderator is arrogant.

Legal release and consent

For some types of studies, it may be helpful or necessary to secure legal release from respondents. This should be done when the company needs safeguards against respondent liability or copyright claims. Situations which may require the signing of legal release or consent forms prior to the conduct of research include:

- Projects in which new product ideas are generated or refined.
- Research involving underage minors, particularly if the topic is somewhat sensitive, such as those involving personal hygiene.
- Research on sensitive topics such as criminal behavior or health treatments.
- Projects which require interviewers to enter respondents' homes.
- Projects which require videotapes or other research products to be exhibited to external audiences (such as distributors or retailers), in which respondents might be identified.

The requirements of legal release and consent as well as potential risks and liabilities should be carefully reviewed with counsel before any particular form is used. The use of consent forms does not eliminate the need for insurance coverage. (See the Appendix for samples of forms.)

Research ethics

Ethical considerations related to qualitative research demand adherence to a number of principles and practices surrounding the selection of participants and interactions with subjects. These are goals and ideals that should pervade every aspect of the research encounter.

- *Respect* Respondents should be treated with the utmost respect and consideration. They should be regarded as valuable allies and confidants rather than as objects.[13]
- *Safety, no harm* Respondents should expect that no aspect of the research process will harm or offend their person and dignity. This includes techniques used in the research, questions, exercises and probes, which should cause minimal pain and not be offensive, defamatory or insulting in any way from the perspective of participants.
- *Privacy* Respondents have the right to know and control the ultimate use of their words and image. Their names should not be disclosed to outside parties particularly on the basis of information disclosed in the interview, and they should not be solicited individually for sales or marketing activities by the client.
- *Informed consent* If any aspect of the research process is questionable as to considerations of respect, privacy and safety, the respondent should be informed in advance of any potential issue or problem and given the freedom to decline.
- *Transparency and disclosure* Respondents should be informed about all details of the project as long as they do not threaten objectivity or bias results. These include research objectives, auspices and techniques, among others. If any aspect of the research cannot be divulged, it should be described as such and not covered up with a lie. As much information as possible should be revealed. For example, if the sponsor's name may not be disclosed, it should be described as a 'major manufacturer of breakfast cereals'. If a 'strategic lie' is part of an exercise, this information should be revealed as early as possible.
- *Non-discrimination* Unless there are segment dynamics that need to be studied in isolation, respondents should not be excluded from research participation on the basis of racial, ethnic, religious, national origin, gender, health or disability status, marital status, age or sexual preference characteristics that are not intrinsic to segment targeting.
- *Right of refusal* Respondents have the right to decline to answer any question, refuse to participate in any exercise or terminate participation in the session – without penalty – if they find that any question, procedure or practice offends their person or dignity.
- *Legality* It is unethical for researchers to promote violation of any applicable national or local laws. It is further inappropriate to use research

to promote violating the ethical precepts of any profession involved in a business transaction.

- *Appropriateness* It is unethical to use research to promote the use of products that are inappropriate for the targeted segment because of age, health status or other concerns. For example, research should not be conducted to promote cigarette smoking among those who may not legally smoke.

Final inspection and briefing

This section describes all of the details that should be checked by both the moderator and research manager just before the research is conducted. Members of the management and research team as well as the moderator should always arrive at the facility at least one hour before the start of the first focus group or in-depth interview so that a final inspection and briefing can be conducted. This also guarantees that the team will be present when respondents begin to arrive.

- *Confidentiality* The facility should be given a list of observers attending the sessions prior to the evening of the groups. Anybody not arriving with the moderator should be identified by name only or by the name of the research company rather than by the sponsor. She should not mention the name of the company or the research topic as identification as this might tip off waiting respondents.
- *Host(ess) introductions* The project's host or hostess for the evening should introduce himself to all members of the observing team. This is the person to whom all requests should be directed about meals, sound, temperature and so forth.
- *Catering arrangements* Arrangements for meals and/or snacks for client observers and respondents should also have been made prior to the conduct of the groups; however, many clients prefer to select among menus from nearby restaurants for a last-minute meal decision. Make sure that all catering instructions, for example, special dietetic or kosher meals, have been followed as the final inspection is performed. The hostess should be informed regarding the time meal service is desired.
- *Special services* Any other special arrangements – videotaping, video-conferencing, note taking, translations – should also be checked at this time. Videographers should be briefed about special requirements such as close-up shots of body language during the session.
- *Supplies* Make sure that both the conference room and the observers' room has sufficient quantities of any supplies that may be needed during the interviews, such as easel pads, marking pens, note pads, pencils, collage materials.
- *Communication during the interview* The moderator and observers should make arrangements for communicating during the interviews, if necessary. For the most part, notes to the moderator during the session should be avoided. Instead, it is best for the moderator to step out and quickly 'huddle' with observers in the viewing room at various agreed-upon points during the interview that may be declared as a 'recess'. Notes passed into

the focus group room during the discussion can be very disruptive to the flow of the session and can compromise the moderator's authority.

- *Rehearsal* At some point, hold a final briefing or 'run through' of the discussion guide with the moderator and observers to make sure that everyone has achieved consensus on how various issues will be handled during the session. At this point, the amount of time that is to be devoted to each aspect of the discussion should be confirmed.
- *No last-minute changes* It is important to avoid last-minute changes in the discussion guide or stimuli used during the sessions. The moderator should be given as much lead time as possible to become familiarized with concepts and prototypes that are to be tested in the sessions. Any bright ideas for a new stimulus or set of questions should be suggested in the debrief following the session.
- *Comfort* The moderator should make certain that the lighting, heating and cooling systems are comfortable in both the viewing room and focus group room. Observers should be shown how to adjust the sound in the back room.
- *Final screener check* Obtain the completed screeners for the arriving respondents from the hostess and review them to confirm that participants have been recruited to specification. Sometimes, for everyone's convenience, the facility will prepare final summary sheets based on the screeners.
- *Re-screening* Check on arrangements for re-screening respondents. Sometimes, security, sensitivity or other demands make it necessary to have a member of the research team or the moderator handle the re-screening herself. Normally, only 2-5 critical questions are asked rather than going through the entire screener with each respondent. Some moderators prefer to informally chat with respondents during the re-screening so they can consider dropping inarticulate recruits.
- *Final culling* Determine the maximum number of participants that will be accepted into the interview session since the facility is likely to have over-recruited to account for no-shows. (The standard practice is to recruit 12-14 for groups of 8-10.) If all recruited participants have shown up, it may be necessary to 'pay and send' one or several of them. Research manager input is needed to determine which respondents are the most expendable without biasing the respondent mix. Make sure that the facility handles this responsibility of sending away recruited participants with care and sensitivity. If re-screening has determined that any of the invitees do not match specifications, now is the time to send them off as well.
- *Collection of pre-tasking materials* If they have not already been collected, there is a need to review how pre-tasking materials will be assembled. It is usually best to collect items in advance of the session so that embarrassment and misunderstanding is avoided during the interview if anyone has mistaken the directions.
- *Name tags* The moderator should make sure that she and all the participants have had name tags made. The form of address should be appropriate for the culture and social status of the participants, for example, some may prefer to be addressed as 'doctor', 'mister', 'señorita' or by their first names.

If all the pre-interview planning has gone well, you should now be ready to start. *Good luck.*

Table 7 Final inspection and briefing checklist.

Item	✓
Arrival at least one hour before the start	
Facility given a list of observers	
Host/hostess introduced	
Arrangements for meals and snacks	
Special arrangements	
Videotaping	
Note taking	
Translations	
Other	
Supplies for interviews	
Easel pads	
Marking pens	
Note pads	
Exercise materials	
Pencils	
Other	
Arrange communicating during interviews	
Final briefing or 'run through'	
Comfort conditions	
Lighting	
Heating/Cooling	
Sound	
Completed screeners reviewed	

Item	✓
Legal release/consent forms secured	
Re-screening arranged	
Maximum number of participants decided	
Name tags	
Pre-task materials collected	

3.2 The Qualitative Researcher's Frame of Mind

The qualitative researcher is not detached from the process of data collection. He or she is a critical resource that guarantees that valid and reliable information is being derived from participants. The moderator also is involved in a process of continuous analysis throughout the interview, during which hunches and tentative hypotheses are checked and respondents are probed for accuracy and details.

Conducting qualitative research is an important responsibility which requires a unique frame of mind. It demands concurrent attention to both the front and back rooms. The researcher must project several personal qualities in order to facilitate respondent acceptance, to sustain rapport and to collect valid data. Simultaneously, consultants need to keep the client's objectives in mind and continuously process verbal expressions in a manner that exposes meanings and insights consistent with strategic goals. The research manager depends on the moderator to serve as a channel between the brand and its consumers.

Above all, qualitative research consultants should be passionate about their work and intensely curious about 'what makes people tick'. Moderators also need to be quick learners, assimilating information about the brands and categories. They should be excited about leveraging their intellectual skills and making connections between knowledge and strategy.

Listed below are several personal qualities that the researcher should assimilate and demonstrate while conducting an interview.

- *Objective* The qualitative researcher should be aware of and set aside her own beliefs, attitudes, expectations and prejudices. Moderators should also insist that client observers reduce their personal ego stake in specific outcomes. Ideas and concepts should be allowed to fail or get radically revised without penalty to anyone's career or integrity.

- *Direct and specific* Questions and the thrust of the discussion should be clear and thought provoking without being rude or derogatory. Even tough questions should be asked without equivocation. Inappropriate humor, sarcasm, seductive chumminess and ambiguity make the moderator seem weak and lacking in confidence.

- *Non-judgmental in attitude* The moderator should stay emotionally neutral about respondent attitudes while being accepting and provocative. Judgmental reinforcements, such as 'that's good', should be avoided. Be careful of words and phrases that encourage defensiveness, such as, 'Why didn't you do that?'

- *Good listener* The moderator should establish and maintain strong rapport. He should avoid talking more than necessary and instead help respondents to speak and reveal themselves. Moderators should be supportive whether or not respondents react positively to stimuli. Responses should not be channeled to support the expectations of product management.

- *Sensitive to body language* The moderator should be acutely aware of her own as well as the respondents' body language. She should maintain eye contact with participants, present an open and relaxed posture; lean in toward respondents while speaking, rather than sit back in her chair. Moderators should be adept at 'speaking' without words, by using their hands, eyes and posture. They should be able to vary their tone of voice as necessary and command the geography of the interviewing environment.

- *Friendly and open* Moderators should be lighthearted and non-threatening. The encounter with consumers should be marked by a sense of safety and security. Moderators should be relaxed and easy with smiles and friendly gestures. They should be the kind of people that invite confidentiality and disclosure – everyone's best friend – while avoiding seductiveness and insincerity.

- *Professional* On the other hand, moderators should maintain a degree of professional distance from respondents. They should avoid expressing their own opinions or acting like a participant in the discussion. Instead, they should make connections and draw implications of participants' utterances, continuously checking and confirming their own observations. They should make sure respondents understand the moderator's role and responsibilities.

- *Reciprocal* A good moderator has a 'giving' personality. These types try to make research a good experience for the respondents. They validate the importance of participation and provide psychic rewards for valuable time and effort being expended by respondents.

- *Respectful* Good moderators show respect for the feelings and opinions of subjects. Naomi Henderson (1991) likes to use the Rogerian concept of 'unconditional positive regard' or UPR in describing the kind of approach moderators must practice: 'accepting the worth of each participant, respecting individual points of view and receiving all divergent viewpoints as relevant to the topic under discussion'.

- *Flexible* Good moderators can adjust themselves to different personalities and respondent types. They're not rigid nor do they ever rush respondents about time schedules or other expectations. They can change the course of an interview quickly if respondents' attitudes demand such a change.

- *Creative* Good moderators project creativity. They are prepared to see familiar activities in new ways, draw new implications, envision new futures. They encourage creative leaps in others.

3.3 What Are We Looking For

Qualitative researchers should be good students and analysts of human behavior. They should have considerable insight into the intricacies of interpersonal communication – how people express themselves, interact with and influence others. They should be conversant with perspectives and concepts drawn from a wide range of learning and academic disciplines – psychology, sociology, anthropology, literary criticism, fine arts, linguistics and economics.

Social scientific literature provides qualitative research with several ways of describing and understanding behavioral patterns. This section draws upon this tradition of scholarship to provide a series of issues which may help researchers achieve focus in creating questionnaires and conducting research.

The primary patterns we look for in any research study can be described as *behaviors*, *meanings* and *tools*. These fundamental concepts will be used to organize the perspectives that should guide the moderator's exploration of consumer patterns.

Behaviors

Cultural *behavior* refers to all human actions outside of biologically imposed conditions (such as sleep and digestion) that are enacted in daily life. Behaviors can be conscious and purposeful or subconscious and non-goal-directed. Here are several examples of behaviors.

- *Rituals* are patterned behaviors, usually performed without thought, that are repeated by force of habit or belief. Examples include one's own particular pattern of personal care in the morning or manner of cleaning the bathroom each weekend. Marketers may be interested in rituals because they want products to match consumers' accustomed ways of completing tasks or because they want advertising imagery to reflect consumers' true practices.
- *Roles* are behavioral sets through which persons enact a status in relation to other members of a group. Being a boss or a father are examples of roles. Marketing roles may include decision maker, influencer, negotiator and critic. The roles that consumers play in their homes or workplaces largely determine the product categories as well as the brand-associated features and benefits that will be of interest. For example, the principal family food preparer in a household may be interested in speed and convenience as a benefit because this work role occupies a disproportionate amount of personal time.
- *Practical activities* include work, shopping or anything else that is oriented to accomplishing a goal. Every culture provides a set of patterns for completing practical activities. These should be understood in creating and

promoting products because they may create opportunities for better meeting people's needs. For example, ethnographic research reveals that Turkish women sort their laundry by sex of the wearer – a pattern not found in the US or Western Europe. This may suggest the feasibility of differentiated products that better meet the expectation for cleanliness in men's vs. women's clothing.

- *Performances* are patterned behaviors that are staged for the benefit of an observer. Many product brand usage situations involve some level of identity performance, for example, wearing a Versace™ suit, driving a BMW™, smoking Marlboros™. In each case, there may be elements of product satisfaction produced by technical features; however, the main benefits associated with usage may involve the reactions induced in others.
- *Play, games and diversions* are behaviors believed to induce personal relaxation or bonding between individuals. They also can provide the basis for various social relationships, for example, when the boss invites a junior employee to join in a golf outing. To understand the emotional connection of many product categories and consumers it may be necessary to involve an appreciation of the idea of 'play'. For example, in visiting a fast food outlet such as McDonald's™ or White Castle™ even an adult's motivation may reside less in satisfying hunger and gaining nutrition than in experiencing the fun and diversion of trivial food.

Meanings

Meanings are the ideas, emotions or beliefs that we attach to an object, a behavior or to another idea. Researchers make sense of behaviors by trying to understand the meanings behind them. Cultural standards provide the reservoir for the everyday experiences that hold or convey meaning. As Durgee suggests:

> Symbolic anthropologists focus not only on what respondents say and do but more importantly, on what their statements and actions mean symbolically. I might like Dr. Pepper™ soft drink, not only because I like its sweet taste but also because it means that I am 'part of an original crowd'. (1992: 36)

Specific meaning-laden patterns include those listed below.

- *Symbols* are things that stand for something else. They can include simple shapes or marks, such as a cross which stands for Christianity or the crucifixion, or they can be quite complex, such as a corporate logo. Brands want their logos and associated design elements (golden arches, red-white-and-black package) to be both instantly recognized and associated with (symbolize) a set of values and attitudes that comprise the brand image. Associating the brand with a famous spokesperson can effectively borrow equity because the celebrity symbolizes some higher value – Tiger Woods represents youthful excellence, Cindy Crawford epitomizes maturing beauty.

- *Signs* are markings that point to something in the environment. A highway sign, for example, directs the driver to an exit. The Amoco™ sign provides direction to refueling for both the car and driver.
- *Archetypes* are broad character types that may transcend culture in illuminating the human experience. Cooper and Patterson point to the 'trickster' representing 'our wishes for exaggeration, seduction and the absurd' (1999: 2) as providing a useful guide for emotionally loading advertisements in a way that supercedes rational faculties and appeals to inherent subconscious meaning.
- *Language, jargon and slang* are tools for communication. However, words have emotional connotative meanings beyond their basic communication value. A clear example of this is sexist language – for example, referring to an adult woman as a 'girl' can be either insulting and demeaning or tender and affectionate depending on the source and context. Since words are redolent with meaning, it is important to analyze how products are named and described. Referring to McDonald's™ as 'Mickey-D' stimulates interest in young consumers who have created this nickname. Federal Express™ found it beneficial to rename its overnight delivery brand to reflect the affectionate consumer term 'FedEx'™.
- *Beliefs and values* are meaning filters or standards of truth – a set of principles for conducting everyday life. They provide legitimacy to personal behavior and help one tell right from wrong. Personal values such as thrift or industriousness may thwart acceptance of premium brands or various luxury categories. A health orientation may lead consumers to a variety of products such as vitamin and mineral supplements, fat-free cookies or breakfast cereals containing oat bran. Sometimes expressions of beliefs may be inconsistent with other values or observed behaviors; for example, consumers who want ecologically safe home cleaning liquids are disappointed by the performance of 'green-positioned' products in meeting their cleanliness standards.
- *Attitudes and opinions* express a point of view toward people, things and events. They can range from positive to neutral to negative. They can be intensely upheld or maintained with minimal salience. They are important sometimes as rational explanations of purchase behavior but, just as frequently, may serve as *post-facto* rationalizations.
- *Interpretation* is how we make sense of things that are communicated to us. Two people may see the same advertisement or read the same novel but interpret them differently. Interpretive patterns may be influenced by the culture as a whole or by the unique perspectives of age-related or other sub-cultural groups.

The process of interpretation is critical in assigning meaning to behaviors that are observed within the context of a research study. Dickie (1997) reports that in the course of an observational research project on the usage of new 'pay at the pump' gasoline dispensers, he found that some consumers approached the pump intending to obtain a fill-up and left quickly without their intended purchase. It took some time to realize that the departing customers were not wearing their reading glasses while driving and could not decipher the instructions – a bit of real world context that was overlooked when consumers evaluated the concept and prototypes in a laboratory setting. Later versions of the equipment managed to adjust for customers who would not be wearing reading glasses.

- *Feelings* refer to the emotional values that we attach to people, behaviors or ideas. They are people's inner response to the external world. Sometimes they can be justified, most often they are based upon deep experiences and sensations that defy rational explanation. Feelings such as attraction, jealousy, greed and hatred may lie behind behavior toward products and brands.
- *Relationships* are socially constructed ties between things and/or individuals. The ways we are bonded into relationships – for example being part of a family, nation or club – have a tremendous impact upon our daily life, our work habits and our beliefs. They also have a great deal to do with how we select restaurants, brands of cognac, toilet tissue and financial services providers. Perhaps Mom or Grandpa used that brand; it may have saved Uncle Jack from financial ruin; maybe it was first used and recommended by a fraternity brother.

Tools

Tools are culturally produced devices – both objects and ideas – that expand human powers. Tools can help us live life more comfortably or securely; they can help us perform our work, defend ourselves and organize our social ties. Most products offered by clients of market research are tools that are offered to facilitate and enrich the daily lives of consumers. Broadly conceived, examples of tools can encompass:

- *Physical space* or the constructed environment which can include our homes, workplaces, and cities.
- *Technology* from low to high. This is the conventional meaning of tools. Anything that expands human powers, from paper clips to super-computers, are examples of technology. People are continuously looking for ways to make things faster, more abundant, more reliable and personally satisfying.
- *Rules* which provide a systematic framework for an organization or a body of knowledge. They guarantee that everyday life proceeds with some degree of predictability and security. A simple company policy statement, the rules of baseball and the US Constitution are examples of tools that help us carry on our lives. The rules of grammar or a dictionary assure that written expression can be decoded.
- *Techniques* or ways of doing things. These are the 'how-to's' of our daily lives. Techniques work hand in hand with technologies to advance human potential. They can be diminutive in scope or grand in scale – how to screw in a light bulb or how to finance construction of a commercial development. Techniques may reside in the knowledge base of craftsmen, technicians, professionals or average people.

Viewing our own or others' behaviors, meanings and tools with objectivity is very difficult. We take so much for granted and expect that our own patterns are the 'normal' ways of getting things done. However, when we conduct research in a different culture, we have to step outside our own routines and expectations in order to see things clearly. To achieve a higher truth, the researcher must suspend his own values and try to understand the consumers' perspective – to walk in their shoes, so to speak. This search for empathic insight is an essential principle of qualitative research. Acting like a stranger even in your own culture is a stance that can produce new understanding.

It is also very easy to misinterpret the meaning behind various behaviors. If the context of an act – the cultural meaning, its history, its intentions, the behavioral sequence leading up to it – is poorly understood, the observer may get its true meaning all wrong.

3.4 Thinking Creatively

Good moderators demonstrate creativity in their own thinking and inspire creativity among respondents. Studies with exploratory and developmental objectives require an extra measure of creative energy. The guidelines presented in this section are offered as a starting point for achieving breakthrough thinking.

Qualitative research requires what Edward de Bono (1970) has called 'lateral thinking'. This involves looking for new pathways rather than merely working within accepted boundaries – and going for more even when you believe you have finally found something. Lateral thinking is provocative – it asks for what is next, what is better. Lateral thinking is not unimodal, it makes leaps· backwards and forwards. It looks for new ways of defining, naming and classifying things. Instead of going where everybody is going, lateral thinking takes you to minority viewpoints. It invites risk and does not guarantee answers.

Roger von Oech's book *A Whack On The Side Of The Head* (1983) describes creativity as a thought process that can be achieved after several barriers that thwart creative processes are broken. Moderators should be conscious of the 'mental locks' that von Oech describes and take steps to overcome them in working with interview subjects.[14] Some suggestions for moderators are listed below.

- We've been taught to look for the one right answer. That's fine most of the time but thinking that way in marketing research leads us away from alternative answers. A good moderator validates diversity and allows many different points of view to emerge. She pushes respondents to be imaginative and take risks.

- Logic has its place when you need to plan or get organized. When you're trying to be creative, excessive logic can be a hindrance. Good moderators are ready to use and invite the use of abstractions, metaphors and ambiguity. Probes that invite a move away from logic may purposely introduce contradictions, for example, 'What would make you hate this brand?' and, 'Who should not be buying one of these?'

- Following rules too rigidly can lead to dead ends. Good moderators are ready to innovate and break rules if the situation requires this kind of flexibility. This may involve dramatically shifting the direction of the discussion in order to pursue a worthwhile lead. Clients that prohibit innovation and require strict adherence to a discussion guide may be losing some of the most valuable insights.

- Valuable ideas may not seem practical at the outset – they only become so after considerably more ingenuity and effort. Good moderators don't judge everything by the standard of practicality because that can be a trap which locks participants into a single pattern of thinking. Creative thinking requires going into a 'what if' mode. How to make findings actionable may not be apparent from the content of any single interview but may emerge from deep thought and imagination after all the sessions have been completed.

- We have learned to avoid ambiguity because, most of the time, we need to be precise to communicate clearly. Good moderators searching for new ideas, however, encourage a dose of ambiguity which allows participants to explore alternative solutions. Consumers may hold apparently contradictory feelings simultaneously – about the wish to follow a diet, for example, while continuing to seek the indulgence and gratification that snack foods provide. This ambiguity led a creative marketer several years ago to fashion a characteristically paradoxical ad slogan: 'Enjoy the guilt'.

- Moderators who fear errors and mistakes will seek out only 'safe' solutions rather than breakthrough innovations. Creative marketers learn from trial and error. If you're not failing every once in a while, you're not being innovative. Clients that place financial pressures on consultants based upon some arbitrary standard of success risk missing the essential truths of the qualitative research experience.

- Good moderators encourage participants to play, have fun and act like children when the situation calls for innovation. A spirit of lightheartedness will free participants' minds for creativity. Group interviews may sometimes seem like they are drifting between anarchy and control – good moderators know how to manage both for the benefit of client objectives.

- Specialization is a fact of life but it can also make our thinking banal and rigid. Good moderators are not afraid to learn from people who approach problems from alternative perspectives.

- Conformity, also known as 'groupthink', or 'the way things are done around here', has a deadening impact on creativity. Good moderators are able to reduce conformity to group pressures and give participants the courage to stand out. They validate individuals who express their own opinions from the beginning to the end of the session.

- If participants don't think they are creative, it becomes a self-fulfilling prophecy. Good moderators are inspirational and reassuring. They give everyone a shot at a breakthrough idea. They set high expectations which may startle or upset participants initially yet provide encouragement as effort is expended to meet demands.

3.5 Creating and Using Discussion and Observation Guides

The basic tool for conducting a focus group or in-depth interview is the discussion guide. Before the discussion takes place, the guide is a statement of intent about how the sessions will proceed in terms of topics to be covered, the sequence of questions, probes or exercises to be introduced and the amount of time to be spent on each topic.

Discussion guides

Constructing an effective discussion guide and understanding how to use this tool is an essential step in the research process. It is important that the research manager and the moderator reach agreement about all aspects of the discussion guide well in advance of the research because it will serve as a 'map' for the conduct of the sessions.

Listed below are guidelines for writing and using the discussion guide.

- *Be sure that the discussion guide conforms to the ebb and flow of the interview.* It should begin with exploratory and factual questions and become more focused and opinion-seeking later in the session. Moderators should avoid diving into the heart of the matter until they are confident that understanding and a productive conversation flow have been established. Early questions should avoid sensitive issues, excessive probing or imaginative exercises which should all be saved until a degree of rapport has been established.

- *Use the discussion guide as a topic outline, not a questionnaire.* It should include the issues that management wants addressed – not necessarily the questions someone believes should be asked. The moderator should have the flexibility to raise issues in a manner appropriate for the respondents and the situation. Some matters need to be approached indirectly, for example; other issues need to be addressed several times so that hunches and hypotheses can receive support.

- *Write the guide as a tool to provoke peer discussion.* The discussion guide should not encourage just a two-way dialogue between interviewer and subjects. It should provide for issues to be approached as a group so that conditions, limitations and the meaning of behavior are explored. The moderator should avoid the role of constant inquisitor.

- *Ask questions that are 'open-ended' rather than requiring a 'yes/no' response.* In focus groups and depth interviews, they should stimulate discussion and exploration among respondents rather than just demand reactions to the moderator. If statistical information about attitudes and usage is required, the study should apply a different research methodology.

- *Structure the discussion from general to specific.* In constructing the discussion guide, within each topic area the discussion flow should go from general issues to specific concerns and probes. For example, an early topic question may be, 'Let's talk about how you do dishes'. Later questions under this topic can focus more tightly on specific aspects of the process or experience such as the fragrance or viscosity of dishwashing liquids or the difficulties in eliminating some types of stains.
- *Follow the respondents' indications of interest.* In a survey study, the interviewers must make sure that all the questions are being asked in the same way at the same point in every interview. This is not the case with a discussion guide. The moderator should be expected to follow the respondents' interests, sentiments and language. He should take cues from the matters that respondents are most conscious or passionate about.
- *Establish a logical flow of conversation.* Try to make sure that the discussion follows a logical flow. Sessions that are disjointed are hard for participants to follow and make them feel cut off. At the same time, moderators should be permitted flexibility and encouraged to digress when necessary as long as the interview's evolution is consistent with research objectives.
- *Don't read from the discussion guide during the interview.* Attention to the instrument can detract from eye contact with respondents and this can disrupt rapport. A thoroughly briefed moderator essentially memorizes the guide in preparation for the interview and only consults the written page to make sure all details have been handled.
- *Don't insist upon too much detail in the discussion guide.* The moderator should use markers and key words that will jog memory during the discussion and allow her to maintain active and interested interaction with respondents.
- *Don't make the discussion guide too long.* Three double-spaced pages are normally sufficient. Make certain that the discussion can be completed in the allotted time; otherwise some topics may be rushed or shortchanged and respondents will feel that their opinions are not valuable or important. Less is more. If the moderator and research manager believe that completing the guide will be difficult within the given time period, they should agree in advance on discussion priorities and what can afford to be dropped.
- *Remember these rules for the desired discussion flow.*
  - General to specific
  - Facts to opinions
  - Impersonal to intimate
  - Talk to activities
  - Rational to emotional

Observation guides

Observational research and ethnographic studies make use of an observation guide to direct attention and participant interaction during this type of research encounter. The guide is a 'map' of anticipated behaviors that will be systematically observed across a range of respondents during the research project. Most rules for constructing an observation guide are identical to those for a discussion guide. Here are some additional tips to structure a study whose main approach is watching.

- *Make sure that the behaviors to be observed can be watched without being too intrusive.* Excessive encroachment makes participants self-conscious and less spontaneous about their behavior.

- *Break down anticipated steps.* Each behavioral area under study and being observed should be broken down and elaborated into all of its logical components in creating the guide. However, the ethnographer should allow for unanticipated surprises and original patterns of completing an action. For example, the act of brushing teeth can be broken down into multiple steps.

  - Removing toothbrush from storage
  - Removing toothpaste from storage
  - Preparation of toothbrush
  - Preparation of toothpaste
  - Preparation of mouth
  - Application of toothpaste on toothbrush
  - Method of brushing
  - Length of time devoted to brushing
  - Ease of access to rear teeth, backs of teeth
  - Rinsing teeth
  - Expectorating
  - Cleaning toothbrush
  - Returning toothpaste to storage
  - Returning toothbrush to storage

- *Define probing points.* Observational studies can range from those applying 'pure' observation in which the ethnographer has little or no interaction with the respondent, to 'participant' observation, which can involve considerable interaction. In the latter case, at any point while observations are being made, the respondent can be probed regarding thoughts and feelings around any behavior being observed. In making a probe, the ethnographer should be careful not to render the respondent overly defensive or sensitized to the behavior being watched. It is much better to ask, 'What are you thinking right now?' or, 'What are your intentions as you're doing this?' rather than, 'Why didn't you put the cap back on the toothpaste?'

3.6 Guidelines for Observing Research Sessions

It is very difficult for marketing and research managers to be good listeners when observing a research professional conducting interviews. Many bring an emotional investment or ego to the process, such as ownership of a particular strategic idea or advertising execution. There are political dynamics that may cause tension between consumer insights and brand management specialists within a marketing organization or between specialists and the advertising agency. This may result in inappropriate feelings of embarrassment, shame and blame when consumer reactions are not as expected. Sometimes the moderator may get caught in the middle of contending political players and subtly persuaded to muddle research conclusions.

While some clients are overly political during the course of research observation, others are tempted to turn the entire matter into a party or sporting event complete with loud cheering for winning concepts. In either case, the result is an inappropriate back room atmosphere and a failure to maximize the usefulness of research observation.

In spite of these threats to productivity, research managers should make the effort to gain and promote effective listening skills in order to maximize the usefulness of qualitative research projects. Taking charge of the back room and structuring the activities, perceptions and reactions during interviews are among the most important shared responsibilities of the moderator and research manager.

Who should be invited to observe

Research managers should be careful in issuing invitations to research observers. Having too many personnel in the back room can become distracting. Inviting observers with no compelling reason to be involved detracts from the seriousness of the research and leaves the back room vulnerable to excessive frivolity – a feeling that this is a form of entertainment rather than serious work. On the other hand, colleagues in creative and strategic roles who implement decisions based on exposure to consumer information can benefit from the encounter. People in the following roles, consequently, should be considered for the invitation list as long as participating will clearly inform their responsibilities.

- Research and consumer managers
- Brand/product planners and managers
- Senior management
- Technical product development staff
- Sales personnel

- Sales personnel
- Account managers and creative personnel from strategic consulting firms, advertising and public relations agencies

It is unethical for personnel from a competing research company or consulting agency to attend as an observer with the intention of capturing the business by subverting the incumbent.

Observer schedule/logistics memo

The moderator is generally responsible for submitting a schedule and logistics memo for the benefit of observers. The research manager should ascertain that everyone invited to observe the sessions receives a copy in both paper and electronic form within sufficient time because the memo should contain information essential to the success of observation.

The memo should detail the following:

- *Project schedule* including days and times of all research activities according to targeted segments and location of each session. It is helpful to have this in both table and calendar formats.
- *Directions* to all facilities from local airports. This information is routinely supplied by the facilities themselves.
- *Information on local hotels* and restaurants according to price, class of service and distance to the facility.
- *Local contact information* about the moderator. In case the moderator has to be reached at the last minute, it is useful to provide name, address, phone, fax of hotels or other local arrangements. Cellular telephone and e-mail addresses if usable should also be recorded. Clients should be discouraged from contacting the facility directly about substantive changes in the project without clearance from the research consultant.
- *Facility protocol information* including:
  - Lead time necessary for arrival and check-in.
  - Dress code. It is a good idea to discourage observers from wearing white shirts or bright jewelry when videotaping because these are sometimes reflected in the back window.
  - Check-in procedures. Some facilities require security precautions such as business identification. It is advisable to encourage clients to identify themselves by the consultant's company name or by the study topic since waiting respondents may overhear the name of the client company and become subtly biased.
- *Information on catering arrangements* for clients who may have special requests such as vegetarian or kosher meals.
- *Briefing and debriefing schedule* that includes observers. Client observers are less prone to run off at the conclusion of a group discussion if they know in advance that a debrief will take place afterwards.
- *Orientation information for novice observers* including general information about maintaining objectivity, focusing on meanings and thought processes,

reading cues in body language and looking for the big picture. These may be helpful to novice observers who cannot attend a briefing.

Backroom briefing

Many qualitative research consultants believe that it is a best practice to conduct a backroom briefing prior to the first, several or all groups. The purpose is primarily to reaffirm mutual expectations and responsibilities. During the backroom briefing, the moderator, research manager and other observers have a final opportunity to review study objectives and research techniques. At the very least, a summary of norms and etiquette for inexperienced observers may be helpful. Some moderators prepare a formal orientation and others may have specific task assignments for observers.

It is helpful to provide copies of the topic guide and the respondent information sheets to all observers so that they can follow the progress of the discussion and review details about participants throughout the session. Sufficient note paper and writing instruments should also be distributed.

Observers should be encouraged to look for diversity in opinions and practices as well as areas of consensus. Often, the hardest part of being an observer is to avoid concentrating on a particularly negative, positive or vocal respondent. Thus, some consultants encourage observation 'exercises' which promote active listening skills.

An observation room exercise advocated by some moderators, for example, is to assign one or two participants to each observer. In addition to listening for the overall thrust of the discussion, the observer is expected to be the advocate for 'his' respondent during the debrief.

Another option is to have observers differentiate their observations by 'confirms' vs. 'challenges' that correspond to things known about the brand's consumers. Yet another practice is to have listeners segment their observations according to the strategic value of the information, for example, 'choice process', 'benefits sought', 'reasons to buy', 'tonality expected', etc.

Bad habits

Listed below are some bad observation room habits which create problems for the collection and interpretation of useful qualitative information. Practicing moderators have experienced most or all of these.

- *Failing to be dispassionate and objective.* Since some observers arrive with a stake in the outcome of the research, they cannot resist seeking only consumer input which confirms their expectations, or they deny or explain away rival perspectives. Members of creative teams may do this quite unconsciously; as Jim Spanier says, 'They're not being disingenuous; they truly hear more of the positives' (1993: 33).
- *Drawing general conclusions that are inappropriate for qualitative research studies.* For example, estimates of market share or global conclusions such as 'Americans love this flavor'.

- *Talking too much.* Rendering opinions and judgments while the session is in progress disturbs other observers eager to hear consumer input.
- *Disparaging the moderator's style or methods without really understanding qualitative research techniques.* Qualitative research consultants vary in their approaches to moderation and, in any case, place their emphasis upon strategic conclusions rather than showmanship in demonstrating their value. Observers should not try to 'improve' the moderation. If there are legitimate complaints about the moderator's style or techniques, these should be resolved affirmatively afterwards in a less pressured and tense environment or they should be reviewed in the moderator's evaluation at the conclusion of the engagement.
- *Dismissing the subject matter as being uninteresting.* Again, this boorish criticism presumes that the function of observation is entertainment. Good focus groups have many silent spells and periods of confusion.
- *Avoiding difficult or ambiguous material.* Some observers inappropriately skip the introductions and return only for the concept screening or some other component of the session. This course of action misses essential details which set the context for understanding consumer reactions to stimuli.
- *Allowing distractions to occur.* Some of these might include getting over-involved with the food or snack service, napping, making phone calls from the observation room or attending to other business while the discussion is in progress.
- *Making inappropriate demands on the hostess or the research facility while the session is in progress.* The hostess is not a personal secretary or messenger. Because of other commitments, it is usually not possible for her to type up new concepts or perform other unanticipated business services.
- *Listening only for details and nit-picking.* Greenbaum urges observers to 'focus on the macro rather than the micro issues raised during the group' (1995: 50). Observers should allow their preconceptions and assumptions to be clarified and challenged.
- *Taking a positive or negative attitude toward various speakers.* That is, playing favorites and selectively ignoring what some participants have to say – especially because they don't dress well, or lack a desired level of articulateness. Like them or not, these are the brand's targeted consumers.
- *Taking notes selectively to reinforce one's own prejudices.* Martha Wilson suggests that clients are prone to ignoring various assertions when 'the participant has expressed a common complaint that the client feels powerless to rectify' (1994: 16).
- *Making inappropriate demands of the moderator.* It is not helpful to insist upon instant changes in components such as the discussion guide, exercises or interview sequence while the group is in session. These items should be based upon research objectives and developed well in advance of the interview. If there is a legitimate need to redirect the study based upon conclusions from early portions of the sessions, this should be arranged in consultation with the moderator after the sessions have been completed.

Guidelines for effective listening

Most of the preceding problems can be managed and the effectiveness of qualitative research can be maximized if observers follow these guidelines.

- *Examine the entire record of interviews.* Look at the total context before reaching conclusions based on the research. Don't jump to conclusions on the basis of the first sessions in a project. Be patient and let the findings evolve over the entire set of interviews.
- *Stay balanced.* Pay proportionate attention to both positive and negative feedback. Don't get swayed by persuasive, articulate or dominant respondents. On the other hand, if one person's opinion in the session makes everyone change his or her mind about buying a product, make a careful record of what was said.
- *Appreciate group process.* It takes time for a group to coalesce and work in harmony. Moderation requires careful staging and management of different character types and roles.
- *Listen for and analyze the 'big picture'.* Pay attention to the main ideas and central concepts and don't let anyone get distracted by details. These big picture issues include but are not limited to the following:
  - What respondents like and dislike overall.
  - Which consumers expect to use the product.
  - How they expect to use the product.
  - The benefits that the product offers.
  - Communications elements that are persuasive or not persuasive.
  - Ways in which the concepts can be combined or adjusted.
  - The product's advantages and disadvantages relative to its competitors in the marketplace.
- *Focus on the speakers' meanings, motivations and intentions rather than on just their words.* Sometimes, when people say, 'I hate all mouthwashes', they really mean that they have not found one yet that matches their desired flavor, intensity or expected benefits.
- *Don't expect consensus.* Pay attention to the negotiation that goes on between participants. Try to understand the range of feelings or practices.
- *Don't be distracted by the respondents' clothing, demeanor, grammar or similar personal characteristics.* These individuals have been recruited to the sessions because they are the brand's customers.
- *Try to understand the thought process through which respondents are reaching their judgments.* Sometimes, opinions are situational and are generated as the discussion proceeds. If something gets respondents to change their minds quickly – for example, being challenged by another member of the focus group or learning new information about the product – take note of that process.
- *Don't expect every moment of the discussion to be meaningful.* Don't expect great verbatims for every point in the discussion. Don't expect all questions to work as expected.
- *Record notes objectively and thoroughly.* Include points that you don't immediately understand or that sound ambiguous and contradictory. Record consumer language. Make note of all respondents' work-arounds,

dissatisfactions, and wishes because these are clues to needs. Use the discussion guide as a resource that can be filled in as respondents are speaking.

- *Pay attention to non-verbal cues as well as to what's being said.* Be sure that there is general consistency between expressed opinions and body language.
- *Don't expect the consumer to do the planner's, strategic marketer's or copy writer's job.* Consumers can only describe their practices, feelings, hopes, aspirations, frustrations, disappointments and so on. It is the marketers responsibility to leverage these through the filter of their own insight and intuition to produce the tangibles of a marketing campaign.

Passing notes and communicating during the interview

The best practice in conducting qualitative studies is to brief the moderator thoroughly and provide sufficient flexibility so that communication during the interview can be minimized. Research managers should avoid trying to over-direct the moderator by passing notes into the interview room. This practice tends to be disruptive and compromises the moderator's authority vis-à-vis the respondents.

If you must pass a note into the interviewing room, be sure that it is brief and legible. Forcing the moderator to become distracted breaks the rapport that he or she has established.

Most moderators prefer to leave the interviewing room at one or two points during each session to ask observers if any points need to be pursued further. In this case, too, more than one or two departures can break rapport and should be avoided.

If the observers are in the same room as the respondents, the best practice is to wait until the very end of the session and open the discussion to questions from observers in a manner that allows the moderator to preserve authority.

Research associates in the viewing room

In order to improve client service, manage backroom contingencies and further leverage the effectiveness of their work, many consultants now assign associates to serve in the viewing room. This practice is fairly common in Europe and is slowly catching on in North America. Someone proficient in the project's objectives and execution details is well-equipped to handle issues raised by observers and provide support for the moderator. The back room associate is also valuable as an analyst who can take notes about the main discussion while listening in on reactions and participating in spontaneous discussions occurring in the back room. Reyn Kinzey argues that this type of input has greater validity than a transcript produced by a non-involved support person and produces faster report turnaround.[15]

3.7 The Stages of a Research Interview

Interviews go through a relatively predictable sequence of stages. Understanding these stages can help you appreciate effective moderation. Respecting this cycle helps the moderator ensure favorable interaction with respondents, which leads to collecting richer data. In composing the discussion guide, the moderator should make certain that the question sequence conforms to the stages described in this section.

The stages of an interview correspond to the well-known stages of a group experience. They can be seen as similar to stages in the life cycle.

- Infancy
- Childhood and adolescence
- Young adulthood
- Mature adulthood
- Old age

Let's take a closer look at each of these stages. (NOTE: The time allotments for each stage are approximate and based on a two-hour focus group.)

Stage 1: The introductory stage (infancy)

The primary issue at the outset of a research experience is for the moderator to greet respondents and help them get oriented to the new relationship and situation. This is the time to explain the purpose and the ground rules of the research and to allow the moderator and the respondents to get comfortable with each other. (5-10 minutes)

Stage 2: The role taking and rapport building stage (childhood and adolescence)

In this stage, the moderator's main tasks are to establish rapport, set an appropriate tone, and gain the confidence of participants. Group members try out their roles and take their first steps toward productivity. At this point, respondents are expected to begin speaking. Some moderators initiate this phase of the discussion by having respondents discuss some neutral topic such as their occupations, neighborhood or family composition. (10-15 minutes)

Stage 3: The general questions stage (young adulthood)

In this part of the research process, a constructive pace is being established. The moderator asks general questions and seeks statements of fact about usage experience or general attitudes toward the category, for example. (15-20 minutes)

Stage 4: The specific questions and activities stage (mature adulthood)

After gaining a basic understanding of factual issues and the participants' perspectives, the moderator should be ready for higher risk kinds of questions. At this point you can probe and challenge for deeper feelings and emotions, ask more pointed and specific questions, delve into sensitive issues, involve the group in various exercises and ask creative and 'what if' questions. (60-70 minutes)

Stage 5: Closing (old age)

This is the wind down stage. It is the research team's last chance to gain factual information, feelings, projections and intentions from respondents. Many moderators use this time to review and summarize attitudes and feelings that have been shared and validate the perceptions and hunches that have emerged during the session. The moderator must also anticipate the end of the experience, make the respondents feel good about their contributions and break off the relationship in a positive and constructive manner. A closing exercise is very helpful at this point. (10-15 minutes)

An important fact: These stages are exhibited in any form of research. They are true for brief telephone interviews, focus groups or lengthy ethnographic field studies. Researchers who fail to respect these stages risk alienating their informants and damaging research validity.

3.8 Playing the Moderator Role

The moderator's role is comparable to that of the orchestra conductor. He or she is the central figure in the implementation of the research and responsible for assuring that all elements of the process are coordinated in a manner consistent with project objectives. These details include:

- *Managing all of the logistics and contingencies* for the sessions. Keep the research manager informed of all specifics, supervise the recruitment and other required services. Make sure that all services are delivered according to specifications, on time and within budget.
- *Taking charge of the interviews.* Make participants feel comfortable, establish the correct tone and definition of the situation. Develop rapport with respondents. Promote comfort and openness among members of group discussions. Create a relaxed and accepting atmosphere. Demonstrate unconditional positive regard.
- *Maintaining a high level of interest* and motivation among respondents. Keep up the enthusiasm necessary to keep participants involved. Maintain a high energy level. Start at 120 per cent and never allow anyone's energy to dip below 100 per cent. Demonstrate leadership in managing various personality types and group roles, including dominant and reticent respondents.
- *Guiding the discussions and interviews* in a manner that permits spontaneity and self-expression. Encourage respondents to show respect, consideration and validation for each other.
- *Keeping the discussion focused* on the project objectives. Always remember the strategic needs of the study and continuously check and obtain feedback about how successfully the interviews are matching objectives.
- *Analyzing responses continuously.* Probe for validity and fill in gaps while the discussion is proceeding.
- *Making sure that all participants in the discussion group have a chance to express their opinions* regardless of their content. Put respondents in charge of monitoring their own participation in a manner that shows deference to their peers' wishes for participation. Keep a mental list of expressed opinions and check the evolving discussion against what respondents have said earlier.
- *Being the time keeper.* Move the discussion along in a quiet, non-invasive way. Give everyone a chance to participate in roughly equal proportions. Do not allow time pressures to stifle discussion and full disclosure.
- *Playing the role subtly* so that the moderator's personality or behavior does not overwhelm the focus group or depth interview.

Listed below are some additional tips for learning and continuously improving performance of the moderator role. The moderator should:

- *Take a critical and analytic approach to his own behavior.* Objective self-monitoring can yield insights into how one is perceived by others. Earlier, we discussed several personal qualities that need to be modeled by the moderator such as friendliness, non-judgmental attitude and objectivity. For each one of these qualities, determine which words and behaviors reflect what is desired.
- *Solicit feedback from colleagues and observers.* Be open to constructive criticism. Some moderators cultivate peer review relationships with other practitioners. Multiple moderator agencies usually benefit from regular discussions and project assessments.
- *Inspire confidence and openness by being confident and open.* By being comfortable with yourself, accessible, modest and frank about your own shortcomings, you can encourage others to share their feelings and anxieties and to learn from your example.

Role models

There are appropriate variations of the moderator role. Different individuals can be effective with distinctive types of personal affect and styles. Good practitioners can adjust their presentation of self for the type of group being conducted. On the other hand, respondents react badly if they suspect insincerity or fakery. Moderators should never present themselves as something they are not – unless it is obviously in a spirit of play or purposive naiveté.

There are also various 'role models' in the larger culture that can help moderators learn different ways to elicit openness and confidence in others. Good moderators learn from other occupations and roles to adjust their situational behaviors.

- The *clergyman* can inspire others to a higher truth and can help us reveal inner thoughts.
- The *doctor or therapist* is devoted to helping us and uses a scientific and clinical approach.
- The *best friend* is always supportive, accepting and a good listener.
- The *journalist* is always after another 'scoop'.
- The *detective* attempts to link discordant pieces of evidence into a coherent story.
- The *explorer* is seeking novelty and discovery.

Inappropriate roles can threaten respondents and close off discussion and disclosure. When there is an exploitation of the power relationship, when the moderator fails to show respect, or when personal drives at variance with research objectives manifest themselves, the project suffers. The voyeur, seducer, bully, or cop are examples of roles that are likely to distort findings because they make respondents feel used or threatened.

Table 8 Moderator role checklist.

Item	✓
Managing logistics	
Making participants feel comfortable	
Establishing the correct tone	
Developing rapport with respondents	
Maintaining a high level of interest	
Keeping up the energy	
Guiding the discussions	
Keeping the discussion focused	
Continuously analyzing responses	
Probing for validity and gaps	
Giving everyone a chance to express opinions	
Keeping dominant participants under control	
Bringing out shy respondents	
Being the time keeper	
Managing contingencies	
Playing the role subtly	
Managing logistics	

Developing rapport with respondents

The process of developing rapport starts immediately when the moderator begins to interact with respondents. Rapport refers to a feeling of comfort – a sympathetic relationship between the moderator and respondents. It involves becoming accepted by informants, gaining their confidence and trust so that they reveal themselves with minimal hesitation. Maintaining rapport also requires the researcher to be sensitive to time pressures and to respondents' needs. It requires exhibiting sensitivity, acceptance and positive reinforcements for continued cooperation.

Rapport is promoted if respondents are turned into allies and experts rather than guinea pigs and objects of experimentation. Providing enough correct information at the start of the group promotes feelings of affinity and common purpose. Therefore, the introduction should not be minimized or glossed over.[16] The points to be discussed during the introduction include:

- Purpose of the discussion.
- Background and role being played by the moderator.
- Explanation of the ground rules.
- Reassurance that respondents' contributions are important.
- Reassurance that respondents' can speak their minds.
- Reassurance that there are no hidden agendas.

Here are several recommendations for conducting the first two stages of the interview in a manner that maximizes building rapport.

The introductory stage

As the respondents are led into the interview room, the moderator should stand at the doorway and greet each person individually. It is helpful for the moderator to make eye contact with each person, shake respondents' hands or touch their arms and say things like, 'Welcome', 'Thank you for coming', 'Nice having you here'. The moderator should be sincere in her welcome. This creates a transition from public space to the structured interview environment and reinforces that the moderator is setting the agenda.

Seating

Most moderators permit respondents to select their own places around the table. The ecology of the table, however, sometimes attracts particular character types to selected locations. For example, confrontational respondents may set themselves up on the opposite side of the table from the moderator. In order to discourage personality clashes, some practitioners prefer to assign seats by randomly placing name cards around the table and having respondents sit behind their cards. (Some respondents may object to the absence of choice since they may want to be close to the moderator or write more easily with their left hands.) The moderator should make sure that all the respondents' names are visible to all others in the room. That can be accomplished by writing names on both sides of the 'tent cards'.

The moderator's own name card should also be visible to all respondents. The form of address used by the moderator should be socially appropriate to the situation and the participants' status. The etiquette of various cultures and occupations should be followed. If everyone is using first names in a focus group, it is usually helpful for the moderator to use hers as well unless it is culturally inappropriate or destructive of rapport and authority.

Introductory message

Focus groups, depth interviews and site visits are always initiated by an introductory message. As moderators gain experience, they may modify their introductions to suit their personal styles or the characteristics of the group being interviewed. The introductory message has several regular components: introduction and explanation of purpose, disclosures, permissions, participation ground rules and conclusion. A good general purpose opening is provided in the Appendix.

Part 1 The moderator identifies herself by name and briefly describes her credentials and experience as deemed appropriate for the audience. Then, she describes the purpose and overall agenda of the session in a general way, for example, 'We're here to look at some ideas for an advertising campaign for breakfast cereals' or, 'We're here to have some fun and come up with ideas for a new type of credit card'. In some countries, back room observers are brought in and introduced to respondents as well. In general, it is inappropriate to define the back room as 'my clients' or 'my boss' as this tends to weaken the perception of moderator authority. It is better to identify observers as 'colleagues' or 'members of the research team'.

Part 2 The next part of the introduction requires disclosures of the conditions and technology associated with the session such as microphones, videotapes, observers and two-way mirrors. Being honest about these features of the research facility actually enhances the trust that participants place in the moderator. In any case, they should not be ignored because respondents will notice things and possibly become alarmed if their curiosity is not settled. A brief explanation helps respondents understand why recording and observing are important. Stating '...so that we don't miss any details' or, '...so you only have to react to a single moderator' helps to alleviate a possible impression of privacy loss. The Appendix contains a brief disclosures message that can be used as a model.

Part 3 Afterwards, the moderator continues with permissions. Some respondents may want to know if smoking is permitted – a practice disappearing in American facilities. In general, respect local custom and the preferences of other participants in determining whether smoking will be allowed. Reassure participants that they may get another snack or beverage during the session if they so desire. Some moderators inform participants that there will be one or several bathroom or cigarette breaks in the middle of the session.

Part 4 The final part of the introduction should deal with participation ground rules. Here are several items that might be mentioned.

- That participants should feel free to join into the discussion as they wish and not wait to be called upon.
- That everyone is expected to contribute and that participants should manage their own contributions so that everyone has a roughly equal chance to express opinions.
- That the moderator will alternate who gets to speak first after a topic is introduced.
- That some exercises will require a written reaction before anyone speaks.
- That only one person should speak at a time and that side conversations should be avoided.

- That everyone has the right to voice his or her own opinion regardless of anyone else's views.
- That varying opinions are welcomed and that everyone should remain accepting of alternative perspectives.
- That everyone should speak loud enough so that their voices are picked up on the recording equipment.

Part 5 The introduction should be concluded by reviewing the importance of everyone's participation. A general statement about the social or higher level significance of the research also helps to promote a sense of bonding and common purpose; for example, 'This is your chance to let corporate management know how real customers feel' or, 'Corporations can make big mistakes if they don't listen to consumers'. Participants should be invited to ask questions if any of the ground rules are unclear. If the moderator's explanation has been effective, there usually are no questions at this point. Sometimes, respondents may want to review some point of procedure, such as bathroom break rules.

Pointed questions

Occasionally, some participant may ask a pointed question during the introduction or early in the discussion which the moderator might not want to answer for fear of biasing the discussion. For example, they may ask, 'Which company is sponsoring these discussions?' or, 'Are they having trouble with those ads they showed on TV last year?' This situation needs to be handled tactfully and in a manner that does not spoil rapport. A quick explanation and diplomatic escape may be the best way to move on, for example:

> *I can't answer that question right now because it might influence the way some respondents answer questions. If you're still interested at the end of the discussion, I'll let you know.*

The role taking and rapport building stage

The next step is to allow respondents to introduce themselves to the group. The moderator usually goes around the table and has everybody identify themselves by first name (the name they prefer to be called) the town or neighborhood in which they live and something about their household composition – spouse, children, pets. Many moderators also like to have respondents reveal something personal about themselves, unrelated to the discussion, in order to promote the rapport building process. Examples include, 'What is the most interesting thing about your job', 'What do you like to do most in your free time' or, 'Where would you like to spend your next vacation'.[17]

The purpose of the introduction routine is to:

- *Get everyone speaking at the proper voice level.* Some respondents with gentle voices may have to be reminded sensitively that they will have to adapt. 'Your voice is fine for everyday life but we're taping here and it may not pick up what you say if you don't speak louder – and I don't want to miss anything you say'.

- *Let respondents spontaneously discover commonalities and differences amongst themselves.* The moderator can promote rapport between participants by reinforcing these common characteristics and it will model the role she will be playing in the session. Some examples: 'So that makes three of you with cats and two with dogs' or 'It looks like we're evenly split between singles and marrieds here'.
- *Give the moderator a chance to cultivate rapport with each participant.* Eye contact, warm smiles and authentic welcoming expressions to everybody communicate that their efforts are important.
- *Maintain introductory banter.* The moderator should react positively and warmly to respondents and thank them again for agreeing to participate. A bit of back-and-forth small talk at this point which reveals facts about the moderator also helps to stimulate rapport.

   Participant: My name is Marge. I live in Green Hill with my husband and two daughters, aged 16 and 19. We enjoy going to South Padre Island for vacations.

   Moderator: I also have a 19-year-old daughter. It's great to watch them grow. Thanks again for coming over tonight.

Seating chart

As everyone is going around the table with their self introductions, it is a good practice for the moderator and observers to write down names and pertinent information on a seating chart. This helps to remember names and supplies the moderator with information such as brand usage, household composition or occupation that can be referenced during subsequent probes.

Sequential vs. group questions

Sequential or 'round robin' questions are those that need to be addressed by everyone in a focus group; group questions are addressed to no one in particular and may be picked up spontaneously by anyone. The moderator should model both types of questions during the early stages of the session. The first substantive question asked of a focus group may be asked in 'round robin' fashion. This should be a simple and factual question such as, 'How often do you purchase bath soap?' or, 'What are the main things you use your Palm Pilot™ for?' However, after the introduction, sequential questions should be strictly limited because these inhibit group interaction and will make the session seem like a series of individual interviews rather than a group discussion.

Setting up discussions

When a topic is opened for discussion, it should be introduced with a phrase that encourages individuality and diversity such as, 'Let's talk about...' or, 'I'm interested in your different attitudes toward...' or 'I'm curious about the different ways that people...' This will make it seem more like a discussion and less like an interview. It will also validate individual feelings and reinforce that the moderator is looking for a range of responses rather than a collective group opinion.

Rapport building review

Before moving on to additional moderation techniques, let us review some of the most important rules for moderators building and maintaining rapport in a focus group.

- Explain as much as possible about the purpose of the session and its ground rules.
- Maintain eye contact with everyone in the group.
- Be friendly in greeting and acknowledging respondent contributions.
- Show concern for participants' comfort, feelings and integrity.
- Show 'unconditional positive regard' in your reactions to participants' contributions.
- Tell a little about yourself – as long as it is not related to the topic of discussion – so that respondents can see you as a real person too.
- Demonstrate high energy and interest.

3.9 Understanding Respondent Motivations

For the most part, respondents in a focus group, depth interview or site visit are there to help the moderator and the client company. They want to answer questions honestly, pay attention to the rules, try their hardest to complete exercises and have a good time in the process. They are generally accommodating, and working with respondents should not be regarded as a contest of wills.

Nevertheless, there are several factors which can either inhibit or facilitate honest and open discussion in a focus group or other research exercise. Moderators and research managers need to keep these factors in mind as an interview session proceeds.

Inhibitors

There are interpersonal dynamics, situational factors and psychological forces which can inhibit free flowing talk and open revelation.[18] Moderators and research managers should avert or minimize the following:

- *Time pressures* These include pushing the discussion too quickly, not allowing participants to complete their responses or rushing through a discussion guide that is too long. Staring at your watch too often implies impatience. Complaining to respondents about elapsed time tends to raise anxieties and leads respondents to question the worth of continued participation. Don't say, 'We have only a half hour left and ten more topics to cover'.

- *Ego threat* No one wants to be put on the spot. Asking participants to disclose things before they are ready, being judgmental and failing to control judgmental group members all contribute to mute expressions. It is also wrong to use terminology that is too abstract and technical or to ask questions in a way that forces respondents to admit a weakness, for example, 'You're not very familiar with spreadsheet software, are you?'.

- *Inhibiting etiquette* Respondents may feel that it is impolite to elaborate, challenge or disagree with statements by members of the group. This problem may be particularly severe in sessions with professionals because they may normally defer to a senior participant. This was evident in a recent focus group involving ophthalmologists in which younger practitioners were reluctant to demonstrate knowledge of emerging technologies that was superior to their senior colleagues. Additionally, some respondents believe that certain 'politically correct' attitudes must be expressed in public. They may pull the moderator aside after the session, as one actually did, and say, 'I don't really believe in all this environmental mumbo-jumbo'.

- *Trauma* Compliance may be diminished by having subjects describe an unpleasant experience or asking them to participate in exercises that are threatening. Respondents may resist writing an imaginary obituary – this is particularly true among Asians for whom this is considered bad luck. Describing an unhappy service encounter, criticizing an employer and disparaging a formerly favored brand can create equally unpleasant confrontations for otherwise avid participants.
- *Forgetting* Many respondents simply forget the precise ways they have done things in the past and are unwilling to admit that to an interviewer or peers. They may, consequently, falsify, embellish or deprecate their response.
- *Confusion* If respondents are unsure about the ground rules or the topic being discussed it can inhibit full disclosures.
- *Unconscious behavior* Many consumer acts and product usage behaviors are largely unconscious – ritualistic, habitual, illogical and emotional. Probing for a rational account of an opinion or behavior that is unconscious only encourages improvisation, rationalization and falsehood. Projective techniques are usually needed to bring these patterns into better awareness.

Facilitators

As humans, we seek pleasure and avoid pain. Listed below are some of the psychic rewards sought by research participants. Leveraging these rewards will facilitate honest disclosure in research interviews.

- *Expectations* If the moderator has high expectations for the session's outcomes and provides continuous reminders, respondents will follow her lead. Reinforcements about meeting expectations – without sanctioning the specific content – helps to keep up the productive flow, for example, 'Thanks for coming up with so many definitions' or, 'I appreciate your honesty about that'.
- *Recognition* Respondents participate in research studies because they seek recognition and validation. They are flattered when major corporations seek their advice. When moderators show positive regard, they help respondents achieve this reward.
- *Altruism* Participants respond in research studies because they want to make a contribution. They are excited that their responses will impact company policies, help develop new products, create new advertising campaigns, etc. Letting respondents know that, 'You may turn on the TV and see how the ideas generated here have turned out' helps them feel that their efforts are worthwhile.
- *Sympathy* Sometimes people participate in research because they are looking for sympathy. They may have had a negative experience with a product category and are now looking for a receptive listener. They may have an unmet need in a category that means a great deal to them – a drug with fewer side effects, a detergent that handles their child's soiling – and are delighted that someone may do something about it.
- *Catharsis* Similarly, some participants just want to get something off their chest. They are encouraged when peers hold the same opinion or when they

are given a compassionate ear. Moderators are often cheered to hear respondents say, 'I'm glad that somebody in management is listening' or, 'I never knew that others go through the exact same thing every morning'.

- *Meaning* Respondents appreciate being able to see things in new ways and learn about others' feelings. The opportunity to hear new perspectives encourages participants to share their own feelings. This is particularly true in senior executive, medical or professional group interviews where the chance to hear about another company's risk management practices, database software packages or disability compliance policies may constitute the most important inducement for attendance.
- *New experience* A focus group, ethnographic encounter or depth interview can be an exhilarating experience for a first-time attendee. Even experienced participants enjoy discussing new topics or being involved in different product categories. The chance to socialize in a safe atmosphere and make new friends can be mobilized for session productivity. The novelty of various elicitation techniques or trying out new concepts for a familiar product create enthusiasm and interest.
- *Extrinsic rewards* Of course, participants ultimately are encouraged to follow the rules because they are being paid an incentive fee at the end of the session. However, researchers should never rely only on the cash to encourage openness, nor should respondents ever be reminded about payments during the session or threatened with withholding the fee for any reason whatsoever. The latter practice makes participants feel 'used' and poorly respected; consequently, it can backfire and produce invalid data.

Market research participants are not only individuals reacting from their own needs and drives, they also become members of a spontaneous group. Effective moderators must consider participants' individual needs as well as their reactions to becoming part of a group. The next section deals with managing group dynamics in a manner that supports open disclosure.

3.10 Using Group Dynamics Effectively

After the first two stages of a focus group research interview, a collective consciousness slowly emerges and suddenly the whole is larger than the sum of its parts.

Getting the sense of the group

A group interview is unique because, if managed correctly, respondents should be reacting and responding to their peers as well as to the moderator. This produces findings which have a higher level of richness and validity. Most people are likely to be more honest and open with a fellow peanut butter user sitting next to them than with an anonymous call from a peanut butter company.

On the other hand, time is limited. In a typical two-hour focus group, there may be only an hour and a half of discussion time remaining after all the formalities have been addressed. That leaves about 15 minutes for each respondent – not nearly enough time for each to react thoughtfully to every issue on the discussion guide. Therefore, the moderator must strive for achieving a sense of the group as a whole. This requires listening for the main thrust, continuously confirming the accuracy of impressions being gained and checking against competing dynamics that may distort what is being heard.[19]

Various interpersonal dynamics and roles spontaneously evolve in groups, including leadership, hierarchy, competition, cooperation, negotiation and coalitions. These should be tracked and mobilized to advance research objectives. Otherwise natural group processes may thwart the successful collection of valid information.

The general questions stage

During this stage of the focus group, it is the moderator's responsibility to start mobilizing group dynamics in managing the discussion. Listed below are several tips for guaranteeing that group dynamics work in the moderator's favor.

- *Regulate eye scan.* The moderator should regularly conduct an eye scan of everyone in the group. Keeping visually in touch with every single participant contributes to a sense of cohesiveness and joint purpose. It keeps participants from feeling that other persons or opinions are favored. Persisting with the eye scan helps to monitor lagging attention and monitors non-verbal reactions that may need probing.
- *Use inclusive opening discussions.* When discussion on an issue or topic is initiated, the moderator should look at no one in particular or, alternatively,

make an effort to scan the entire group at once. She should resist the natural temptation to favor the first person on the right or left or the person directly opposite the table. While awaiting the first response, the moderator should do an eye scan of group members. If the group has assimilated the instruction to alternate participants who start the discussion, they should naturally take turns. If this does not occur naturally, the moderator should make an effort to call on alternate participants. In any case, it is necessary to discourage dominant respondents who like to be the first to voice their opinions.

- *Manage personality disputes.* Several situations that should be avoided include allowing personality disputes to develop in the group and letting the same respondents continually take opposite sides in a discussion. If that happens, other respondents at the table are often tempted to sit back and watch the jousting. Moderators should play down the competition by being sure other respondents carry on the discussion and by not reinforcing antagonists.

- *Use group leaders.* Sometimes, certain participants will become natural leaders of the group. They may have more experience, advanced knowledge or higher sophistication. The moderator should leverage the insights of group leaders, but not let them compete against their own authority or monopolize the discussion. Normative group participants are often inhibited about contributing if they discover that one or several of their number can speak with greater depth about a topic. On the other hand, knowledgeable participants' views should not be suppressed because they may naturally possess greater interest, experience or passion about the topic at hand. Thus, moderators are hard pressed in these situations to open the discussion in ways that bring out the less knowledgeable respondents without their being educated or pushed aside by the group leaders. It frequently pays for the moderator to acknowledge the variety of backgrounds in the group that validates the diverse levels. For example:
  > *It seems like we have a range of experience with oral surgery in this room and I would like to hear from those with 20 plus years of experience as well as those who just finished dental school.*
  > *It looks like some of you have been frequent flyers on just American Airlines™ while others bring some experience as frequent flyers on many other carriers. I need to listen to both types of respondents.*

- *Avoid playing favorites.* The moderator should not play favorites. It is tempting to block out those who are less articulate or less colorful in their imagination, but this is a mistake. The moderator's body language and verbal reinforcements should be accepting and respectful of all opinions.

- *Encourage diversity of opinion.* It is important to ask questions and probe in a manner that encourages diversity and opens the discussion to alternative perspectives. On the other hand the moderator must continuously confront the question of how divergent opinions fit with the sense of the group – is an opinion idiosyncratic or does it suggest a range of valid possibilities? Proper phrasing of probes must affirm the likelihood of alternative viewpoints and partially test for whether or not these are normative.

Does anybody agree or disagree with that statement?
Have I heard all the different points of view on that issue?
Does everybody go along with that remark or do some of you feel differently?
Do you all do things in that way or do some of you do things differently?
Did you have the same or a different reaction to that word?
Did you all have similar encounters or were some of you treated differently?

- *Promoting consensus.* In most cases, the moderator wants to uncover a range of opinions. However, it is also necessary or valuable to achieve consensus or an impression of overall feelings as a way of closing a section of the discussion or to summarize the sense of the group. The moderator should seek consensus in a way that does not squelch individuality. For example:

    I know there's a range of opinion here, but I'd just like to get a sense of the group's opinion of which ad execution is preferred.
    I've heard lots of ideas today but I want to know which you think would be the top three priorities for the bank.

3.11 Asking Questions Fairly

Asking respondents for information is not a simple process. Collecting accurate and reliable data requires that the moderator is careful about asking questions fairly. This involves paying attention to the structure, phrasing and intonation of both the question and reaction to the answer.

Naive outsider role

Whether or not the moderator is more knowledgeable about a product or category than the participants, it is natural for them initially to feel that he is an 'expert'. This problem is slightly lessened when the discussion revolves around technical issues than when an everyday product category is under examination. Even heavy users do not consider themselves experts on cheese spreads or insecticides.

Respondents are also likely to take for granted product attributes that are part of everyone's stock of knowledge. They view the moderator as a fellow user and regard it as unimportant to mention what they take to be obvious – and sometimes moderators may seem unwilling to probe for what everybody takes to be natural and expected. This can be very problematic for research interviews.

Thus, it is important for the moderator to play the role of a 'naive outsider' convincingly – to get respondents to reveal details no matter how unsurprising they may seem. Going after things from the participant's point of view requires the moderator to suspend or suppress her own knowledge and leave the initiative to participants – to treat them as authorities regardless of their initial self concept. Here are some guidelines for how moderators can maintain a stance of strategic naiveté.

- *No assumptions* The moderator has to assert frequently that he is coming into the discussion without assumptions. It may be helpful to say something like:
  We all use toothpaste but talk to me as if I am someone using toothpaste for the first time.
  I know it's hard to believe that someone knows absolutely nothing about laundry detergent, but when you're responding, please treat me as though I'm completely ignorant about this product.
- *Prefacing* Asking questions by starting with, 'Can you help me out?' or, 'I would like to learn about…in your own words' or something similar puts the respondent into an authoritative position and helps with rapport.

Natural language

The moderator should learn consumers' natural language and terminology as quickly as possible. This will allow her to call things by their 'right' names and avoid imprecision about what respondents mean. Consumers' terms should always remain the framework for questions. The following questions aim for natural language:

> *If you and your friends were talking about this at home, what words would you be using?*
> *What words would you use to describe someone who owns a...?*

Moderators should avoid using business or marketing jargon, such as 'white goods', 'SKU', or 'strategy brief', which have no meaning to consumers. Similarly, they should not be put into fantasy roles that suggest marketing expertise, such as 'creative director'. Respondents who are too comfortable with marketing concepts and terminology should be excluded from future research participation because they have ceased to be everyday consumers.

Moderators should show sensitivity to cultural, regional and social class differences in language usage. Certain expressions may have different connotations and meanings and this could have a broad impact on the implications derived from the research. Words can create social distance, be poorly understood and create confusion. Moderators should choose their words carefully and make certain they fully understand what respondents mean exactly by the words they use.

Composing a question

Questions asked in a research study should be phrased clearly and fairly. Moderators should also be sensitive to the underlying structure of the questions and watch their tone of voice as they speak. Listed below are several guidelines for asking questions.

- *Focused interviewing* The main principle behind the interviewing strategy is to ask fairly general questions and allow the responses to stimulate further questions and probing. The result is a spontaneous discussion-like encounter rather than a strict recitation of questions and answers.
- *Open-ended questions* Qualitative research interviews rely primarily on open-ended questions which allow the respondent to shape the answer as much as possible. Normally, the use of 'yes/no' or closed format questions that provide a limited number of response categories is minimized.
- *Contextual questions* 'What', 'which', 'how' and 'when' questions about factual matters or opinions encourage respondents to offer explanatory answers that provide context. For example, 'What are your regular practices for eating breakfast in the morning?' and, 'When are you most likely to feel you need a sleeping aid?'
- *Active verbs* Prefacing questions with active verbs, such as, 'Describe...', 'Explain...' and, 'Tell me...' encourages elaboration.

- *Two-tailed questions* The moderator should phrase questions in a way that permits a range of opinions. Sometimes this requires specifying the directions that responses could take, for example, 'Some people like mixed drinks, others take their spirits straight – where do you fit?'
- *Eye contact* Maintain consistent eye contact. Don't break off eye contact with someone in the middle of a response to look down at the discussion guide or elsewhere, because this tends to make respondents feel that they have given the 'wrong' response.
- *Sequence of questions* In order to reduce ego threat, let the question sequence follow the natural stages of the interview described earlier. In the early stages, engage in small talk and ask general questions to get oriented. Save challenging and pointed questions until late in the experience.
- *Controlled release of information* On the other hand, careful release of information is usually necessary in framing questions in order to clarify the issue, define terms, bring unstated assumptions to the surface, and lend context. For example, instead of the general formulation, 'Are you eating more or less breakfast cereal than in the past?' it is best to first provide a time framework, such as 'over the last five years'. It would also be best to clarify and define the object of the question, 'I'm referring to cereals like corn flakes, Raisin Bran™ and Special K™ eaten cold in the morning'. Selective release of information also can be used as a way of testing the impact of various communication elements. For example, 'Now, if I add the word "fresh" to the idea of "glowing", does that make a difference to you or not?'
- *Prefaces to encourage respondents or reduce etiquette* Introductions to many questions require prefaces that give respondents permission to respond in a way that possibly violates norms, admits confusion or reveals something embarrassing. For example, 'Many women find it hard to keep from perspiring at some moments. What are the situations that make you worry about perspiration odor?' Or, 'Nearly everybody experiences some confusion in picking a wine to go with dinner. How do you usually decide what to drink with your meal?'

There are also some things to avoid when asking questions.
- *Words that educate or inform respondents* Moderators can bias a discussion by controlling the information respondents get about a subject. Research managers should be careful not to draw global conclusions on the basis of reactions to incomplete questions or partially explained concepts.
- *'Why' questions* Avoid questions or probes using why even though the main objective for qualitative research is to explain why. As Lazarsfeld has said, 'We cannot leave it up to the respondents to tell us whatever they are inclined. The average consumer is not trained to survey offhand all the factors which determine his purchases and he usually has a very hazy understanding of the *why* question' (1992: 15). These questions also tend to stimulate defensiveness. They restrict the range of responses. 'Why' puts people on the spot, making them think they have to supply a rational explanation immediately. 'Why' questions can be touchy, inflammatory and threatening.

- *Leading questions* Leading questions are those which imply or promote a preferred answer as they are asked. They should be carefully avoided. The worst form of leading questions are those which start with a declaration and then look for confirmation, for example, 'You want to be more productive, don't you?' or, 'How many of you agree that this would be a good product for us to offer?' Others offer subtle biasing information inside the question, for example, 'How do you feel about saving the environment by buying organic foods?'

- *Emotionally loaded words or phrasing* Emotionally loaded words increase defensiveness, shyness and reticence, and should be avoided unless they are applied as a conscious provocation. For example, 'How do you feel about smoking heavily?' (better to say, 'How do you decide when you want a cigarette?') or, 'What makes you think that you need to dye your hair?' (better to say, 'What were your intentions when you first began to use hair coloring?').

- *Moderator opinions* Moderators should avoid injecting their own opinions into the group discussion or depth interview because they might lead respondents who may be seeking the approval of an authority figure. Sometimes this sin may be committed subtly by reading the least favorite concepts with low affect.

Reactions, acknowledgments and reinforcements

When somebody provides a response, it is natural for the moderator to punctuate it with a reaction, acknowledgment or reinforcement. Interviewers need to be careful, however, because they can influence the depth and extent of the response by how they react. Sympathetic reactions in a health study, for example, can induce more reports of symptoms and conditions from patients.

Unlike natural conversation, it is inappropriate for the moderator to respond with judgmental reinforcements such as, 'That's good' or, 'That's too bad'. These reactions communicate subtle cues that may shape respondent attitudes. Instead, the moderator should react with emotionally neutral reinforcements, for example, 'That's interesting to know' or, 'That's new to me' or just, 'Uh-huh'. Non-verbal reinforcements are also important. A smile, a nod, moving the face or body closer to the speaker or widening your eyes shows interest and encouragement without leading respondents in particular directions.

Active listening

In a focus group, depth interview or site visit, the moderator must be an active listener – continuously analyzing the discussion in her own mind while staging a balanced presentation with respondents. The moderator must also offer evidence that she is being attentive and is empathizing with respondent concerns. Sometimes, moderators will rephrase a participant's remark or summarize the 'drift' of the discussion to demonstrate their understanding of the issues that concern respondents.

Showing an interest in the information

Active listening requires both verbal and non-verbal interest. Displaying or withholding expressions of interest sends cues to respondents that they might be 'off track'. Consequently, reinforcements should be continuous and deliberate.

Summarizing and paraphrasing the information

Providing summaries and alternative formulations demonstrates that the moderator is trying to understand, but this process also brings some risks. When the moderator is listening actively, he should avoid putting words into respondent's mouths. The interviewer should not declare or interpret 'what respondents really mean' during the course of an interview since this can send out a negative message. If moderators paraphrase a respondent's remark, they should always double check with the respondent to be sure they are speaking accurately. They should continuously ask, 'I'm not putting words in your mouth, am I?', 'Is this correct?' or, 'Is this what you meant?' if summarizing the direction of a remark.

Data validation

During qualitative research interviews, it is both necessary and useful to validate responses among different respondents in the group. This means checking a response for completeness and honesty and probing to see if this attitude represents a consensus or a minority viewpoint. Rephrasing and summarizing responses are useful validation techniques. Asking a question over again at a later point in the interview and in a different manner is another way to check validity.

Validation questions that confirm the 'sense of the group' or the individual respondent provide a resource for 'instant analysis' that may be useful in the debrief following the interviews.

The specific questions stage

The specific questions stage begins about 45 minutes into the interview. If things have been going well, the moderator has cultivated rapport with the respondents and they have developed a comfortable discussion pattern. The interview is now ready to move into a higher risk mode in order to:

- Delve into emotions.
- Conduct creative exercises.
- Probe more intensely.
- Discuss sensitive issues.
- Ask more 'what if' questions.
- Challenge responses and encourage more intense discussion.
- Experiment with different ways of addressing issues.

Moderator movement

Moderators who stay in one place, seated at the head of the table, through an entire interview session can induce tedium and boredom. Rather than just sitting still, the moderator should stand up and walk around when she asks some questions. She should also vary her stance toward the group by using the easel or a chalk board to record responses or draw diagrams in order to promote attention.

The moderator should also examine his body language. Effective discussion leaders use hand motions and their physical stance to encourage responses. When necessary, moderators get physically closer to respondents in order to enter their zone of intimacy. This induces feelings of confidentiality when sensitive issues are handled. The moderator should also move closer to respondents whose attention may be lagging or who are beginning to dominate the discussion. Being in motion while others are sitting is a technique for exercising group leadership.

3.12 Probing

There's always more to learn after a question has been answered. Good moderators want to understand salience, implications and emotional resonance. Furthermore, because of time pressures or ego threat, respondents may be offering less than a full response. That's where probing comes in. The moderator may ask for elaboration, a definition, a comparison or a context. There is an infinite number of actual probes and good moderators select the best ones for any situation.

It is important to vary probes because it is tiresome to hear the same one over and over and respondents stop reacting well if they keep hearing 'tell me more' after each of their responses. It begins to seem as though the moderator is not listening or just acting ritualistically.

Sometimes the most effective probe is what is known as the 'silent probe' in which the moderator simply uses body language, such as the 'raised eyebrows' gesture, or inward waving of hands to communicate that she expects more than the respondent has proffered.

Probing has many important functions in a focus group or in-depth interview – to check for thoroughness, as a validation technique, to demonstrate active listening, as a starting point for analysis, etc. A sophisticated repertoire of probes distinguishes an effective and mature moderator from an amateur. Here are some techniques and examples of probing.

- *Appropriate language* Remember to minimize the word 'Why?' in probes since overuse tends to make respondents uncomfortable and defensive.
- *Information requests* Ask for elaboration, clarification, definition, context, conditions. These require specific ways of expanding responses.

    Tell me more about that.
    What does ___ mean to you?
    Do you always do it that way or only sometimes?
    Give me an example of ___.
    When was the last time you saw/felt/thought...?
    What/who/anything else?
    Is 'x' a 'y'?
    Give me another word for that.
    What were you thinking when you...?
    Tell me how you...?
    Who else has...?

- *Non-verbal probes*
    - Silent probe – the moderator just keeps listening and expecting more
    - Inward hand waving gestures
    - Inquisitive or puzzled eyebrows
    - Smiling as though more is coming

- *Reflective probes* These involve playing back the moderator's understanding of what the respondent has just said. When using reflective probes the moderator should make sure that respondents don't feel that words are being put into their mouths.
  - *Echo probe* is a fairly exact playback.
  - *Summary probe* reduces what the respondent has said to key points.
  - *Interpretive probe* rephrases what the respondent has said.
- *Confrontational probes* This type should only be used when a high level of confidence and trust has been established. These tend to challenge words or assertions that the respondent has made. For example:

  You don't really believe that?

  Nobody really does it that way any more – or do they?

  Don't give me the polite answer; give me the right answer.

  Don't tell me what everyone thinks, let me know what you think.
- *Creative probes* These probes use imagination, projections and similar tools to elicit further feelings from respondents. Perhaps the respondent can answer the question for someone else or react to 'what ifs'. Here are some examples:

  If you were 70/5/90 years old, what would your opinion be?

  If I wanted to discourage you from buying the product, what should I say?

  If money was no object, which ___ would you choose?

  If you could use/buy/consume any brand which would it be?

  What would you say to someone else about ___?

3.13 Interpreting Body Language

Understanding body language is very important on two levels. It is a necessary tool for interpreting the respondents' attitudes and feelings. Researchers also need to be aware of their own non-verbal communication in order to maximize rapport and to control negative attitudes.

The four dimensions

According to Hall (1976) there are four main channels of non-verbal communications which research managers should understand: body movements and characteristics, non-verbal aspects of speech, proxemic or territorial behavior and temporal or time-related communications.[20]

1. Kinesics, or body movements and characteristics

Various parts of our bodies convey information: eyes, face, body posture, hands, legs. The significance of physical gestures during interviews is probably the most researched and best understood aspect of non-verbal communications. For example, by maintaining eye contact, smiling appropriately, leaning forward while listening and acknowledging respondents as they speak, the researcher quietly communicates that he is open, honest and authoritative. Command of a situation is also expressed by an upright posture and assertive hand gestures to emphasize points. Some other examples of body language that may be observed among participants include:

- *Tightly crossed arms or legs* indicate a defensive stance and represent discomfort or the need to mask an underlying feeling. It is common for interview subjects to maintain this stance while the session is going through its first stages. If rapport is well-established, they are likely to relax and un-clench their arms.
- *Hand-to-mouth gestures* such as obscuring the lips with the hand, are often used to disguise feelings of doubt, deceit or exaggeration.
- *Open palms* facing the listener typically indicate honesty and openness.

2. Paralinguistics, or non-verbal aspects of speech

Voice volume, intonation, quality of voice (tense, growly, sarcastic), pitch and other non-verbal aspects of speech are clues to underlying feelings. For example, an increase in pitch often indicates deceitfulness or tension; lowering the volume of speech can indicate doubt or insecurity. Hurried or unclear speech sounding as though the informant is trying to get through a statement as fast as possible can indicate falsehood or doubt.

3. Proxemics, or people in space and in relation to each other

The manner in which territory is manipulated and managed is an effective mode of communication. Think of the way family members are arranged around the dinner table or how managers take their places around a conference table. Each says a great deal about authority relations and the relative power of the particular individuals taking their places. For example, in Western cultures, the person with authority is at the head of the table. In Japanese business practice, on the contrary, the highest ranking person may sit on the side as a more subtle expression of domination. Additionally, the way personal space is manipulated speaks loudly. We all have zones of intimacy and politeness and set clear rules when allowing others to come close or 'invade' our personal space.

Moderators can read participants' discomfort with a concept or antagonism toward an idea by watching if they back away from the table or regard a product prototype from a safe distance. Moderators can show interest by leaning in and reducing distance from respondents.

4. Chronemics, or inferences about time

How we use and manipulate time is another dimension of non-verbal communication. People's rate of speech and activity, lateness and interruptions can communicate about power and insecurity. Pacing is a way of communicating and regulating mood. A rapid-fire rate of speech betrays anxiety on the interviewer's part and makes respondents tense. A more deliberate pace which respects time demands invokes a cooperative spirit and relaxation.

Reading non-verbal cues

It is easy to be aware of non-verbal cues but hard to interpret them. Dishonesty or guilt typically cannot be inferred from a single gesture. On the contrary, reading body language requires a careful study of people's individual 'natural' patterns of non-verbal communication as well as breaks or disruptions that may occur when specific questions are asked.

- *Attitudes toward the situation* Many non-verbal cues will be reactions toward the discomfort of being interviewed or toward other group members. They should be distinguished from expressions that are associated with the information exchanged within the interview. As Newman has observed:

  It is important to recognize that a quiet respondent may be that way due to some level of discomfort with the group format, or they may have an opinion that is vastly different from the rest of the group. In either case, a trained moderator can use her skill to help overcome these obstacles. (1995: 33)

- *Attitudes toward the information* Interest or disinterest can be gauged from the non-verbal reactions of participants to a question or a concept, and toward statements made by other participants. Moderators need to use these cues in determining who and what issues need to be probed and the type of probe that might work best to elicit a true response. For example, if one respondent averts her eyes and gently withdraws from the table as several group members talk about how much they like a new eye makeup, it might be good to say to that respondent, 'There may be other opinions here. Diane, do you have something to say that is similar or different?'

- *Cultural variability* Non-verbal communication is highly variable across cultures. Consequently, this factor should be taken into account when making interpretations. For example, slowness in reacting to a question may signal evasiveness in most Western cultures; however, in Asian cultures, it may indicate deliberateness. The cultural patterns associated with body language should also be accounted for when making assumptions about natural patterns. For example, Latinos and other South Americans and Mediterraneans have a cultural preference for closer body space than do Anglo-Americans and Northern Europeans.

- *Leaky channels* Body language interpreters look for 'leaky channels', that is to say, inconsistencies between words, eyes, hands, etc. The logic behind this is that it may be possible for a liar or manipulator to control one or several communication channels but hard to manage them all at once. Thus, if a respondent indicates that she likes a product but handles it with minimal affect or eye contact, it may be a clue that her words are false.

- *Reflecting body language* It is important to maintain rapport and positive interaction. Respondents quickly pick up the interviewer's negative affect and may reflect it back. In contrast, skilled moderators try to mimic positive aspects of the respondent's body language, such as their pace of speech or natural stance. This helps respondents feel a breakdown in social distance and empathic listening.

Participants will naturally reflect the moderator's body language. If he is 'up' and enthusiastic, respondents are likely to follow that cue. If he is dull and speaks in a monotone, it will have a negative impact on the interview.

3.14 Exercises in the Focus Group

In just about every focus group and most individual interviews, it is helpful for the moderator to engage participants in one or several pencil-and-paper exercises. These shift the emotional dynamics of the session by producing new opportunities for exploration. These may be used as a way of focusing opinions, expressing personal characteristics that would be difficult to describe spontaneously, or to evaluate the client's positioning or other strategic concepts.

When evaluating concepts, for example, it is best to have respondents react individually with time to frame their own opinions about the idea on paper prior to group influence. Exercises, thus, have several important functions, including:

- Reducing 'groupthink', or the tendency of participants to stifle their individual feelings in order to conform to group consensus.
- Lessening the impact of dominant respondents.
- Allowing individual differences to emerge. This overrides many people's natural tendencies to suppress the possibility of standing outside of a perceived consensus.
- Adding variety to the interview experience and breaking up the tedium of pure discussion.
- Providing an opportunity for the moderator to slip out and meet with observers in the viewing room.
- Helping evaluate concepts in a consistent manner.
- Providing an opportunity for creative explorations.

Listed below are some tips for conducting exercises during focus groups.

- Arrive with pre-printed exercise sheets so that everyone receives identical stimuli.
- Be sure to have enough clean pads and sharpened pencils available.
- Reassure respondents that spelling and grammar don't count but that neatness would be very helpful.
- Reassure respondents that this is not a 'test' (since it may look and feel like one) and that no one will be evaluating their individual responses.
- Be sure that everyone indicates a code letter identifying the time and place of the group at the top of every page. Sometimes it's also helpful to have some demographic information on the top of the page, such as respondent's gender or age.

Individual vs. group vs. subgroup

It is useful to apply some exercises to the group as a whole, while others are better implemented among all group members individually. Still others are best completed by subgroups created when the entire group is broken up into two to four smaller units. The type of exercise, the moderator's preference and the situational group personality that emerges may all influence the proper choice. When she has decided to have an exercise completed by subgroups, the moderator should consider whether to assign members in some random manner, such as right half of the table vs. left half, or to pick participants by design. For example, if group members have divided into divergent opinion 'camps' earlier in the discussion, it may be instructive to have them complete exercises isolated from each other.

Concept exposure

If a research objective involves evaluating a prepared concept statement, give everyone a sheet with each concept and have respondents mark features that they particularly like with a green pen and cross out items they dislike with a red pen. Alternatively, have respondents place checks next to likes and X's next to dislikes. Let them rewrite any aspect of the concept.

Here are some issues that the research manager may want to evaluate about an advertising copy or a concept.

- Is it believable.
- Is it unique.
- Does it increase, have no impact or decrease your liking for the product.
- Does it provoke curiosity and what else do you want to know about it.
- Does it make you want to buy the product.

Here are some issues that may be explored in a test of a new product concept.

- Is there a need for this product.
- Describe who is likely to be interested/not interested in the product.
- For those that are interested, what benefits would they be seeking.
- What would be the main objections of those not interested.
- Would this be a one time purchase or would a pattern of repeat purchase develop. What would be the benefits of repurchase.
- What would you like to hear about the product when it was being promoted.
- Where and in what format would you expect to hear about this product.

Storyboards

Advertisers sometimes prepare these as part of the concept refinement and planning process. Qualitative research is often used to get feedback through consumer exposure prior to final production. Unfortunately, there is often a tendency to reject good ideas because respondents fail to understand the stimulus or are unable to imagine the transition between storyboard and final execution. For this reason, it is unrealistic to give consumers 'veto power' over creative decisions.

When storyboards are exposed, it is usually necessary for the moderator to carefully explain the action sequence. If she is uncomfortable doing this, someone from the creative team who has been briefed on maintaining objectivity in the setting may be a good substitute. In any case, a dispassionate presentation requires control of affect so that doubts and preferences are not revealed non-verbally to participants (Clowes, 1993).

- When there are numerous concepts to review, it is usually helpful to display all the evaluation criteria on a board so that respondents can refer to them consistently and they do not have to be repeated with every concept.
- It is difficult to review more than 10-12 concepts meaningfully in a two-hour focus group. Large numbers of concepts produce tedium and confusion. Alternating the concepts exposed to different groups and individuals, in some situations, provide a better understanding of concept dynamics.
- Vary the order in which concepts are exposed to various groups or individuals. This reduces *primacy* and *recency* bias, that is the tendency for subjects to favor either the item heard first or the one heard most recently.

Product sampling

Qualitative research is useful for obtaining feedback on product prototypes and samples. Depending on the objectives, the clients' brands may be exposed in relation to competing brands or in isolation. Regardless, some attention should be paid to how the product exposure will be staged.

- *Blind test vs. exposed brands* Some circumstances may call for the brand name to be obscured until the first reactions have been received. This allows a clear evaluation of features without having expectations influenced by the symbolism of the brand name. In some cases, it is useful to test for consumers' brand associations by asking them to guess the brand and probing for reasons before the actual mark is exposed.
- *Examination rituals* Structure the steps of the product trial very deliberately so that each prototype gets equivalent time and attention. Otherwise, subtle biases will be introduced which favor one over the other. For example, break up the steps of a taste test into a series of evaluations.
  - Examine product top and bottom – surface and interior.
  - Smell product.
  - Take a taste and evaluate flavor, texture, mouth feel, sweetness, etc.

Pre-tasking exercises

Items produced in a sensitizing activity prior to the sessions can be utilized in the actual interview to elicit further associations and ideas. Participants may arrive ready and enthusiastic or a bit reticent about what they have brought, but at least they have given the issue some thought.

Various ways of using preparatory exercises within the interview include:

- *Product placements.* Experiences with the test product can be reviewed under various headings, such as common benefits experienced, problems and dissatisfactions, adaptations and improvements desired.
- *Diaries.* Written and visual diaries can be shared among the group and used as a basis for exploratory probes that focus on particular elements of the diaries.
- *Stimuli from home.* Photographs of family members, pets, an area of the home that they hate to clean or a particularly soiled item of clothing can be the foundation of an exercise.
- *Media usage, store visits, etc.* Respondents who have watched certain particular television commercials or visited a store not previously frequented can also be debriefed. Evaluation categories may include expectations, initial reactions, surprises, new information learned and intentions for future visits.

3.15 Projective and Elicitation Techniques

Projective techniques are a category of exercises that provoke imagination and creativity. Exercises usually involve having respondents react to an incomplete or ill-defined stimulus and evaluating the results. Alternatively, these exercises may place respondents into an unlikely or unfamiliar role or frame of mind.

Projective techniques are useful for drawing out emotional values, for exploring issues in a nonlinear manner and for bypassing respondents' rational controls. The techniques are also helpful in getting respondents to verbalize unframed, subconscious, low salience or low involvement attitudes. They are an effective validation technique. When there are substantial differences among respondent backgrounds, projective techniques can equalize participants because they don't place a value on respondent experience.

Moreover, projective techniques can be particularly successful and helpful when the respondents feel a deep or emotionally intense involvement with the products, brands or categories under discussion. The applications for projective techniques lie in new product development, image studies, positioning studies, creative development and other areas.

Conditions that promote successful implementation of projective techniques include the following:

- *Use an enthusiastic and experienced moderator* who is allowed sufficient time to design and plan the exercises. Last-minute tasks or projective tools invented in the viewing room are almost never helpful.
- *Carefully link the study objectives* to the research techniques being used. It is incorrect to present a series of poorly conceived projective exercises just to experiment and see 'what it might turn up'.
- *Create an atmosphere of trust and respect* for all respondents. Participating in these exercises may make some respondents feel silly or not helpful. This is particularly true in research among senior executives and professionals. Moderators should be reassuring about the value and importance of these exercises. Similarly, they should be non-judgmental and accepting of all respondents' contributions.
- *Be careful of the mix* during the session. Respondents representing widely different social statuses, educational levels or those who have authority relations to each other may present difficulties for administering projective exercises. Make sure that a respectful tone is established and that reactions and reinforcements are supportive.
- *Conduct the exercises after a thorough warmup* and only during the 'specific questions stage' of the interview. Projective tools as a 'start-up' technique can be confusing and threatening.
- *Use a single one or a series of exercises* but leave enough time so that respondents can fully elaborate their feelings.

- *Do not overuse projective tools* and do not rely upon them at the exclusion of discussion and evaluation. Often the value of an exercise is maximized by verbally debriefing participants about what they were trying to say and getting the reactions from others about new issues that might have been raised.
- *Recruit for creativity* to gain access to respondents who regard themselves as creative or at least disposed toward enjoyment of puzzles and games.
- *Show caution and conservatism* in the interpretation of the exercises. Do not stretch the meaning of these techniques farther than they deserve to be drawn. Place emphasis on the analysis to deliver the *meaning* of the output. Do not just report what people said because it will not immediately make sense.

Imaginative exercises

Presented below is a catalog of projective exercises along with implementation instructions. These generally are used to help respondents verbalize subconscious or unframed attitudes.

- *If X were Y* Have participants imagine that a pair or set of brands in one category were transformed to another. For example, 'If Crest™ and Colgate™ toothpastes were cars, which makes would they be?' or, 'If Nokia™, Ericsson™, and Motorola™ cell phones were colleges and universities, which would they be?' The content of the response and further probes are helpful in eliciting brand imagery. Thus, if one is the BMW™ vs. the Ford™ of the category it may indicate a perception of better product integrity or design. If one is the MIT of the category, another is Cal Tech and the third is UCLA, it may indicate that while the two brands share an image of technical sophistication, the third may be more associated with socializing and relaxed communication.
- *Personification* This exercise is similar to the previous one as a brand imagery elicitation technique. Participants imagine that the brand is a person and then describe demographic or status-driven attributes associated with his or her personality, for example, 'If Marlboro™ (or any other cigarette brand) were a person, would it be a male or female? What university would s/he have attended? What kind of car does s/he drive? Where does s/he live? What is his/her favorite vacation destination? What beverages does this person favor?' and so on. The interpretation is clear if the modal responses are, 'Harvard-BMW™-Westchester-Hawaii-cognac' in contrast to, 'State technical school-Ford™ pickup-rural Georgia-Atlantic City-beer'. One suggests an aggressively upscale suburban lifestyle while the image of the other is more masculine and working class.

- *Authority figure* Have respondents imagine that the brand is an authority figure such as a teacher, author or newspaper editor. Have them first describe the personal attributes of the figure (gender, age, appearance, manner of speech). Then have them submit questions they would want answered and would believe that the authority could credibly address. This is a good test for subconscious elements of brand equity and brand authority in that it exposes doubts and problems associated with the product. It also reveals a great deal about unstated assumptions. For example, Hallmark™ cards might be imagined as a mature matronly figure who can deliver a thoughtful response to a question like, 'What gift should I get my mother-in-law for her birthday?' If this pattern of response was obtained, it would be fair to conclude that the brand was not communicating a youthful image.
- *Role playing* Take respondents out of their everyday reality by having them speak as though they were someone else. Have them play the part of a household member with whom they share a decision, an authority figure, or someone of a higher status. For example, 'Mary, you're a ten-year-old boy and, Suhair, you play the boy's mother. Imagine that you're at the supermarket deciding on a breakfast cereal to pick off the shelf.' The ensuing discussion is likely to reveal unspoken objections as well as those of overcoming resistance to some products that may be favored by children and not their parents.
- *Imaginary universe* Have respondents imagine that the personified brand (the brand fantasized as people) or the brand's users inhabit an entire world or country. Then, have them describe a range of features about that world. Does the planet have a congenial or threatening climate? What are its physical features like – is it a water world or a desert planet? What are its people like? How do they govern themselves? What is the average life expectancy and how good is their health? How do they organize themselves as families? What are their homes like? What do they do for practical activities and leisure? What are their ideals and aspirations? The responses to a full range of questions like these can reveal unspoken beliefs and attitudes about the brand.
- *Visitor from another planet* The experience of encountering something in a fresh way can be provoked by getting respondents to imagine they have just arrived from Mars and are seeing or tasting a brand for the first time – for example, Henessey™ cognac or Dunkin' Donuts™. What are their first reactions? What questions do they have? What will make them try it again?

Creative exercises

These techniques use stimuli that disrupt or undermine patterns of conventional thinking by introducing alternative realities or paradoxes into the discussion.

- *Guided fantasy* This technique tries to get participants into an alternative frame of mind as a way of reducing the impact of conventional thinking, loosening inhibitions and freeing the mind for imaginative leaps. It uses relaxation techniques and quasi-hypnotic suggestion to take respondents into an alternative reality – a beach, a crowded restaurant, a dream. The setup of a guided fantasy exercise needs time. The moderator must have the complete trust and cooperation of respondents as she takes them into a deep state of suggestibility. Then, at a certain point after reinforcing the altered state, she gets them to answer questions from that perspective. This technique is useful for idea generation.

- *Wrong answers* Having respondents provide consistently 'wrong' answers to questions is a means to learning about underlying beliefs. For example, respondents' reactions to, 'What is the wrong way to pick a facial cream?' and then probing to explore what makes the answers 'wrong' reveals assumptions and standards about the appropriate considerations for choosing a product in the category.

- *Ambiguities and paradoxes* This technique introduces absurd or extremely fanciful elements into brand or category evaluation to push the limits of thinking. The idea is to radically remove the brand from its conventional perception. For example, 'If we were to develop a "Tide™ dog food" or a "Marlboro™ brand of breakfast cereal" what would make it unique?' or, 'If we were to create a "L'Oréal™ automobile", what would be its features?'

- *Product obituary* Another way of introducing an altered perception is to get respondents to imagine that the brand no longer exists and then revealing what is lost or missed about the product. The rhetorical structure of an obituary is a useful tool for inducing this set of associations. It begins with a review of the life span and includes elements such as major accomplishments, what is missed, survivors, etc. The end result is an elaboration of possibly unspoken benefits and beliefs about the brand.

Incomplete stimuli

Reactions to partial or incomplete stimuli can help to reveal respondents' inner thoughts about a brand, category or anything else.

- *Word association* Respondents are encouraged to respond without deliberation to another word. The typical formulation is, 'What is the first thing that pops into your mind when I say ____?'

- *Sentence completion* Similar to word association except that the stimulus can be better elaborated, for example, 'People who want to stay healthy will ____ every day' or, 'Women who care about their appearance will ____'.

- *Empty balloons* A picture is presented of people contemplating something or several people interacting (they can be cartoon or stick figures) and empty balloons, as in a comic strip, are connected to them. Respondents are asked to provide dialog by presenting a particular topic that they are discussing or thinking about, for example, 'These two women are discussing their laundry. One uses only detergent and the other prefers a detergent with bleach. What are they saying to convince each other to change their practices?'

  A variation of 'empty balloons' may also be used to explore the gap between 'thinking' and 'feeling' or 'saying' and 'believing'. In this case, the figure has several balloons that represent the underlying behavior and respondents are challenged to fill in the blanks. For example, 'This person is at the store trying to select a multi-vitamin, what is she *thinking* and what is she *feeling*?' This technique allows respondents to reveal underlying emotions attached to product or brand selection.

Sample empty balloons figure

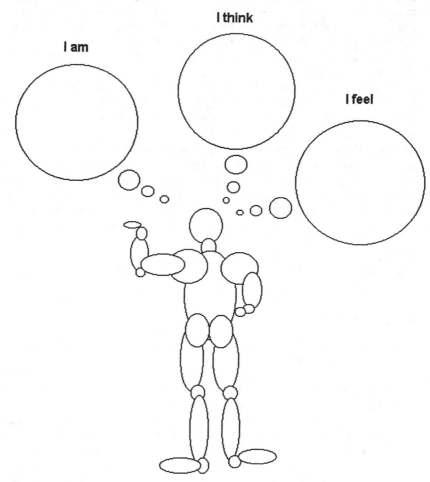

- *Modified TAT (Thematic Apperception Test) or mood boards* Here the stimulus is a picture or drawing – perhaps extracted from proposed advertising images without copy. Respondents are challenged to describe the situation as thoroughly as possible. Alternatively, the stimulus presented can be a collage of images developed by the research team (mood board) and the respondent may be asked to describe their sense of 'all the images put together' or how the images make them feel.

Sorting and ranking exercises

These techniques typically involve advanced preparation, props, game pieces and rules of play.

Product sorts

Actual products or brand names in a category can be arrayed for respondents to sort in various ways. For example, they can be encouraged to arrange the brands into at least two 'families' with roles such as uncle or mother. Then, let them describe what distinguishes the families or what they have in common and what makes particular brands occupy a particular role. If brands of candy were sorted in this way, it would be instructive to find out why one might be considered the grandfather (maybe the brand is tired and needs refreshing) as opposed to the rebellious teenager (maybe the brand needs to overcome objections from mothers).

Attribute or word sorts

This technique is useful in situations where respondents are having difficulty describing brand imagery or emotional connections to a product. Flash cards (index cards or white cardboard cut into pieces the size of playing cards may be used) with different adjectives or attributes printed on each are given to respondents and they are required to select up to ten appropriate words for the product being discussed. This works best if at least one hundred options are provided and the words represent paired antonyms, such as hot-cold, young-old, lazy-energetic, happy-sad and so on. Further discussion and probing can elicit more words and reasons why the particular subset of words was selected.

Picture sorts and collages

This exercise is similar to the word sort except that pictures of persons, products or objects are used. Visual stimuli sometimes help respondents frame their ideas or get over inhibitions experienced when thoughts have to be put into words. People depicted may occupy a wide range of roles including different work, leisure activities or at-home responsibilities. (Be sure to vary racial, gender and age characteristics.) Products or brands pictured may represent a range of upscale vs. downscale, young vs. old or traditional vs. novel, for example. As the appropriate images are selected to represent the brand, they may be arranged in a collage. Then, respondents may discuss why specific images were chosen. The finished collages make excellent support materials when the final report is presented to the client.

Separate collages may be used to represent the various competing brands in a category. Respondents may then be invited to elaborate their perceptions of the differences between them.

Another way of implementing this technique is to provide participants with a range of magazines and have them search for the images to select. They may be invited to also choose words or phrases from headlines to further elaborate the collages. The results can be stunning in their color and pithiness. Anastas, who advocates a variation of this technique, reports:

> To explore the benefits of chewing gum among teenagers, we set up a wall of photos that teenage gum chewers had clipped from magazines (supplemented with additional photos that we had selected). I especially remember one introverted fellow in Mesquite, Texas. You know him, he's the one with the turned-around baseball cap who speaks only in monosyllables: 'Yup', 'Nope' and 'Don'know'. His whole demeanor changed when I asked him to select two or three photos that showed what he felt when he chewed gum. He talked for seven minutes straight, without probing, about his picture and his gum and his routine and his outlook on life. I have it all on videotape. (1994: 15)

Component or benefit sorts

If respondents have difficulties describing the features and benefits desired in a product, it could be helpful to push them along by forcing several choices. For this sorting exercise, the moderator may array, on illustration boards, a wide range of possible features or benefits associated with brands or categories.

A developer of office equipment, for example, used this technique to look for credible combinations that could be engineered into hybrid products. Flash cards with a range of office equipment categories, including phone, fax, postage meter, scale, copier, printer and desk, were provided to owner/operators of small businesses and they were challenged to create combinations that would be useful to companies like their own. The output of this exercise served as the focus of further discussion about technology needs in the SOHO (small office/home office) market.

Forced choices may also be helpful in elaborating the benefits associated with competing brands or those desired in a new product. Terms used in the sorting exercise may include low price, advanced technology, compact and portable, highest quality, appeals to a range of ages, designed for young people or trendy. (A very wide range of choices works best.) Respondents can then identify the benefits associated with current competing brands and evaluate options that could be designed into new market entries.

Ranking and linking exercises

Word and picture sorts are valuable in their own right but sometimes their impact can be multiplied by challenging respondents to rank or link them in either rational or imaginative ways. For example, 'Which words or pictures would you use to describe yourself?' can be used in exercises prior to having respondents sort the same words to describe brands. Other possibilities for extending these exercises include, 'Which are the top three benefits?', 'Which benefits will people want ten years from now?' or, 'Which components will help users in Alaska/China/Saudi Arabia?'

Spectrum sorts

This technique is derived from the traditional 'semantic differential technique'. Respondents are asked to place a particular brand or several in a category along a spectrum – that is, a continuum of semantic space between two antonyms. Depending on the category, these may include:

male	1	2	3	4	5	6	7	female
unhealthy	1	2	3	4	5	6	7	healthy
luxurious	1	2	3	4	5	6	7	basic
young	1	2	3	4	5	6	7	old
quiet	1	2	3	4	5	6	7	loud
downscale	1	2	3	4	5	6	7	upscale
urban	1	2	3	4	5	6	7	rural

As respondents place brands on successive spectrums, for example, Pepsi™ vs. Coke™, a highly nuanced image emerges. The points in the semantic space occupied by the brands can become a focus for further probing and discussion.

Stimulating the senses

Creativity can be heightened by stimulating all the senses – including taste, touch, hearing and smell – and getting them involved in the discovery process.

Sensory exploration can be implemented in conjunction with a verbal exercise or it can provide the basis of a sensory sort. For example, in conducting a mind mapping exercise on images associated with water for a manufacturer of water purification devices for the sink, a moderator played several pieces from the classical repertoire. His choices included Handel's 'Water Music' and Débussy's 'La Mer', whose composers were inspired by the movement and energy of water. The music functioned to add inspiration as respondents were depicting their mental representations.

During a word association exercise conducted for an imagery exploration of beef products, the client prepared and served several platters of steaks. The immediate tastes, smells and textures respondents experienced while they ate the beef (prepared to their preference) provoked an exciting range of benefits, sensations and metaphors that were used in subsequent promotions for the category.

Sensory sorts

Varieties of textures – silk, velvet, steel wool, sandpaper – presented on panels of illustration boards or scents – flowers, bleach, vanilla, basil, soil, wood, orange peels – presented in a series of small bottles can be used to induce imaginative leaps. This technique is particularly useful in categories which have a high sensory impact, such as beverages or soaps, for which consumers may lack a highly developed vocabulary.

Mapping exercises

The objective in this set of exercises is to develop a written depiction of inherent mental images associated with brands or product categories.

Semantic mapping

A semantic space is created by drawing two axes each defined by the two major dimensions of product differentiation in the category – yielding a two-by-two table; for example, for the mass retail chain category it may be upscale vs. downscale and boutique vs. department store. Respondents are then invited to classify several brand names – Macy's™, Target™, K-Mart™, Bed, Bath and Beyond™, Wal-Mart™, Victoria's Secret™ – within that semantic space. The outcome of this exercise resembles what statisticians might produce in a multiple regression graph.[21] For example, the chart may look like the one below.

Sample semantic map on store image

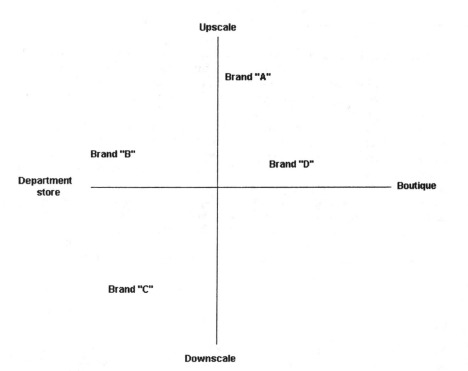

Subsequent probes can elicit details about the meaning and significance of having placed the brand into a particular zone, for example, 'What makes Brand B much more upscale than Brand C?'.

Mind mapping

This technique involves an articulation of mental images elaborated on paper and connected with arrows, lines, etc. The images may include words, drawings, etc. Mind maps are useful for both developing and elaborating concepts.

Creating a mind map starts with placing the main idea at the center of the page. Then, the first subsequent words that come to mind in connection with the main idea are placed around it. Next, the further associations that are produced by these words are connected and a set of idea 'trees' are elaborated until the respondent can go no further. Below is a mind map representing a single person's plans around the main idea of 'vacation'.

Respondents should be encouraged to identify emotions, ideas and brands that come to mind as they create the map. It should represent an image of how they think and react to the issue.

Sample mind map on vacation planning

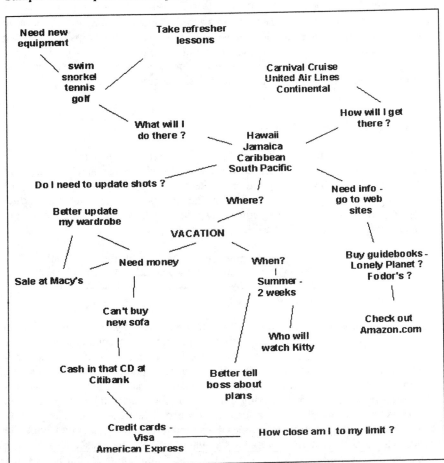

The mind map created above reveals expectations, anxieties and brand associations for various activities. Further probing can elaborate this process and promote insights into the reasons why the various elements are connected.

Automatic drawing or psycho-drawing

This is a similar mind mapping exercise in which subjects are challenged to use found images, words and pictures to describe feelings or attributes related to products, brands or users. Shy respondents may need reassurance that artistic skills are not necessary and stick figures are welcomed.

Time mapping

This technique makes use of the well-known 'time lines of history' and is very useful as an idea generation technique. Respondents are asked to draw a time line representing historical intervals in the past, present and future. Then they are challenged to describe how the category, product or brand – such as the supermarket, toothbrushes, Kleenex™ or recorded music. – has or will develop over the distant time intervals. To release imagination, it often helps to introduce a bit of humor or absurdity into the gaps, for example, 10,000 BC, 1970, the present, 2050, 2510. This exercise releases ideas about benefits, expectations and unmet needs that might be subsequently engineered into the brand.

Laddering and benefits chains

Laddering has become popular as both an interviewing technique and a foundation for analysis and interpretation. This exercise takes the mind mapping process further by having respondents take the depiction to deeper levels of emotion and meaning.[22] It is premised on the means-end principle that product usage has consequences for the consumer and that these drives are ultimately rooted in deeper values, as Reynolds and Gutman put it:

> …Consumers learn to choose products containing attributes which are instrumental to achieving their desired consequences. Means-End Theory simply specifies the rationale why consequences are important, namely, personal values. (1988: 11-12)

Understanding the link between product features and higher values can help advertisers tap into deeper precognitive levels when communicating about a brand. Some criticize the process as being overly rational in its approach and not truly projective. However, it provides a means for approximating the thinking process that lurks beneath conscious choice when purchase decisions are made.

The preferred context for laddering exercises is the individual depth interview, but the exercise is frequently conducted on a group level as well. The process begins with a fairly routine mapping of principal features associated with the brand. Then, the moderator repeatedly uses probes that reach for deeper meanings, for example, 'Tell me why is this important?' and, 'What makes that significant?' as each level is revealed. Eventually no further probes are possible and the assumption is that we have reached the level of values. The output is a depiction of the means-end continuum that describes the intermediate associated meanings as a benefit-chain. The example below illustrates a possible laddering of a headache remedy.

Sample ladder on headache remedies

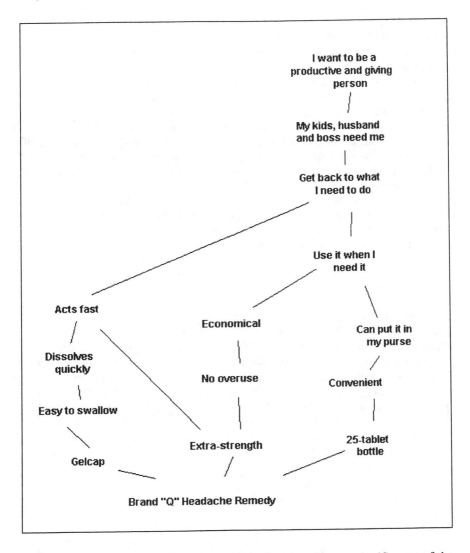

The ladder and benefits chain above reveals that the ultimate significance of the product formulation lies in the respondent's desire to resume the conventional roles of wife, mother and loyal employee.

Idea development techniques

Several techniques are useful for having groups both develop and elaborate ideas.

Ideawriting

This technique maximizes the input of group members while diminishing the impact of the most verbal or insistent participants.[23] It shifts the idea generation task onto paper thus reducing the role of interpersonal dynamics.

It begins with each participant reacting to a creative challenge, for example, 'Describe additional features you would like to see added to your word processing program'. After each participant completes his idea, the sheet gets passed to the next person who is invited to build upon the idea, endorse or challenge aspects of it or create additional ideas on the same sheet. This process is repeated until all of the concepts have circulated to each of the participants. Then respondents are invited to adapt, extend or change their original concepts as they see fit and expose the final product for discussion and elaboration as a single group idea.

By the time the final round occurs, everyone has a stake in each individual contribution and there are no surprises or embarrassments since each sheet will represent a consensus of opinions. The final result is also richer since everyone has had a chance to reflect on all the individual ideas.

Delphi technique

This approach was developed as a forecasting (hence the name which recalls the soothsayers of Apollo at Delphi) and idea generation technique by the Rand Corporation in the early 1950s (Moore, 1987). The Delphi model depends on successive elaboration of information by a group of experts based on knowledge or experience – these can include scientists, physicians or mothers on the subject of infant care. The process can be applied as either a pre-tasking tool in preparation for a focus group or as a group creativity exercise in a single session that is at least a morning or afternoon in duration. As a group exercise, it can adapt some aspects of ideawriting. It can follow an idea generation progression moving along several stages, including:

- Problem identification.
- Solution identification.
- Values identification.
- Prioritization.
- Synthesis.

An example is a study of mothers involved in infant care who were invited to keep a diary of problems encountered in the two weeks before a focus group. Before the conduct of the group all the mothers' contributions were collected and turned into a single anonymous list that everyone received. Then, before starting the group, respondents were asked to conceptualize solutions individually to each of the problems listed. Consequently, the group interview could focus on linking solutions to personal values, prioritizing and synthesizing them without having to expend time on problem or solution identification within the group session.

3.16 Problem Participants and How to Manage Them

Focus group and depth interview participants are individuals. No matter how well our plans are set, there may be personality dynamics in the session that threaten the moderator's authority and the collection of valid information. Respondents who are a bit quirky or who have different opinions are entirely expected and manageable, however there are sometimes those who present an authentic threat to the flow of the session.[24] Every moderator should have a bag of tricks for managing inappropriate behavior among respondents.

Disruptive respondents

Occasionally, a participant will arrive 'high' or drunk. Or, on occasion, someone prone to neurotic behavior such as extreme anger or heavy disruptive sarcasm will have gone undetected during the screening process. Every once in a while, you will get a respondent who does not take the session seriously and is bent on disruption. The moderator needs to remove this individual without starting a confrontation that may make other participants uncomfortable. The main injunction to follow is: *Do not confront the disruptive person in front of others.* The moderator should step out of the room and, with permission from the research manager, should ask the host/hostess to call this person out of the session after a lag of 2-3 minutes.

Latecomers

The research manager and the moderator should decide and confer with the host/hostess about how late in the session latecomers will be accepted. If the weather is bad and/or you need a particular respondent, you can make allowances in the first 10 or 15 minutes of the session (The moderator should bring them up to speed and quickly review ground rules and instructions they might have missed). You have a right not to accept or pay respondents who are late.

Dominant respondents

Some respondents appear so excited and involved in the session that they seem to take over. They don't seem to know more than anyone else but they pop up first every time to answer a question. They frequently challenge other respondents in a dismissive way and don't share the spotlight. They are not necessarily in charge of their emotions – in many cases, these individuals have weak egos and are seeking approval from the moderator by showing off.

This type of extreme dominator should be distinguished from the *natural group leader* who has the respect of peers by virtue of superior knowledge and articulateness. The group leader needs to be heard and channeled subtly while the extreme dominator needs to be controlled.

The moderator should try to control dominators with praise at first, for example, 'Thank you. We've heard your opinion.' Then, withdraw eye contact and use other non-verbal cues, including standing right in back of them when speaking with the group. If the behavior persists, it should help to call attention gently to this person's behavior. For example, 'We've heard a lot about how you feel. Now I want to be sure that others get a chance, so I won't call on you for a while'.

Passive respondents

Some respondents are very shy and passive and need to be given many openings to participate. The moderator should first try to bring them out by calling on them by name, for example, 'Inge, we're very interested in what you have to say'. If a stronger message is needed later in the discussion, the moderator can also call attention, gently, to this respondent's behavior. For example, 'Marcel, we haven't heard very much from you and we really want to know what you think'.

Compliant respondents

Sometimes participants can't seem to muster up their own opinions. They just agree with the last person's response or what appears to be the general consensus in the group. These people are simply afraid to be assertive and voice their own opinions. Alternatively, they might not have well-developed opinions and are fearful of exposing some area of presumed ignorance. The moderator can usually manage this by setting the right tone and offering 'unconditional positive regard' to all participants. If these reinforcements do not work, you may just have to rely on pencil-and-paper exercises or projective techniques to bring out these individuals.

Liars

If the moderator is paying attention to body language cues, he may suspect that a respondent is lying about a feeling or practice. In this case, it is wrong to call something a lie and it is not helpful to point out the inconsistency between verbal and non-verbal expression. The moderator should spend a moment reflecting on what may be producing the disparity – is it a matter of etiquette or propriety ('Yes, I always practice safe sex' or, 'Yes, I always clean my bathroom on Friday') or is the respondent posturing. If sufficient rapport has been established, a gentle confrontational probe may be in order. Otherwise, the moderator should rephrase the question at a later point in a less ego-threatening way. For example, 'We all have trouble sticking to our home cleaning schedule, is it ever hard to stick to yours?'

Rambling, unfocused respondents

These participants just can't seem to follow the drift of the discussion. They may pipe in with an opinion on an issue that was discussed 15 minutes earlier. Otherwise, they can't seem to stay on the subject – bringing in anecdotes about their Aunt Mary in Manchester, for example. They want to participate and they feel good about the session, but they can't seem to get things right. The moderator should look at the positive side and acknowledge their efforts. On the other hand, the respondent should be gently and tactfully confronted by describing what they are doing. Then, their cooperative intentions should be redirected. For example, the moderator might say, 'Thank you, Mario, I appreciate that comment, but I wish you had made it while we were still on the subject of____' or, 'I'm sorry, Marie, we don't have enough time now to let you finish that story but if there's some time left at the end, I'd like to hear it'.

To review, here are some standards for dealing with quirky respondents.

- Be patient.
- Acknowledge good intentions.
- Be firm and stay in control.
- Tactfully describe the problem and redirect the situation.
- Don't condemn or shame anybody.
- Do not display negative emotions such as anger, hostility or cynicism because it may provoke fears in others.
- Do not threaten to eject someone or withhold the incentive. If someone needs to be ejected do not do it yourself.
- Hold to your high expectations.

3.17 Keeping the Discussion Focused

In every focus group or depth interview, the moderator is responsible for *pacing*. That is, she must negotiate between the twin pressures of getting through the discussion guide and allowing each person to have their say. This can create dilemmas – staying focused vs. moving the discussion along vs. maintaining rapport and a spirit of open disclosure.

Moving the discussion along appropriately

Before the moderator closes off discussion on a topic, she should make sure that every opinion has had a chance to be aired. Asking a question like, 'Have we heard all the different viewpoints in the room?' or, 'Is there another point of view out there?' provides an opportunity for closure and lets the discussion move along easily. Another good way to close off a topic is to provide a brief reflective summary, some analysis or an interpretation of what has come earlier. For example, 'It seems that there are three main sources for information about insurance – calls from brokers or agents, newspaper ads, and recommendations from friends. Right? Let's move on now'.

Leadership

Be firm when you are moving the discussion but make sure that no one feels you are cutting them off.

Determining relevance

At every stage in the discussion, the moderator must make a decision about how relevant and salient a particular remark or discussion flow may be. If it's not exactly on target, is it worth a digression or should one return to the issue later on? In either case, the moderator should be positive and open and say things like, 'That's an informative remark, let's pursue it with the group for a minute' or, 'I appreciate your telling me that. Let's set it aside for a minute and come back and talk about it some more'. Or, 'Thank you. That issue is on my agenda and I'll get to it after we finish talking about ___'.

Redirecting the discussion

The moderator should be polite and positive when he has to redirect the discussion. It should be done in a spirit of completion and accomplishment and never disinterest, for example, 'It looks like we've heard all the different points of view about ____. Let's move on'.

Quieting down respondents

Respondents sometimes get so caught up in the heat of discussion that they forget about the ground rules and even their etiquette goes out the window. Several may compete for attention or speak at the same time – a huge problem because this will be blurred on the tape recording. The moderator may have to remind respondents about the problems that multiple voices will make for the tape recording. She may have to reassert authority in the group by saying something like, 'We won't be able to learn about your feelings, unless we approach this one at a time'. She should acknowledge the good intentions and enthusiasm of participants while reaffirming the ground rules, for example, 'Rita and Concepcion, I'm really happy that you're trying to share your feelings with the group – that's important. But I need you both to let the other finish before you start talking'.

3.18 Managing Interview Contingencies

Problems can arise in all research situations. The moderator can be met by hostility, a lack of seriousness, or the 'freeze out'. Respondents may be unable to articulate their attitudes and feelings or they may be dishonest or emotional. The best advice for dealing with contingencies is to remain positive and professional. The moderator should try to reestablish rapport by emphasizing the positive purposes of the study.

Some tips for dealing with common contingencies follow.

- *Lagging interest* If the energy level and interest in the room starts to die down, the moderator should pay close attention to her own actions, body language and energy level. What can she be doing differently? Perhaps she should get up from the table and use the easel. Start an exercise. Redirect the discussion. Ask questions differently.

- *Hostility to the interviewer or the research sponsor* Customers who have had negative experiences with the brand, company or category may carry a 'chip on their shoulder' and the moderator is the most convenient target for their hostility. The participant may vent his hostility and reject all the concepts as 'a typical ripoff'. In order to manage this contingency, the moderator should not deny the validity of the criticism or try to defend the company. It will only make matters worse. Instead, the moderator should acknowledge the problem and move on.

    I understand how you felt to be treated that way by the service department; but we're conducting these groups to learn how to do things better. What would you have preferred?

- *Emotional reactions* When talking about a traumatic experience, respondents may react emotionally – with tears or nervous laughter. Here again, the moderator should show empathy and acknowledge the respondent's special circumstances. He should just try to just listen without reaction. In a recent interview with a cancer patient, she had a tearful outburst when the moderator asked about some side effects of radiation therapy.

    You could never understand how I feel and what I've been experiencing. You don't know the pain I feel or the fear when I'm up late at night...

    MODERATOR: You're absolutely right. No matter how much I listen and want to understand you, I'll never feel what you are feeling. Your reaction is absolutely valid. I want to try hard, though, and get as close as I can. But I'm not sure I ever will. Let me just listen.

3.19 Closing the Interview Effectively

An effective closing is one of the most important parts of the focus group, depth interview or site visit, and planning ahead can have many benefits. Proper closure can help to:

- Provide a sense of accomplishment for participants. It is always important to end the interview on a high note and not just let the energy drop.
- Allow participants to summarize what they have learned or how they have changed as a result of the session.
- Provide reluctant respondents a last chance to contribute.
- Let respondents offer projections for the future, for example, will their buying behavior or decision making habits change in any way.
- Let respondents suggest ways to improve future interviews.
- Let respondents change a response given earlier.

The closing exercise should revert to 'round robin' style as in the introductions. Here are some suggestions for questions that might be asked during a closing exercise.

Here's your chance for a parting shot. What concluding advice would you give the company about how to better serve customers.

Let's have everybody summarize the single most important thing you learned in tonight's session.

If there was a single word or idea that we should definitely include in our next ad campaign what would it be.

How might you do things differently now that you have been exposed to the information you heard tonight.

If you had the president of the company on the phone, what piece of advice would you give him after tonight's session.

After what you have heard tonight, what will be the single most important benefit that will get you interested in the product.

3.20 Maximizing the Usefulness of Creative Brainstorming Sessions

Creative brainstorming (also known as 'ideation') sessions are a variety of qualitative research oriented toward advancing company goals and solving problems. Some applications include:

- Generating line extension ideas or new product concepts.
- Creating competitive marketing strategies and tactics.
- Finding new ways to communicate product benefits to consumers.
- Evaluating and improving business processes.
- Improving internal communication and team-building.
- Maximizing employee productivity.
- Organizational problem solving.

A good creative brainstorming consultant is, first of all, rooted in a consistent perspective or a philosophy of the creative process. Here are several principles that a consultant should follow.

- *Be team-oriented.* Idea generation needs to be a joint effort – interactive and cooperative – a product of mutual inspiration and incremental expansion. The consultant should facilitate a process in which participants are encouraged to learn from each other and to bump against, inspire and expand each other's ideas.
- *Work on quantity first.* To discover good ideas, idea generation and problem solving sessions need to go for large numbers of seed ideas to be screened and refined first. Most ideas eventually will get sifted out, while others will rise to the top. Nevertheless, unless there is a great deal of raw material to work with, the end product will suffer.
- *Separate creation from evaluation.* Ideas flow most freely in an environment which is accepting and non-judgmental. If evaluation happens too soon, it tends to cut off spontaneity and risk-taking and generates ideas that are too safe and cautious.
- *Work in a spirit of play.* A necessary feature of creative thinking is avoiding excessive logic and structure. That means working in a spirit of play, or playing for productive ends.
- *Invite risk.* Creative energy is loosened when brainstorming participants have the freedom to gamble, to be ridiculous, to be wrong, to lose. Just like the stock market or the race track, high risk leaves you open for high gain. The best ideas often sound ludicrous at first and evolve after continued deliberation and development.

- *Use contradictions and paradoxes.* Imposing too many restraints on thinking creates ideas that are predictable and stilted. Breakthroughs are born in contradictions and paradoxes and in combinations and mixes that do not initially seem like they belong together.
- *Invite sensory expansion.* Creative boundaries are enlarged when thinking can go beyond the limits of verbal expression. Pictures, drawings, charts and maps provide added dimensions for stimulation and imagination. Music, sounds, taste and smells can also provide both inspiration and an outlet for creative exploration.
- *Merge different thought processes.* Creative thinking involves merging thought processes that appear at first to be contradictory – intuition and rationality, convergent and divergent thinking, using the left brain and right brain, linear and existential thought processes.
- *Minimize specialization.* The best creative leaps are often made when the perspectives of seemingly incongruous disciplines somehow find common ground. Staying within specialized fields invites rigidity, conformity and confinement.
- *Don't rule anything out.* You cannot initiate a creative process knowing precisely how your best ideas will develop. Be open to paradigm shifts. Expect to be surprised.

Although the specific project management approaches of various firms will differ, the consultant should be following a variety of steps.
- Gaining background information on the category and brand as well as the organizational culture, if it is unfamiliar.
- Formulating clear and measurable objectives.
- Developing a project plan that describes the mutual responsibilities of client and consultant.
- Selecting targeted participants that represent the appropriate mix of internal and/or external participants who will be needed for achieving project goals. Members of internal teams may include senior executives or managers drawn from sales, marketing, technical R&D, manufacturing, advertising, public relations or customer service departments, for example. External participants may include customers, experts or trend leaders such as people involved in cutting edge pursuits or creative professions (software developers, artists, designers, performers).
- Developing creative exercises to stimulate thinking.
- Managing and facilitating the ideation experience.
- Reporting and presenting results.

Some firms offer services beyond ideation in actually producing marketing plans, or product prototypes.

3.21 Maximizing the Effectiveness of Observational Research

Here is some additional advice for undertaking observational research studies that offer the greatest benefit to your marketing program.

Consultant selection

Make sure to select a trained and experienced consultant who is familiar with observational and ethnographic techniques as practiced by anthropologists, sociologists and psychologists. Not all qualitative research practitioners have the requisite background; only a select few do.

- Expect to pay a premium for this kind of research.
- Determine in advance how much participation and interaction will be conducted between observers and subjects as opposed to pure observation.

Participant selection

Observational studies may have both aware or unaware participants, or some combination of the two. An example of an observational study using unaware participants involves the researcher in 'mystery shopping' to test whether service delivery or a sales encounter is proceeding according to specified expectations.

For aware participants, make sure to recruit individuals who will be cooperative and not intimidated by the extra demands and intrusiveness required by observational research studies. Sometimes recruited participants in observational studies demand a higher than average incentive fee.

You may conduct observations in either a public or a private space. Restrictions against observing in a public space are minimal. On the other hand, if you are conducting observations in a private space, make certain you have the necessary permissions and authorizations. Gatekeepers for private spaces, such as a store manager, also may require that an incentive payment be made.

Be sure that the data recording method is consistent with project objectives. You may use the full range of open or surreptitious recording methods, including:

- Written notes.
- Photographs.
- Open or concealed audiotaping.
- Open or concealed videotaping.
- Time-lapse photography.

NOTE: Sometimes analysis of a particular site requires multiple cameras, special lighting or other equipment.

Determine the nature and extent of client co-participation and how this will be structured. For example, what will be the client's role at the site vis-à-vis the respondent.

Consider the reporting format that will best suit the needs of internal clients. Observational studies easily lend themselves to visual documentary reports.

Allow a good deal of extra time for coordination and management of all the details. In particular allow for a good deal of time in the field because on-site visits can be difficult to schedule.

3.22 Maximizing the Effectiveness of Research with Special Populations

Certain population segments sometimes require special consideration or an adaptation of specifications in executing the research. This section is devoted to an analysis of reasons for modifying the details as well as recommendations for producing optimal results with special populations.

Children and teens

Children represent an important market for goods and services whose value as market research respondents should not be disparaged. In the USA, kids under 12 are responsible for $15 billion of their own discretionary spending and have a further influence in $165 billion of their parents' spending each year (Kaladjian, 1996). On the other hand, children's sensitivities and vulnerabilities must be considered in planning and executing the research.

Children and teenagers under the age of 18 tend to be very self-conscious about age and anxious about appearing 'immature' relative to their age-related self concept. Consequently, it is advisable to recruit by *school grade rather than by chronological age* since that provides a better 'consumer-defined' standard for peer relationships. Limiting the age range of group participants to no more than two school grades also helps youngsters see fellow group members as age equals. Mixing a 7-year-old with a 12-year-old in a session risks profound inhibitions, cynicism and embarrassment even if they are both devotees of Dragonball™ or the Backstreet Boys. Other recommendations before structuring groups with youth respondents include:

- Limit the length of session to one hour if possible, one and a half hours at the most with older children and teens. Children have limited attention spans and even the most compelling discussions will quickly produce boredom and torpor.
- Limit the size of the group to six or seven. Youngsters can become very animated and rambunctious in group sessions particularly if their attitudes are at the extremes – highly positive or negative about the concepts or categories. High energy can produce disciplinary problems if there are too many participants around the table.
- Segregate by gender most of the time because of the differential physical and verbal skills that commonly develop between boys and girls of the same age.

Some research managers maintain an erroneous belief that only female moderators should conduct interviews with children and teens. In contemporary

Western societies family roles and custodial norms have changed sufficiently so that it is no longer to be assumed that women are more adept at nurturing and intimate roles. Furthermore, youngsters have a wide range of male significant others, such as fathers, teachers, uncles and grandfathers, who provide a precedent for intimacy with males as moderators.

Moderators must guard against speaking down to young participants – even in jest. Childish language and social distancing, for example talking about 'you kids' can appear condescending. Adults also should not try to emulate youth jargon because language changes meaning very quickly and across boundaries of region and social class. Young people easily can expose and disrespect phonies who use inappropriate, outdated and irrelevant terminology. In contrast, youngsters appreciate moderators who are up front – offering detailed explanations and preparation for next steps in the session and being taken into confidence.

It is a best practice for the moderator personally to re-screen and build rapport with each child individually for several minutes before combining participants as a group. The experienced moderator can plan and adjust her own approach to various group participants based on her assessment of each child's personality and affect. Important things to remember during the session include:

- It is natural for youngsters initially to perceive the experience of group participation as something like a school classroom, but this needs to be challenged from the outset. Without conveying an image of negative authority, the moderator should spend some time explaining and reinforcing the differences between school and research. For example, children may need reminding that most rules of classroom etiquette – not cutting others off and challenging others' opinions politely – remain in force. Nevertheless, children's expectation to mimic and comply with the adult authority figure should be diminished.

- Some degree of irreverence appeals to kids' sense of humor and reassures them that the research exercise is not school. Karen Forcade (1996) reports having had children place a pair of shoes brought from home on the conference table – in violation of etiquette rules – to loosen them up for a discussion of footwear.

- Children react well to stimuli that are concrete – such as visual, taste and touch tests – as opposed to those which are conceptual. Under age eight, they have highly limited abstract and verbal skills.

- Young children tend to feel more comfortable in a community-based living room setting or viewing facility that can be arranged in such a manner. Floor seating can also be cozy. They appear absurdly mismatched to an oversized corporate conference table, and are likely to become overly compliant and inhibited when placed in such an environment.

- Interviewing techniques that use games, play and creative exercises involving clay, crayons, paints, song, verse, etc. usually work well with children.

- Interviews with children scheduled on the weekend rather than a weekday are likely to help both the 'show rate' as well as group dynamics. Children and teens tend to be over-scheduled, and after long school days are likely to be tired or have competing commitments to extra-curricular activities.

Weekends, on the other hand, may sometimes interfere with religious responsibilities so it may be difficult to find a happy medium.

Despite the pitfalls, research managers should value the high productivity of children as respondents. As Forcade points out:

> Children are more skeptical than adults. They question the whys, the reasons, the choices. Children are completely sincere and will share their feelings and beliefs. Children are more truthful. Although it takes more time to set the stage and get the kids to relax, they are indeed more truthful than adults. If they don't like the idea or if they love it, children get very excited and completely animated. You can even hear their voices reach a higher pitch. Children are not restrained. They are not inhibited by thoughts like 'this might be a foolish idea' or 'this could cost too much money'. Kids will talk and talk. And when asked to stay within certain bounds of reality, they comply. They can do that too. (1996: 31)

Seniors – the mature market

The point at which a mature adult becomes a 'senior' is open to interpretation. Some brands have a tradition of defining the shift at age 50 or 55. Others rely upon some other official age marker, economic transition or qualification for social insurance benefits, for example, the 'retirement age' of 62, 65 or 70.

Social gerontologists agree that there are very wide variations among people classified as seniors in terms of self-image, health status and labor force participation. Little should be inferred from knowing just someone's age and employment status. For example, many retired adults supplement their income with part time jobs, income-producing crafts or by performing various services. A recent focus group of 'retirees' included men earning income by repairing small appliances, selling goods at local flea markets, consulting to small businesses and performing temporary child care services.

A major division in the senior market is between the 'young-old' who are still very active and vital and the 'old-old', a relatively smaller group limited by poor health and immobility.

Inferences about economic status and social roles should also be made with caution. It is wrong to stereotype the mature market as economically disadvantaged and uninvolved in child care. Older adults can be relatively affluent even though their consumption styles may betray the thriftiness learned by living through wars and depressions. Additionally, a variety of forces including women's return to the labor force, delay of childbirth and high divorce rates are giving grandparents a greater impact upon child rearing and other family decisions than in the past.

Seniors are enthusiastic market research participants even though they sometimes need help to overcome the heightened suspicion they have about outsiders trying to take advantage of them.[25] Their sense of responsibility once recruited often leads them to arrive one hour or more prior to the interview's start. Below are some useful considerations when working with seniors.

- If some or all senior research participants are likely to be disabled, the facility used should have adequate provisions for their comfort. Can wheelchairs and walkers navigate around conference tables? Are bathrooms accessible to the disabled?

- Bathroom breaks are necessary if interviews or focus groups last longer than one hour.
- There is often a 'language gap' between generations. Terms reflecting popular culture or new technologies may not be completely understood by seniors and should be limited.
- Seniors can be very sensitive to safety and security. They are often reluctant to travel long distances and are likely to decline research sessions that end late in the evening. They often ask to have someone accompany them to the facility.
- Seniors are joiners and are likely to be affiliated with a wide range of social, fraternal and religious organizations. These associations can serve as a convenient entry point for recruiting older adults. Conducting interview sessions at local community facilities or a familiar shopping mall is also likely to put seniors at ease.
- Many older adults follow restricted diets. Consequently, fresh fruits and vegetables and unflavored drinks, tea and coffee are preferred refreshments over sugared sodas, candies, cookies and salty snacks.
- Seniors expect to be treated in a mature fashion. They hate to be babied and patronized. They are not your own grandparents. Seniors will dismiss efforts to be chummy and cuddly as blatant condescension.

Women

There is no evidence that women differ fundamentally from men as qualitative research participants. However, one may speculate that within various cultures or age groups, it may be relatively easier for women to communicate about emotions or to establish rapport with other women more readily than men might with each other. In most Western cultures, women should not be thought of as delicate or easily offended. Legitimate questions may be raised, on the other hand, about whether it is appropriate to mix genders within the focus group when certain topics are being discussed. Additionally, matching genders – the suitability of male moderators conducting sessions on feminine products (such as fragrances or menopause products) and/or sensitive subject matter, such as pregnancy or sexually transmitted diseases – should be carefully considered. Several guidelines listed below may help the research manager.

- Gender mixing should be avoided if culturally based rules or age-related norms suggest that respondents would feel shamed, inhibited or prone to posturing in the presence of the opposite sex. In some cases, for example, discussing alcoholic beverages or fashion trends with mixed groups comprising young men and women of dating age may lead to talk filled with bombast and lies intended to impress others. Additionally, in some non-Western cultures, women are socialized to yield to men's opinions in public so they may suppress contradicting opinions after a man has made statements. In interviews with recent immigrants from Asia or Latin America, concerns about female deference may require segregation of the sexes.

- Most moderators are women – the membership of the QRCA in the United States is approximately two-thirds female, for example – so it normally does not require a stretch to match a female consultant with a group of women. When opportunity or experience suggests a male might be able to handle an assignment, the research manager should be confident that proficient male moderators generally are able to maintain a thoroughly clinical stance when confronting sensitive issues with females. Nowadays, women are generally not inhibited about discussing sensitive issues with men in other contexts, for example with a physician, counselor or minister, and they bring this degree of comfort to the focus group. When the tables are turned and women are in the authoritative position, men normally are accustomed to discussing sensitive issues with members of the opposite sex as well. Nevertheless, this situation always requires a high degree of poise, confidence, objectivity and suspension of judgmental opinions.

- In some situations, an experienced moderator can leverage gender difference to appear more objective and naïve in furtherance of complete disclosure. As Rebecca Day points out, 'In many cases, we have noticed that a female moderating a group about a topic that is considered traditionally male tends to get more complete responses because the (male) participants feel somewhat compelled to "explain things". With a male moderator they tend to believe that he knows what they are talking about' (1993: 47).

- It goes without saying that moderators should avoid sexist language or assumptions in conducting interviews.

Racial and cultural minorities

In most circumstances, members of racial or cultural minorities should be integrated into general market studies. There is no valid reason to exclude them as a matter of course if they are assimilated into a society's commercial culture. They should not be excluded automatically as purchasers of products available to the market as a whole on the basis of invalid assumptions. Several years ago, for example, a research manager suggested that participants of the Jewish faith be excluded from a series of focus groups on Christmas cards. She had to be reminded that Jewish people, though they may not adhere to the religious celebration of Christmas, nevertheless participate in the seasonal festival and are likely to purchase numerous Christmas cards and exchange them with friends and business associates. Their category participation, in fact, is important in helping to define the religiously neutral cards that a large segment of the general market prefers.

The rapid rate of growth of diverse populations in Western societies and the concentration of ethnic groups in the younger population cohorts indicates a market phenomenon that producers of goods and services can ill afford to avoid. Ethnic groups are important as consumers of the larger society's goods and services and as a fountain of innovation for the larger society. Socialization into the dominant society's consumer patterns is an ongoing feature of immigrant acculturation (Peñaloza, 1994). Simultaneously, the styles and tastes of minority communities, especially in such areas as food, popular music and the fine arts, although they may seem exotic and foreign at first, eventually become adopted by the dominant society's avant-garde and often become entirely assimilated into prevailing norms. In the United States, for example, salsa has outpaced ketchup as the tabletop condiment of choice. In France, couscous has become a household staple.

Significantly, defining ethnic markets, understanding their media usage patterns and influence structures and gaining access to ethnic communities to obtain market information are complicated by their varying degrees of visibility, assimilation, language issues and matters of cultural traits and values.

Defining the target, for example, is complicated by the dominant culture's tendency to see ethnic communities as undifferentiated masses. Majorities are indifferent and ignorant about the subtle features of ethnic identity. The view from within, in contrast, is highly diverse. Established Cuban-American communities in South Florida, for example, share little with recent Mexican-American immigrants in Southern California other than linguistic similarities and the US Census label of 'Hispanic'. Even regional differences among immigrants from a single country can create problems that affect research validity. Migrants from indigenous areas of Southern Mexico, for example, may have poor Spanish fluency, leaving them as bewildered in New York City as they might be in Mexico City.

There are several legitimate reasons to conduct specialized studies of racial and cultural minorities. Special attention and effort should be extended, for example, when there are separate marketing campaigns focused on ethnic media, such as special versions of advertisements to be placed in Spanish language or African American focused publications. Product developers may find it useful to study ethnic communities to discover potential mass market trends or to identify special needs and opportunities produced by diverse cultural characteristics. The variety of situations and marketing occasions that require marketers to speak directly to members of ethnic sub-communities include the following:

- Products that appeal directly to the cultural distinctiveness of ethnic sub-communities. These may include greeting cards for Dewali, the Hindu Feast of Lights, or foods and ingredients that are common in ethnic diets.
- Public health messages intended for sub-communities that are differentially affected by particular conditions. The Puerto Rican community of New York City, for example, has rates of asthma considerably higher than other groups. Similarly, Eastern European Jews are subject to relatively higher rates of genetic conditions such as Gaucher's Disease and may consequently be targeted for pharmaceutical products for its treatment.
- Products and services related to the ethnic sub-communities' ties to the home country, for example, education, travel, telecommunications and cash remittance services.
- Products and services that benefit from personal selling by fellow members of ethnic sub-communities because sales require high levels of trust or explanation in native languages. These may include security, banking, insurance and brokerage services.
- Professional services that are required for accommodation in larger society, for example, immigration law, real estate brokerage and financial services.

- Categories in which members of ethnic sub-communities represent a significant proportion of the marketing channels, such as Korean and Arab grocers on the East and West Coasts.
- Mass market products that may be beneficially positioned or distributed in respect to the specific needs of ethnic sub-communities.

Culturally-sensitive tactics are often the preferred discovery technique for information about community norms and preferences that can yield strategic insights. These may take a variety of forms, including:

- A 'community-based' approach which emphasizes cooperation with ethnic community leaders and organizational structures.
- In-home interviews and encounters at social gathering places such as restaurants, churches and local community centers.
- Ethnographic observation and interviewing to understand the cultural context of ethnic group behavior in a way that avoids presuppositions about their attitudes and preferences.[26]
- Matching of respondents with moderators by racial, language or cultural features is often necessary. Careful attention should be paid to matters of subculture, dialect and accent in these cases.

Even within an ethnic cluster, avoid treating participants as an undifferentiated mass. Expect considerable human variation within the segment, based on variables such as social class, self image or aspirations.

Business executives

Qualitative research with business executives usually requires an extra measure of thoughtfulness and consideration. Executives are busy and already over-committed and thus may be difficult to recruit. They can be opinionated and domineering during the interview or, on the other hand, in some business cultures may be tight-lipped and cagey – eager to hear what others are saying but reluctant to make their own contributions to the discussion by revealing their own practices. These recruitment and other operational issues create major challenges for even experienced moderators.

Recruitment for senior executive studies focusing upon business-to-business products should be by function and decision making authority – not just by title. Day-to-day responsibility for various tasks such as setting up benefits programs, developing the corporate web site or acquiring sales transaction software is not likely to reside with the senior-most person bearing a human resources or information technology title. Recruiters need to search for the precise person with a particular job and spending authority.

Many research managers tend to overestimate the value of the corporate CEO as a research participant. Most CEOs of major companies serve as inspirational and strategic team leaders who interact primarily with the financial and investor community and exert little supervision over operations. Most operational aspects of corporate management are delegated downward to divisional and business unit leadership.

The desire for peer interaction and airing of views is an important motivator for executive participation in research. Thus, in many cases, group interviews can be the preferred methodology. Several years ago, participants in a technology focus group discussing conversion from military-focused sales to the civilian economy arrived an hour early and were already deeply engaged in the topic when the moderator arrived, because this was a hot topic of the moment.

Alternatively, in cases where executives might be reluctant to discuss their vendors or decision making structures in public, or when the prospective respondents are highly dispersed geographically, individual depth interviews may be the preferred approach. Here are some useful ideas to keep in mind when working with executives.

- A special report summary for participants that outlines major findings from the research may be a useful incentive for senior executives. This document need not address issues that the client considers strategic or confidential, nevertheless, it can provide an overview of views expressed by anonymous study participants.

- Research directors should consider holding senior executive interviews outside the confines of professional research facilities. A session conducted in the private dining areas of a fine restaurant or major hotel can be more gratifying for many senior executives and other high income respondents.

- Research sessions conducted at breakfast or lunch are often effective in motivating senior executives who are highly likely to work late or have long commutes home in the evening.

- The amount of moderator preparation required for senior executive interviews should not be underestimated. The interviewer should be familiar with corporate trends, technical terminology, and decision making structures as well as buzzwords and jargon common in management discussions.

- Some clients are under the mistaken impression that senior executives are 'insulted' by the offer of cash compensation for research participation. Nothing can be further from the truth. Not only do they want the cash, they expect an honorarium in proportion to their salaries. In cases where gifts are offered in lieu of cash, their value should be equivalent or greater than the cash that might be offered.

Physicians and other professionals

Physicians and other professionals such as attorneys, engineers or photographers can provide valuable strategic information to marketers who target them. However, these respondents also present special challenges for recruiters and moderators.

Like senior executives, physicians and other professionals are motivated to participate in market research by a desire for peer contacts and the opportunity to learn what colleagues are doing, such as prescription patterns or the software packages that are being selected to solve common problems. They are pleased to learn that their input will have a significant impact on the development of new products and services and in the implementation of advanced technologies. They appreciate the feeling of being insiders in the marketing plans of companies who supply the goods and services that help them perform their vocations.[27]

Because there is a greater demand for physicians and professionals in research studies than those willing or available to participate, research volunteers are likely to become overused. Without irony, a pediatrician who had already attended several focus groups with the author in Philadelphia once said, 'You're a much better moderator than those others'. Repeated research participants tend to become overly educated about the research process and take on a 'consulting' role that competes against their product user role. In other words, they cease to describe their own needs as customers and start to speak as marketing specialists (Greenbaum, 1992).

Special care is required during recruitment to guarantee that the functional responsibilities of the participant match the usage roles required for product decision making. Professionals become notably specialized in their fields; consequently, nothing can be taken for granted about their actual daily routines. Academic cardiologists may not have routine patient practices or may only consult on severe cases. As a result, they might need to be excluded from research about first line therapies such as medications for hypertension or elevated cholesterol. Senior professors of literature almost never teach the 'Lit 101' survey and would be the wrong decision makers about the features desired in introductory texts. Senior litigating attorneys usually depend upon junior associates in their law firms to conduct case research, so their input on a data retrieval package may not be as valuable as the ones actually working with the software. In many situations, the precise functional responsibilities are delimited by state or national regulations. For example, optometrists may be permitted only in a limited number of states to conduct laser surgery for vision correction. The following guidelines relate to recruiting and conducting sessions with professionals.

- Like business executives, professionals are often protected by receptionists and assistants who keep their bosses shielded from unwanted contacts. Research recruitment requires a strategy for getting past these gatekeepers.
- Professionals also expect cash incentives roughly in proportion to their employment compensation. They cannot be expected to offer their time for the public benefit.
- It is sometimes difficult to find concentrations of available specialists within limited geographic confines. This usually requires the project to reserve a high travel budget for the interviewer. Alternatively, the project can provide an opportunity for telephone or online focus groups. A third alternative which is often adopted is to recruit participants at conferences or conventions targeted to their specialty. Professors of English who make decisions about textbook adoptions may be hard to reach in far-flung college towns but concentrations of them may be found at the annual meeting of the Modern Language Association or similar conferences. Research managers recruiting at conferences should be careful not to schedule interviews in conflict with major presentations or social events during the conference. Here, too, breakfast is sometimes the most convenient time of the day.
- The form of address to be used during the session needs to be carefully considered. In some cultures, the use of honorific titles such as 'Doctor',

'Herr Doktor', 'Monsieur Professeur' and 'Professor' are an expectation while in others, there is some flexibility about forms of address. What is appropriate may be a matter of the moderator's age, experience, self-image and her own professional credentials. Some professionals expect that they will be addressed by titles among outsiders, while within a private setting among groups of their peers, they are likely to revert quickly to the more intimate use of the first name. This may shift if a colleague is a former teacher or a leader in the field.

- Group sessions with professionals are vulnerable to competitiveness, disciplinary politics and distinctions between various contending schools of thought in the field. The moderator is sometimes hard-pressed to permit an airing of diverse views when participants hold one another's opinions to be illegitimate, obscure or obsolete. The divergences in a group discussion also may lead the researcher to question whether the extreme positions may be accommodated by a single product or service – for example whether a single textbook can reflect both critical and traditional perspectives on American history.

Sensitive topics

Sensitive topics generally encompass research discussions of matters which might be shameful, embarrassing or uncomfortable to discuss in a public setting or with strangers. Normally this is understood to include matters of sexual behavior, personal health and bodily functions, but discomfort goes far beyond these subjects. Discussions of family finances, politics, law violation and religious practices may be regarded as equally sensitive. Depending upon the context, even the discussion of legal and relatively benign matters such as usage of adult media, gambling, smoking and drinking alcoholic beverages may be difficult to discuss in public. Matters of family status such as divorce and adoption can be problematic, too. Even discussions of relationships, personal care and child rearing can have their sensitive moments.

Sensitive topics require an extra measure of acceptance and validation on the moderator's part. Moreover, they require thoughtful consideration through every stage of project execution to guarantee that no hurtful offense will be inflicted upon cooperative respondents and to assure that respondents will find it easy to tell the truth and feel good about it.[28] Several helpful guidelines are listed below.

- The topic's sensitivity should be acknowledged during recruitment. Prospective respondents should be given an opportunity to affirm their willingness to handle the subject matter in a research context, for example, 'Do you feel that you can be open and honest speaking with a group of other men about erectile dysfunction?' At this point, personal inhibitions should be validated if they exist and the prospect should be given the opportunity to decline or be interviewed individually.
- Many respondents appreciate the opportunity to share feelings and experiences with groups of people that share their problem. Being able to help others in a similar predicament can be appealing and highly motivational to participants. An AIDS patient serving as a focus group

participant once said, 'I'm alone in my apartment all day. This gives me a chance to turn my condition to some good'.

- Sensitive topics require a lengthy warmup period which gives respondents a chance to become comfortable with the setting and moderator.
- Transitioning to the core issues often requires some gentle humor or an expression of empathy, for example, 'I know it may be hard to answer this question but we need to know...' or 'Now it's time to get to the heart of the matter...'
- Questions should be direct and unapologetic. The interviewer should avoid hesitancy and the 'ums' and 'uhs' which reveal his own discomfort or embarrassment.
- Language should be direct, unambiguous and mature. Using baby talk and circumlocutions only adds to the anxiety and discomfort of the discussion. The question, 'What does vaginal dryness feel like?' is preferable to, 'What happens when you get the scratchies down there?'
- Questioning strategies required in various circumstances include the following:
  - *Acknowledge the respondents' special qualifications* as the 'experts' on the subject matter or 'ambassadors' for their peers.
  - *Reduce ego threat* by acknowledging several valid reactions and opinions and not forcing extreme positions.
  - *Reduce the etiquette barrier* by using 'street talk' and the vernacular.
  - *Use chronological reconstruction* to focus on stimulating memory rather than moving to questions of feeling and emotions directly.
  - *Use projective questioning* to give respondents the chance to pass off their own repressed worries and feelings onto others, for example, 'How do you think most people feel about this?'
  - *Use two-tailed questioning* which outlines some of the possible directions of the response as gleaned from earlier interviews. For example, 'Some people expect to have their bowel movements at the same time every day while others may experience an upset stomach if they haven't used the bathroom. Are your reasons for using a laxative similar or different from these?'
  - *Try couching* to initiate the discussion of a sensitive matter in a non-sensitive context. For example, place the issue of menstruation into a general discussion of adolescent changes. After respondents have talked about social and intellectual development, they will be better prepared to start dealing with physical changes.
  - *Use probing* including the 'silent probe' and body language to encourage respondents to elaborate their responses.
- Moderators need to be ready to handle interview contingencies in a confident and sensitive manner.
  - *Hostility to the interviewer or manufacturer/marketer* Respondents in a vulnerable situation are likely to lash out at the nearest target – sometimes for very legitimate reasons. They may voice complaints about how well they are understood. They are likely to protest exploitation. The legitimacy of these feelings must be acknowledged and validated by the moderator. There is little to be gained by

confronting the respondent or trying to prove that the client is truly virtuous.

- *Lack of seriousness and drifting from the subject* Excessive giggling and joking, rapid movements, fidgeting and drifting to another matter after cursory responses are natural reactions to nervousness and anxiety. A certain amount of this must be accepted in discussions of sensitive topics; retreating momentarily to allow venting of tensions is necessary at several points. However, it may be necessary to redirect this attitude by urging respondents to 'get serious again for a moment'.

- *Inability to speak* Sometimes despite good intentions, respondents simply freeze and cannot say what is on their minds. Having the moderator show a bit of patience and a kind hearted glance, or react with an expression of validation such as, 'I know it's hard to talk about that' can go a long way here.

- *Suspicions of dishonesty* At various points, the moderator may suspect that a response is incomplete, misleading or not factual. The respondent may give off clues like blurting out an answer, speaking in a slow or calculating manner, averting eye contact or blocking the mouth or face that arouse the doubt of an experienced moderator. In this instance, little is to be gained by confronting or challenging the assertion. Asking the question again in a carefully couched way later in the interview and using non-verbal techniques such as eye contact and leaning into the respondent may be the best ways of dealing with suspicions of falsehood.

- *Emotional reactions* Respondents may become emotional about their own predicament or the topic may recall a traumatic memory or association. A discussion of health maintenance, for example, may trigger a recollection about a recent death in the family. The result may be tears, anger, inappropriate complaints, etc. A measure of human warmth and sympathy are necessary at this point. It may also be useful to question how the association was made and what the linkage might be to the topic under discussion.

- Allow a cooling off period. Ample time should be left at the end to wind down the discussion and manage emotions that might have been raised. Sometimes a bit of a cool down is helpful even during the discussion so that respondents can regroup and regain confidence.

SECTION 4

Qualitative Analysis, Reporting and Internal Communication

- Collecting data
- Reporting
- Developing persuasive presentations
- Closing the engagement
- Advancing the research function

4.1 Collecting Data

In conducting qualitative research, data analysis occurs at the same time as data collection. The moderator and observers should look for patterns while respondents are speaking, and the evolving discussion should focus on confirmation and exposition of those patterns. During interviews, probing with validation questions are used to generate evidence for generalizations and hunches about consumer attitudes and practices. Thus, analysis should be considered a continuous and evolving process rather than one which takes place entirely at the conclusion of data collection.

Debrief meetings

After finishing the interviews, the process of data analysis and review continues. Debrief meetings between the moderator and observers are generally conducted as soon as possible after interviews are completed to accomplish the following goals:

- To share impressions.
- To make sure everyone has heard similar opinions from participants and to resolve discrepancies if they have not. If these splits cannot be resolved, the report may have to reflect the diverse impressions.
- To make sure that observers at the sessions do not leave with disputed impressions.
- To suggest areas of the taped record that should be reviewed in-depth during the analysis.
- To review changes in the discussion guide or information gaps that should be pursued in subsequent sessions.

Debrief meetings are usually conducted at the discretion of the research team. If there are no compelling reasons to hold them or if it is too inconvenient to convene (for example, if the moderator and observers are fatigued, or if there are no disputed impressions) then the meetings may be foregone.

Some qualitative research consultants turn debriefing exercises into brainstorming sessions designed to review findings and conclusions as well as to determine implications and business strategies indicated by the research.[29]

Members of the research team and moderators should be careful about analysis that is too hurried. Moderators should not be pressured to draw conclusions immediately after a series of interviews. Analysis that takes place within the context of the debrief should be regarded as tentative, pending completion of written deliverables.

Good qualitative analysis depends upon some degree of reflection and further examination of the documentary evidence. Quick reporting tends to be impressionistic, rather than systematic, and lacks the richness and nuances that are the hallmark of high quality qualitative analysis.

Qualitative data

Data that is normally available for analysis following the conclusion of a project can include all or some of the following materials:
- Audiotapes of the discussion.
- Videotapes.
- Notes taken by the moderator during the interviews.
- Notes taken by observers.
- Ideas that emerge from the debrief.
- Written or visual exercises and attitude statements completed by respondents.

Qualitative data at the start appears unordered and phenomenological. It takes a good thorough analyst to make sense of the disparate information. All of the evidence collected should be utilized in conducting the analysis. Otherwise, subtle biases and selective attention may cloud the conclusions.

Several best practices regarding data collection and assembly include the following:
- *Everything is a potential source of data.* This includes observations of gestures, voice intonations and mannerisms, as long as it reasonably represents respondent feelings and it can be meaningfully integrated into the study's conclusions and recommendations.
- *Avoid voting by a show of hands in the focus group.* This is very unreliable as quantitative data and virtually meaningless as qualitative data. The problems associated with this practice are many.
  - Respondents are generally not chosen through random methods.
  - Samples are too small.
  - Questioning is too unstructured.
  - Attitudes are extremely vulnerable to interpersonal influence.
  - Attitudes may be educated by false information or hearsay.
  - The 'head count' is inimical to the purpose of qualitative research.

  This practice forces respondents to take a stand inappropriately and may consequently influence their attitudes. It is also a poor means of learning about respondent purchase plans or pricing expectations because the situation and context are very artificial.
- *Implement an orderly system for labeling information.* All items should be marked with the group name, location, date and time of the interviews. It is difficult to recollect when and where something was said after some time has elapsed.

Note taking

Note taking during the conduct of a group can be a problem. It can be both distracting to the moderator and subtly biasing to respondents who may perceive that some utterances are more important than others. The moderator should not spend much time and attention on note taking during the interview and should not rely upon notes as more than a memory jog. Additional details can be filled in from firsthand recollection after the interviews have been completed. Listed below are several tips for moderator/interviewer note taking.

- The primary purpose of notes during the interview should be to jot down issues that will become the focus of later probes, and for items to be reviewed at a later point in the interview or during the subsequent data review.
- In taking notes, the moderator should use only key words and marks. Since every sentiment cannot be recorded in moderators' notes, they should be written economically and quickly.
- The moderator should avoid looking at her notes when respondents are addressing her because it discourages rapport.
- Notes should be made for observations that will assist in the analysis. These might include notes about body language when a particular topic is being discussed, or hypotheses that are going to be explored in greater detail through probes later in the discussion.

Listed below are several tips for note taking by observers.

- Use signs and markers to distinguish between different types of notes. An arrow can indicate your own observation, a quotation mark for a direct quote, 'R' for something a respondent said, 'B' for an observation of gesture or body language.
- Use diagrams to describe processes or sequences.
- Avoid generalizations based on the sentiments of a few respondents or only some of the sessions. It is appropriate to suggest hunches or hypotheses; however, final conclusions should be based on the full string of interviews.
- Be sure that your perspective alternates between gaining a sense of the general sentiments of the entire focus group to those of specific respondents.
- Pay attention to patterns of influence in the group and how respondents' attitudes change when new information or the opinions of peers are discussed. These are useful clues to strong marketing propositions.
- Record what you don't understand and come back to it. Everything will not make sense to you immediately. Sometimes a brief period of reflection and review helps you make sense of things.
- Share your notes and observations with the moderator. But, expect that there may sometimes be disagreements based on your different perspectives. In general, you should trust your moderator's judgment or at least suspend your own until she has had a chance to review all the evidence.

Audiotapes

Audiotapes are the key source of qualitative data. Audiotaping of interviews is mandatory and a basic service expectation in viewing facilities. Moderators normally review them in preparing the analysis, but sometimes a 'topline' summary is prepared based only upon interviewer and observer recollections.

Even though interviews are routinely tape recorded at most research facilities, a backup set of tapes should be made on your own if you do not feel that your suppliers' services will be reliable. If there is ever a dispute about what was said in the groups, the taped record is indispensable. Professional quality cassette tapes are the standard recording format.

Videotaping is generally optional. However, a good set of videos will help the moderator analyze body language and interpersonal influence, which is difficult to assess using only audio. The video record is also helpful for non-attendees who want to gain richer impressions of research results.

Taping is quite necessary for recording highly unstructured interviews or exercises.

To guarantee that tapes are usable after the sessions, the research manager and the moderator should exercise some degree of quality control over the taping process. Here are several tips.

- Make sure that the taping is being done with high quality professional taping equipment.
- Make sure that the microphones are centrally located and designed to filter out ambient sounds. They should also be separated from heating ducts, air conditioning units or anything else likely to make noise during the session.
- Fresh tapes should be used for every session.
- Make sure tapes are labeled with the date, time, brief topic name ('toothpaste study') and principal distinguishing characteristics of the group ('male, heavy users').

Transcripts

Review tapes carefully after the groups to see if they confirm your hunches and hypotheses. In order to work with the recorded interviews, it is usually helpful to have audiotapes converted to a written form. There are two standards for converting the tapes:

- *Transcripts* represent a detailed and exacting rendition of the oral record. These should be made if the discussion is highly nuanced or technical or if many verbatim responses will be reported.
- *Field notes* refer to briefer and less specific depictions of the oral record. They may contain summaries of the 'drift' of a conversation and only the most critical quotations.

Some moderators have a set of notes or transcripts made while the interviews are being conducted. Although this may add to the cost of research execution, it is worthwhile if the analysis and reporting need to be rushed.

Moderators who base their conclusions on a detailed analysis of the transcripts and field notes are likely to 'code' various responses according to analytic categories that are posited at the outset of the project or that emerge and are clarified from the research data. Since answers to significant research issues might come at any time during the interviews, coding the responses helps to chase down relevant verbatims.

Exercises and tools

Qualitative findings are commonly based on the products of exercises or games conducted during the sessions. Exercises might be depicted literally in the report or they may be subjected to interpretation through some perspective. Best practices to make the process most effective include following these steps:

- Discuss how exercises will be interpreted before they are carried out. In most cases, counting hands should be avoided since this method is difficult to interpret in any substantial way.
- Interpretation is important – results of written and verbal exercises should not be reported literally unless they are used for illustration. For example, it makes little sense to describe the results of a brand image exercise as 'Two participants felt the brand was like a Porsche™, three like a BMW™ and three like a Mercedes™'. Instead, it is much more meaningful to say that the brand is perceived as premium and European.
- Be sure that the exercises are properly formatted and labeled.
- For pencil and paper exercises, ask respondents to label their papers by a group code (Group A - Denver) before handing them in. This will help you identify the written responses by group during the analysis stage.

4.2 Reporting

Following the completion of data collection and analysis, the written report is the final deliverable for the research project. The report should be composed as the authoritative record of the project for both immediate and long term needs. It should not assume that all readers will be familiar with the context of the project; rather, it should provide sufficient detail so that future readers or those not involved with the project will be able to fully understand the methodology and meanings of the research.

Although the researcher must approach the data objectively and dispassionately, the elaboration of conclusions and implications is highly subjective. These conclusions draw upon not only the interview record but also upon the marketer's experience, intuition and judgment. Since the research consultant is retained as an independent voice for inputs into marketing decisions, his ability to propose unique insights and unconstrained views should be appreciated and defended.

The market research report is somewhat different from other types of written analyses, such as academic or journalistic reports, which for our discussion can provide a frame of reference and with which many researchers are familiar.

How market research reporting is distinctive

Market research reporting is distinctive in its focus, style, purpose and stance. Here are several features that should be expected in a market research report.

- *Focus* The focus of a market research report should be the implications for the business units that have commissioned the work. The analysis should make clear how research findings illuminate issues or support decisions.
- *Style* Academic or scientific language is generally inappropriate in a market research report unless it is clearly explained and relevant to the objectives of the study. Industry or business language appropriate to the product category is the preferred style of discourse. Many qualitative projects also detail consumer language in describing a brand or category.
- *Distribution* Market research studies are confidential and for internal distribution only. They are not designed for publication in academic journals, monographs, conferences or in the newspaper. Research managers should make sure that their findings are not being recycled through inappropriate channels. On the other hand, if a particular methodology or tool has been especially useful in producing benefits to the client, moderators and research managers should consider preparing a version for presentation at professional conferences and publication in industry magazines.

- *Purpose* Qualitative market research reports should be written in support of marketing objectives. They are not a contribution to scientific discourse or public information.
- *Stance* Research reports should take a point of view. They should take a consulting, authoritative, partisan approach in support of marketing objectives and findings. They should not take a detached, scientific or conditional stance.

Formats

Consultants and research managers should discuss the precise reporting format that will be most helpful to the commissioning business unit. Three formats – the topline, summary report and full report – are generally available as written output of qualitative studies. Visual reporting formats are also becoming popular. Determining whether to require one or another is usually based upon considerations of time and budget as well as the client's substantive requirements for elaborating, distributing and archiving the information. Project specifications at the start of the project should detail reporting expectations.

- *Topline* Provides a research summary at most 2-5 pages in length which reviews major findings and implications. The topline is typically written within 48 hours of the last group and contains core ideas and impressions gained from the group experience and the debrief. It is usually not based upon a full review of documentation from the interviews and must therefore be regarded as tentative if there are any disputed or unclear findings. Because effort to complete the topline typically competes against that necessary to produce a fuller report, the topline is declining in popularity.
- *Summary report (also called the management summary, synopsis report, highlight report, summary of findings)* Provides a brief 15-20 page analysis of major findings and conclusions based on recall, notes and a limited review of tapes. A small number of verbatims may be provided in the text to illustrate key points. The summary report offers a selective analysis of key issues and may not cover every single topic covered in the discussion. Preparation usually requires about a week.
- *Full report* A full report is usually at least 30 pages in length to an average of 45 pages and is based on a thorough review and detailed analysis of interview record.[30] It is expected to cover all of the topics covered in research interviews and contains a thorough review of verbatims to illustrate most or all points. Full reports normally take about 2-3 weeks to complete.
- *Oral presentation* The increasing popularity of presentation software programs, such as 'Microsoft™ PowerPoint™' and 'Aldus™ Persuasion™', has led to the widespread adoption of 'bullet-point' style summaries of key findings. European and Australian consultants have come to expect the in-person oral presentation as a basic service requirement and Americans are increasingly moving to this practice. Although normally presented in person at the client's or research consultant's office following the conclusion of data collection, the written documents prepared in conjunction with the

presentation have become popular as deliverables in place of or in addition to other report formats.

- *Video presentation* Since viewing facilities or freelance videographers are increasingly required to create a video record of interviews, video reports are growing in popularity. Creating a detailed review of the video record has been supported by the spread of digital formats and easy to use video editing programs for the desktop.

At least one or two weeks are normally necessary to review the visual record and compile a report outline. A fairly sophisticated finished product can be produced which highlights major findings using a narration overlay or text titles and offers video clips to support conclusions.

Regardless of the type of report commissioned, research managers should remember that there are few ways to automate or hasten production. Companies can sometimes add personnel to the project to speed up data review, analysis and writing but this normally requires a supplemental fee for extra personnel who may have to complete tasks over weekends.

Components of a research report

Qualitative market research reports generally follow the organization described below, with individual variations in the ordering and naming of components.

- *Review of objectives* An overview of the research questions that led to the commissioning of the study.
- *Methods* A review of the project's implementation steps which recreates the experience of the study, including:
  - Project plan, which lists the number and types of interviews and where and when they were conducted.
  - Participant specifications, recruitment criteria.
  - Interview sequence, techniques.
  - Limitations of methods.
- *Executive summary of findings* Also called key findings, highlights, or implications, and includes:
  - Conclusions.
  - Recommendations.
- *Detailed findings* The body of the report which may include verbatim quotes, tables, charts and graphs and other utilities to enliven and color the report. Bullet points, underlining and boldface which help to distinguish key elements of the analysis have become popular in business discourse.
- *Appendices* A discussion guide with tools and concepts included for reference.

The 'limitations statement' is one of the most controversial components of the qualitative report since the manner of formulating the statement can undermine the significance of research findings. Sometimes the research limitations statement insists that, 'Findings are hypothetical until confirmed by quantitative research' – which seems extreme. Others frankly describe the limitations of data collection procedures by stating, 'Subjects were not selected according to random procedures' or the limited purview of the research with the words, 'Conclusions are advisory and not definitive'. This book's Appendix contains a sample limitations statement which tries to highlight the qualifying factors of qualitative methods without denigrating the importance of the approach.

Organization and process

Qualitative market research reports should be organized according to objectives and strategic issues. They should be written in an authoritative manner and avoid a chronological description of the individual interview or group discussion. For example, 'Women are swayed by the depiction of the perfume bottle' is better than, 'Jane felt the bottle was attractive and Kirsten said it would entice her to try the product'.

- *Take a stand in a qualitative report.* Advocate a particular point of view. Even though they are not scientifically definitive, qualitative reports should stand as the current state of knowledge about the brand or product category.
- *Highlight key themes, impressions and ideas.* As Langer and Sabena urge, 'Reports should not simply state consumers' behavior or attitudes (they like a particular store), but have to explain why, their conscious and unconscious reasons' (1997: 24). Qualitative reports must illuminate the targeted market and describe what has been learned about their needs and preferences as a result of the study.[31]
- *Don't belabor the obvious.* Don't restate facts about human nature or brand preference. Pontificating about how much people love their pets or children in selecting products on their behalf provides little insight.
- *Be careful with surprises or bad news.* Information that challenges preconceptions, that the client does not believe or accept usually requires extra supporting information. At the same time, a defensive or apologetic stance weakens the consultant's authority.
- *Utilize other authoritative sources.* Research studies do not take place in a vacuum. If the consultant is aware of other information that illuminates a finding, such as demographic data or publicly available product usage information, it is helpful to provide that context. If the consultant has worked for the same client over some period of time, it helps to situate the findings into the framework of the brand's history.
- *Make sure reports are actionable.* In other words, they should advocate a course of action or decisions that could be based on the research evidence. If information gaps remain, a strategy for filling these should be recommended without leaving the impression that the consultant is just trying to feather his own nest.
- *Determine whether it is best to elaborate the results by topic or by segment.* It is generally better to organize the report by topic and explain segment behavior under each heading. Reports organized by segment sometimes seem like separate reports with little comparative analysis, however, these may be helpful when the recommendations involve highly differentiated marketing strategies.

- *Follow a hierarchy of significance.* Elaboration should proceed from general to specific, respecting the logical flow of the discussion guide, as follows:
  - Points should proceed from overall reactions – the headlines, the thrust – to the details. For example, 'Respondents are very enthusiastic about the idea of a premium breakfast cereal. However, macadamia nuts and dried papaya chunks are more consistent with their perception of what constitutes "premium" than are walnuts and dried apricot pieces'.
  - Discuss the positives before the negatives. This shows balance and fairness. Many clients will not give credence to reports that they conclude 'trashes' the work of creatives and product developers.
  - Present high interest ideas or concepts before those that receive merely polite interest or disdain. Discuss issues that draw intense emotions before those which elicit apathy.
- *Distinguish assertions that are highly meaningful as motivations or barriers to purchase from those which make little difference.* Complaints about some product features, for example, are simply characteristic of the category and are not significant to brand selection. Condom users always moan that the product reduces sensation and is inconvenient to put on; nevertheless, consumers select and use the products for reasons other than natural sensations and convenience.
- *Determine which interventions will make a difference.* Are consumers looking for more information, better persuasion, a different product experience? Avoid tired and clichéd recommendations that may have no impact. For example, many research participants insist they will purchase if the price is reduced, and when the product is sampled or couponed. This may or may not be true; it may be highly conditional; it may be too expensive or impractical to implement.

Analytic strategies

Qualitative researchers look for the modal responses and patterns that are found in the data. They describe the generalizations that can be made about consumers as a result of the research. These generalizations can be translated into various levels of analysis.

- *Descriptions of newly inferred market segments or types of consumers* Perhaps the research has discovered that there are 'traditional' vs. 'insurgent' consumers or 'high concern' vs. 'moderate' vs. 'apathetic' segments. Is the product's performance or experience appreciated equally by each of the discovered segments. Are there implications for new product development or brand differentiation that will broaden appeal to less satisfied segments.
- *Elaboration of processes or sequences in brand decision making or product usage* Qualitative research is very good at discovering behavioral processes and the structures inherent in market dynamics. Understanding the ways in which consumers select products gives marketers insights into possible interventions at key 'turning points'. Knowing how consumers use products

offers insights into areas of dissatisfaction, frustration and consequent opportunities for the astute marketer.

- *Hypotheses about causal relationships or conditions that predispose consumers to particular habits or preferences* We think of a cause as something that precedes a behavior in time and has some implicit logical reason for bringing about that behavior. For example, what makes consumers change their purchase habits or what communications elements dispose consumers positively to a brand. When we say that 'Women's susceptibility to messages about "reducing the effects of aging" becomes heightened between ages 30-40', we are making a causal hypothesis that merits further elaboration.

- *Comparative analysis, or descriptions of similarities and differences between demographic or brand preference segments* Articulating how different 'types' of consumers behave differently in the marketplace provides clues to marketing opportunities.

- *Range of opinions vs. modal responses* Qualitative researchers should be alert simultaneously to the 'typical' consumer as well as the range of opinions or practices common within a group. Exploring within group variations provides clues to changes and evolution in market dynamics.

- *Illustrative metaphors* Qualitative analysis is designed to illuminate as well as explain the consumer's inner experience. Sometimes this process is facilitated by making allusions to the natural environment, history and literature. Be careful, however, not to make the metaphors trite or overblown. Deciding which toothpaste to use is not like Hamlet's quandary over existence.

- *Insight* Qualitative analysis can serve its clients sufficiently by providing firsthand exposure to consumer opinions in their own words and by reconstructing the inner experience of the user. This provides an antidote to the main deficiency of survey polling which requires respondents to force their own feelings into categories created by the researcher. By striving to become the authentic voice of people who need representation when decisions are made on their behalf, qualitative research offers a level of insight and illumination unavailable through other methods.

Process of analysis

The production of qualitative analysis can be highly individualistic and idiosyncratic. There is no single way to make creative leaps, unique discoveries and imaginative insights. Some analysts are very systematic in their approach, mining the transcribed text with great precision and thoroughness. Others can be more improvisational and use the text as a resource. There is generally a four step process in qualitative analysis.

Step 1: Assemble core insights

Start with the most salient insights. Describe what stands out in the study – the major themes. What is new and unexpected. What contradicts that which is previously known or expected. What red flags and alarm bells have come up during the interviews. What are the 5-10 key learnings of the study. What are the most important findings in terms of the study's objectives.

This first step should provide the overall plan and the trajectory for the report. It also reviews the key issues that should be featured in the executive summary or highlights section.

Step 2: Review data

Go through all of the material including notes, transcripts, tapes and exercises. If you work systematically, you may code items – that is, assign symbols or code words to text blocks so that they can be retrieved conveniently – on the basis of the topic outline or in terms of your own analytic categories as established in the review of key findings. Then, create an organizational structure for the entire report. Look for illustrations of your main points and quotations that support the key ideas. Look for contrary examples. Review the text for items that may have been overlooked. Modify or expand your initial impressions as necessary.

At the end of this phase, you should have a thorough framework and most of the raw material for the final report.

Step 3: Illuminate

Add value to the analysis by proposing explanations, principles, conditions and limitations. Summarize and draw conclusions. If you are skeptical about an apparent finding, describe what needs to be done to reach closure. Describe the implications for business decisions – for example, what should be the content and tonality of communications, what product development directions should be pursued.

The report should be pretty well concluded at this point. Now it is necessary to consider the reader and how the client organization will use the document.

Step 4: Edit

Check the style, grammar and syntax. Clarify and streamline the writing. Eliminate redundancies, jargon and bad usage. Make certain that the language is both sophisticated and accessible. Insert reader-friendly devices that help to absorb the report, such as bullet points, underscoring and boldface. Make sure that text blocks are broken up and that there is enough 'white space' on each page. If the final report is to be translated to another language, make sure that both the words and style are followed.

Digging beneath the surface

Adding value for the client requires going beyond what consumers say. It demands that we 'make sense of the research' by looking for wider meanings and contexts. Listed below are several injunctions for provoking imagination and intuition.

- *Words are important.* The language that consumers use – including expressions and the ways words are linked, what is not said and things that are misstated, explanations and rationalizations – offers important clues for both motivational insights and communications strategies. An example is offered by Langer and Sabena.

  > Asked about how they feel about their work, a number of women in a study talked about the importance of earning, the enjoyment of working with people they like, but few spoke of their sense of accomplishment or their need for self-expression. (1997: 33)

- *Body language communicates loudly.* It's not just what people say, but also how they say it. Local culture produces standard expressions of emotions that are visible through body signals and tonality. An effective analyst notes participants' tone of voice, enthusiasm, affect, and their 'hems and haws'. She reports what might have been communicated by averted eyes and stiff postures when examining a stimulus, and pays attention to polite assent as well as ritualistic disparagement. Consumers in the Midwestern US, for example, are likely to look for the good in anything and believe that it is polite to be positive. New Yorkers, on the other hand, may initially greet all new ideas by rudely dismissing them as 'crap, garbage, junk'. Appropriate analysis requires placing both sets of expressions into context and looking for other cues that confirm the initial reaction.

- *Emotions rule.* Look for and describe what creates passion and laughter in respondents. Pay attention to stimuli that provoke memories of childhood, parents, schoolyard companions. In a focus group on beef consumption, a woman who now claimed to avoid the product due to health concerns, broke out in tears as she recalled the warm Sunday dinners at her grandmother's house surrounded by family members savoring the rich beef stew which was regularly served. These emotional expressions helped to generate ideas for repositioning the product.

- *Look for types.* What differentiates various consumers from others. It could be something grounded in their physiological, social, economic or psychological status – men vs. women, East Coast vs. Midwest, high income vs. middle income, risk takers vs. risk avoiders.

- *Check how well perception matches reality.* Keep what is known about the real world as a frame of reference for the analysis. If respondents keep providing incorrect impressions about a product or service, for example, the mix of clothing styles offered by a store chain, or the range of capabilities provided by their cellular telephone, this is likely to indicate a need for new communications or repositioning the brand.

- *Discuss how larger social, political and technological trends impact the findings.* Is there some feature outside the context of the research that can explain participants' feelings even though these factors are not voiced by participants as explanations. For example, the movement of women into the workplace, the evolution of smaller families and delayed marriages and high rates of divorce have an impact on the types of foods, cosmetics, home cleaning products and pet care products that women purchase.

- *Make note of how well the research matches the current state of knowledge.*
  Is there some fundamental change taking place in market dynamics or is
  user behavior characterized by a high degree of stability. How do the
  findings of the qualitative research illuminate findings from previously
  conducted surveys or prior qualitative research which the consultant has
  conducted.
- *Be skeptical about what consumers say in groups to appear socially
  sophisticated or politically correct if it is not matched by behavior.* There is
  sometimes a need to say things because they are perceived as more socially
  acceptable. For example, consumers often tell moderators that they are
  concerned about the environment even though they drive gas-guzzling
  sports utility vehicles (SUVs) to work every day. They complain about the
  harsh chemicals in cleaning products even though they find the poor
  performance of milder products unacceptable. They urge art directors to use
  more 'average people' as models and less provocative sexuality in
  advertising even though these alternatives are usually ignored.
- *Be skeptical about highly conditional usage situations.* Faint praise and
  highly unlikely usage situations are clues that respondents are not reacting
  well to the concepts. For example, 'I'll use it on vacation' usually means, 'I
  can't think of a reason to use it in my everyday life' unless, of course, the
  item is intended for use while traveling. Similarly, 'I'd give it as a gift' and,
  'It's for someone older/younger' means, 'It's not for me'. 'I would buy it if
  it were less expensive' means, 'I see no value in the product'.
- *Be on guard against respondent clichés.* Langer and Sabena (1997: 35)
  review several of these. 'Advertising doesn't influence me' (nonsense). 'No
  one ever wins sweepstakes' (but I always enter just in case). 'I only buy
  what's healthy' (usually asserted while reaching for a cookie). 'I'll buy it
  next year' and, 'When I get more time' are some of the numerous other
  excuses that do not meet the test of real behavior.

Making marketing leaps

Consultant recommendations and discussions of research implications always
add value to the research. Clients expect more than a recitation of facts – they
want guidance and direction. Here are several approaches to making leaps from
information to implementation.

- *Correct deficiencies.* Consumer wishes, fantasies, frustrations, problems
  and work-arounds are all clues to new opportunities. Describe what can be
  done to make the product more appealing and satisfying – reformulation,
  new additives, new flavors and colors. Sometimes the problem inheres in
  what consumers believe about the product and this may call for revitalizing
  the brand communication – new words, copy strategies, tonality and media.
- *Turn a negative into a positive.* 'Not enough' or 'not easy to access' can
  become 'exclusive'. 'Unusual' can become 'unique'. 'Unfamiliar' can
  become 'exotic'. Sometimes the brand does not really need to change, but
  instead needs to know itself and express its character in a way that has
  better resonance with the target.

- *Hop onto the trend.* Adjust the product or communications strategy to where the targeted market is moving socially, economically or technologically. For example, create a web site and information hotline to appeal to twenty-somethings, go upscale in positioning to match rising incomes, create a new package design that facilitates storage in small apartments.
- *Hit the right segments.* Most products that try to appeal to everybody end up satisfying almost nobody. The product may be right for 'traditionalists' but not for the 'independents' who want a different brand. The idea may be appropriate only for trend leaders, the young, professionals, men – be sure that everything is aiming for the right target.
- *Think generationally.* At any given moment, generations with common consumer experiences are in line passing through the sequence of life stages. Does your brand stick with a generation (Levi's™ jeans and the baby boomers) or move on to its successor. What does it take to cross generations and become contemporary – a problem faced by Helena Rubenstein™ cosmetics.
- *Leverage knowledge about the competition.* Learn from what competitors have done right or wrong. Don't remake their mistakes, but build upon their successes. Be careful, though, because consumers – especially young trendy types – often become wary of 'me-too' products.
- *Learn from other categories that appeal to the same target.* Segment dynamics will have similar implications for a wide range of products. If something is valid for how young women will select a fragrance or brand of clothing, it is likely to hold up for how they choose a cigarette brand or a magazine.
- *Build on your own strengths.* Use the attributes that are swaying current customers to draw in others.
- *Link service benefits to the product.* The brand is not just material. It encompasses all of the current, perceived and potential benefits that can credibly be linked to its usage.
- *Look for opportunities in aspirations rather than in current realities.* Consumers keep one foot in the present and the other in the future. They will buy advanced features on their computers, telephones and home appliances not to meet current needs but rather for future possibilities and imagined uses.

The politics of reporting

Research reports are sometimes written and submitted within a highly charged political context.[32] Listening to the consultant's conclusions from a research study is often experienced by clients as similar to receiving a serious medical diagnosis. There is some apprehension. There may be jobs or promotions on the line. Various players in the research process may perceive themselves to be 'winners' or 'losers' in terms of which product development tracks, advertising executions and marketing strategies seem to be most resonant with consumers. Consequently, moderators may be subtly or overtly influenced to obscure or alter research conclusions.

It is a violation of professional ethics for a moderator to modify research conclusions on the basis of client political pressures. If clients do not wish to hear an independent voice which represents consumer sentiments, they should not commission the research in the first place. Since the report is issued under the research company's signature, their integrity and accountability needs to be respected.

The research report should stand as one among several contributions to strategic decisions and should not be the only basis for business directions. In various situations, studies may need to be replicated or triangulated using alternative methodologies before an adequate understanding of consumer dynamics can be achieved.

Tact and professionalism

Still, researcher folklore is filled with stories about clients who are thrown off balance by the delivery of bad news or findings which contradict expectations within the marketing group. Sometimes there is a need to deal with rejection and denial of research findings.

- The consultant should stick to the data and deal sensitively with challenges. Tactful, honest, clear and detailed explanations of how conclusions were derived are often necessary.
- Professional clients respect consultants who stay firm in their convictions. If consultants do not extend this degree of courtesy, losing the client should not be regretted.
- The consultant should remove herself from internal political disputes. It is not helpful normally to sway an argument by mobilizing internal support for your point of view.
- Be ready to justify all aspects of the methodology in a consistent and professional manner. Be ready to offer guidance to less experienced marketers and researchers. Be ready to distinguish your own views from the research conclusions.
- Many criticisms voiced in anger and disappointment go to the heart of technical issues that should have been settled when the study was commissioned and designed in the first place. It is unfair to invoke these as explanations for unexpected findings: 'This was the wrong method', 'We talked to the wrong people', 'The wrong questions were asked', 'It's all just subjective'.
- Some criticisms suggest that the client has an incorrect understanding of the moderator's role or the purpose of qualitative research. Complaints that many consultants have heard include, 'We're not going to let ten housewives from New Jersey tell us how to run a $100 million business!' (They should not – qualitative research should be one of many inputs into decision making. Besides, these women represent your consumers. Ignore them at your peril.) 'The moderator didn't do a good job of explaining the product's technical features!' (They should not have to – the moderator is not supposed to 'sell' the concepts to respondents. Consumer misunderstandings often betray a barrier to market entry.) 'Respondents

were wrong about our product!' (Perception is reality. That is what qualitative research is looking for.)

- Criticisms are often directed toward the nature of interviewing techniques. 'You let a dominant respondent take over the group and change everyone's mind!' (In fact, if a passionate participant is able to sway sentiment positively or negatively in a focus group, the astute marketer should use this as a guide to what could possibly happen in the marketplace.) 'The objections were not thoroughly probed'. (While that might be a fair criticism, it usually betrays a client who expected that nay-sayers would be challenged by the moderator.)
- Langer and Sabena offer a range of useful tips for 'being tactfully truthful'.

> If respondents 'hated' the product/idea, state that they 'rejected it sharply'.
> Instead of saying that the packaging is outdated (you can say that respondents thought this), observe that 'times have changed' and the package needs to be reconsidered.
> Do look for any positives. Is there anything the client can build on by modifying the product, the communication. If there isn't, there isn't.
> Put positives before detailed negatives. Examples: a discount store now out of business – the only thing the respondents liked was the Santa Claus. (They even disagreed about this.)
> Put the negatives in perspective: Are they minor, changeable or seemingly insurmountable. What, if anything, might improve the product, concept.
> Look for negatives as opportunities for further improvement and increased market share.
> Use language which is not emotionally loaded, such as 'shafted', 'trashed', 'ripped off', 'bullshit'.
> Do not be condescending or sarcastic. Do not state or imply that this was a dumb idea to begin with! (1997: 44)

Writing skills

The value of qualitative research outcomes is seriously compromised if reports are turned in without impeccable spelling, punctuation, language and grammar. Copy editing should be a standard step in report production prior to submission. Listed here are some characteristics of a well-crafted qualitative report.

- Paragraphs should be brief and headed by a topic sentence which introduces the main point.
- Write brief declarative sentences in the present tense using the active mode and avoid overuse of the passive mode. Write, 'Men prefer strong flavors while women choose sweet varieties' instead of, 'Strong flavors are selected by men while sweet varieties are chosen by the women'.
- Write assertively. Avoid stuffiness and academic conventions which reinforce the hypothetical and conditional nature of the findings, such as, 'Evidence may support the contention that men prefer strong flavors; in contrast, it is possible that women prefer sweet varieties if they are presented with a choice between strong and sweet'.
- Use consumer segments in general as the frame of reference ('heavy users insist...', 'traditionalists prefer...', 'working mothers wish...') and avoid continuous references to the conditions of the research unless specifying

them adds value to the conclusions. For example, avoid, 'The men in the users segment said they preferred the strong flavors while the women in the same segment said they preferred the sweet varieties'. On the other hand, make judicious references to meaningful events during the interviews that amplify the findings. 'When the sweet varieties were removed from the package, the women's eyes widened as they smiled and sat up in their seats'.

- Do not pretend that this is a quantitative report using code words for numerical estimates. Avoid statements like, 'The majority of men in the group picked "strong" while a few picked "sweet" while virtually all of the women picked "sweet"'.
- Do not try to be folksy, cute or humorous. Your efforts will be misunderstood and resented.
- Use descriptive words that clarify, nuance and color what respondents believe, say or feel. Helpful words include: question, confirm, claim, prefer, object, observe, insist, recommend, advise, recall, wish, demand, assert, deny, argue, wonder, declare, complain, urge, praise and so on.

Computer-assisted qualitative analysis

In recent years, several computer programs have become available to help automate the process of qualitative analysis. Most of these programs use text analysis algorithms to support coding, retrieval and summarizing of the interview transcripts.

Computer-based analysis programs facilitate the process of data coding by providing menu-driven formats for entering information and assigning categories for analysis. After the data is coded, the programs allow for rapid retrieval and sorting of responses through logical processes often supported by artificial intelligence.

Examples of available qualitative analysis programs include:

- Atlas.ti™, for visual qualitative analysis of large bodies of text, graphics, audio and video inputs.
- BEST™, for observational research.
- C-I-SAID™.
- Code-A-Text™.
- Decision Explorer™, a cognitive mapping tool which facilitates model building.
- The Ethnograph™.
- HyperFocus™.
- HyperRESEARCH™, available in Macintosh™ and PC formats, able to integrate text, graphics, audio and video.
- FocusReports™.
- QSR NUD*IST 4™.
- QSR Nvivo™, links any type of data source with rich text formatting and analysis tools.
- winMAX™.

Advantages of computer-assisted analysis include:

- Ability to expedite analysis and report writing, thus reducing project time cycles among experienced users.
- Analysis format is consistent and objective and can provide added value to clients.
- Software is increasingly flexible and easy to operate.
- Various packages are able to qualify findings easily by demographic variables, usage patterns and researcher-derived categories. They can answer questions like, 'Are heavy users likely to describe the brand differently from infrequent users and triers/rejectors?', 'Do women employed outside the home see similar or different product benefits than home makers?', 'Does learning particular functions of the mobile phone result in different patterns of usage?', 'Does misuse of a product, for example, not waiting for a cleaning solvent to be absorbed, result in particular forms of product failure and disappointment?'
- Packages may allow integration of researcher observations, annotations, notes, visual source materials, tape recordings, video clips, etc. with the respondent transcripts so that all these may be analyzed simultaneously.
- Some packages can create logical linkages between various data components that can be useful in charting and diagramming the findings.
- Several packages can be easily linked to statistical analysis programs thereby making some types of quantitative hypothesis testing feasible.

Problems associated with computer-assisted analysis include:

- Investments in training and practice are necessary to leverage their benefits for productivity.
- Many programs are better adapted to the needs of academic researchers with expansive volumes of field notes than to applied business research.
- Automated analysis can lead to inappropriate quantification, for example, counting frequency of quotations and words.
- Text elements need to be carefully coded, otherwise they are treated as equal without regard to context or intensity. Thus, the analysis can be vulnerable to distortion by dominant respondents.
- Programs may not be compatible with popular operating systems, data formats or sources of web information – such as Macintosh™ OS, Palm™ OS, SPSS, HTML – and thus require time wasted on conversion or re-entering the data.
- It may be difficult to integrate visual, sound and video information on some programs.

Computer-assisted qualitative analysis is currently used by only a handful of consultants. However, technological advancements and new software programs should be carefully studied. It is reasonable to expect that this resource will have a larger impact in the future.

4.3 Developing Persuasive Presentations

Oral presentation of qualitative research results is becoming more common and frequent because of easy to use computer-based presentation software and hardware. These technology tools automate the process of presentation construction and add impact in communicating findings.

This trend is also being felt in the ways consultants are producing written deliverables. Increasingly, reports are expected to follow the visual conventions of the presentation. It is no longer appropriate to ignore page design and composition in creating reports. Visual clutter, poor use of images and the lack of graphic elements that aid reading and understanding all weaken even the most cogent findings. No one has the time or energy to wade through reports seeking hidden gems. Some tips for presentations can also support the production of written reports that rely on computer-based formats.

- Choose classic and discreet type styles (fonts). Sans-serif type fonts such as Helvetica and Arial tend to be more effective than fonts with serifs, such as Times New Roman or script-like styles, when projected. Do not overuse uppercase or underscoring.
- Keep background elements simple. Avoid images such as sunsets, marbling, vibrating colors or pointless animations so that nothing distracts from the information.
- Leave enough 'white space' on each slide or page. Avoid filling up each slide with information that cannot easily be read at a distance. Avoid complex charts that are spread across several pages. Remember that intricate diagrams are extremely confusing when projected.
- Leave margins of at least a half inch or one centimeter so that items are less likely to fall off the screen.
- Write in headlines only. Don't use the visuals to communicate details or explanations which should be handled in the oral presentation of findings or in a lengthier report. Use italics or boldface sparingly to add impact.
- Each slide or chart should contain one primary assertion or point of information. Bullet points underneath the assertion should outline supporting or clarifying information.
- Avoid sentences with more than 7-9 words. Avoid more than six bullet points per slide. Avoid more than thirty slides in a 25-30 minute presentation.
- Do not read the slides during the presentation. Use them as launch points for your own impromptu analysis.
- Print copies of your slides as handouts to be distributed in advance so that your audience will not have to take notes while you are presenting.
- Always bring along a backup version of the presentation on transparencies in case the hardware fails or is incompatible with your files.

4.4 Closing the Engagement

After the engagement the research manager is responsible for ensuring that responsibilities toward research consultants have been managed in a fair and proper manner. Final details generally revolve around supplier evaluation and closing business details.

Supplier evaluation

Few corporate research organizations conduct systematic supplier evaluations. And those that do, commonly keep that information within the group. Most often, qualitative research consultants are judged through gossip, hearsay and innuendo which can produce both unwarranted praise and unjustified censure. Research productivity generally gains when there is a consistent and continuously applied evaluation procedure. Many research companies hear only the complaints but are never told about successful engagements. Consultants profit by receiving fair and balanced reports about service delivery rather than having to guess why someone may be happy or dissatisfied.

Criteria normally applied in the evaluation process are listed here.

- *Responsiveness* Has the consultant thoroughly familiarized himself with the business issues stimulating the research. Has she made the effort to explore unstated issues. Has she taken the views of various stakeholders into account in designing the study. Is there a cooperative attitude toward making changes and adjustments as research questions are refined in the course of the study.
- *Process management* Have all the details of project execution been handled responsibly – selection of subcontractors, screening, discussion guide development, information and orientation of research managers and observers, debriefing, reporting.
- *Interpersonal skills* Is the consultant adept at handling a variety of statuses within the sponsoring organizations. Is she humane, professional and balanced toward clients, respondents and suppliers alike.
- *Intellectual skills* Has the consultant made an extra effort to learn about the category and its special marketing issues. Has he delivered added value by conveying insights derived from professional experience as well as knowledge of human behavior, business trends and current affairs.
- *Moderation skills* Has the research organization maximized interviewing skills in a way that generated insights into consumer attitudes.
- *Timeliness* Have all the tasks associated with project execution been accomplished in a timely manner without unnecessary delays.

- *Overall value for fees* Are billing procedures clear and understandable. Are all billed items accounted for in the original budget. Have services been commensurate with fees charged.
- *Overall quality* Rate the overall quality of the researcher's contribution on this assignment.

A sample evaluation form based upon the principles listed above is located in the Appendix.

Final business matters

Upon the submission of final deliverables, the consultant is responsible for submitting the final invoice. The research manager has the job of reviewing and auditing the invoice and must assure prompt payment as stipulated in the initial agreement. There is no excuse for late or incomplete submission of the invoice to accounts payables. If there are special corporate procedures or auditing policies, for example, the need for a purchase order number or vendor registration number, or the requirement to submit multiple copies, the research manager should make the consultant aware of these before the invoice is submitted.

Additionally, if the client organization has payables practices which will elongate the standard 30-day terms, the research manager should inform the consultant of these policies in advance.

Adjustments to the invoice

As long as costs are within the contingency limits agreed upon at the time of contract, the invoice should be paid in full. Nevertheless it is appropriate to question any budget items that are highly disproportionate to what had been outlined in the proposal. It is also acceptable to require submission of receipts for reimbursed expenses.

It is unethical, unprofessional and questionably legal to unilaterally withhold or reduce the final payment as a way to express dissatisfaction with the consultant's service. If any aspect of project services has fallen below expectations, this should be discussed well in advance of invoice submission and some consensus about adjustments should be reached. If there is a perceived legitimate cause for reducing payment, the research manager should guarantee that these are not on account of disappointments with research findings and that the research consultant has been given sufficient opportunity to explain her position in the dispute and provide alternative means of resolution, such as redoing an interview or focus group.

Some situations that often lead to requests for adjustments include the following:

- *Rescheduling and cancellation* If project activities are rescheduled or called off after they have been authorized and initiated, the contracting party should expect to pay for services already rendered, expenses incurred and a fee for time reserved for the project, sometimes gruesomely called a 'kill fee'. Marketing research takes place in a highly competitive and pressured environment; consultants who reserve time for a project correspondingly become unavailable for other work required at the same time. Since they have also already contracted and committed funds to other agencies for the provision of necessary project services, it is unfair to make the consultant financially responsible for cancellation. The percentages of estimate and effective date of cancellation fees are subject to individual company policies and to negotiation.

- *Responsibility for inappropriate recruitment or 'no shows'* In this case, too, the consultant is acting as the agent of the client in securing the services of other suppliers. If a respondent has falsified her status or practices in order to participate or fails to appear despite having been confirmed – possibly for reasons of weather, child care arrangements, traffic tie-ups – financial responsibility for the offense should not fall on the consultant or the recruiter. This is a risk that the sponsor must absorb as a cost of conducting the research. On the other hand, it is appropriate to question recruitment policies or procedures that may have contributed to the mistake and to request some adjustment that may be passed along to the client.

- *Inadequate receivables* The type and degree of reporting should be negotiated at the start of the project. The consultant should not be expected to submit a full report where only a summary report was contracted or to offer a free in-person presentation if her company policy treats this as a paid service. If the time available for report production is shortened, many companies require a 'rush' charge to compensate extra staff or to perform services on weekends. The depth and type of analysis should also be discussed at the start. It is inappropriate, for example, to request quantification of attitudes, practices, projective exercises and demographics in a qualitative study and threaten to reduce payment if this is not performed.

- *Expenses* It is acceptable to expect explanations and justification for travel and project expenses. Some research companies add a fee or 'mark-up' to the expense summary. It is inappropriate for the client to expect the consultant to absorb any particular category of project expenses, including restaurant meals at which project details are discussed or travel for briefings, as 'marketing costs'.

4.5 Advancing the Research Function

The qualitative research project has been completed successfully. All of the vendors have performed to specification; the respondents have provided meaningful insights. The deliverables have been developed in an appropriate manner. At this point, the astute research manager and consultant should make sure to maximize the usefulness of the qualitative research.

- *Communicate* At the end of a successful project, make certain that research results have been communicated in appropriate formats to internal audiences that may benefit from the knowledge gained. The research manager should consider adapting the research conclusions along with verbatims to alternative outlets. Interesting findings, for example, may be detailed in brief memos, on the company web site or listserve or through the company newsletter to members of the sales organization, other subsidiaries, other product groups, senior management and the board of directors. Approval from corporate communications and press relations groups is essential for both internal and external dissemination.
- *Follow up* Make sure that the results are used as anticipated. Monitor the information dispersion process to guarantee that research findings are having significant impacts. Determine how to improve services to internal clients.
- *Obtain/provide feedback* Measure internal satisfaction with the research process and outside vendors involved in the research program. Offer feedback to consultants about service delivery and the value of research findings.
- *Seek continuous improvement* Always look for ways to make the research process more efficient and meaningful. Many marketing organizations sponsor regular internal seminars and 'vendor fairs'. Invite consultants who have demonstrated their value within the organization to make presentations to other brand groups. Invite research specialists to conduct internal training seminars on new methods and techniques. Create a system of awards to recognize significant research contributions within the company. Participate in the award competitions sponsored by major research organizations, such as the American Marketing Association and the Advertising Research Foundation which recognize the value of the research function to the organization.

Continuing education, intellectual growth, recognition of outstanding service, contributions to the trade literature and to professional associations are all required if we are to continue advancing the value and usefulness of qualitative research.

Appendix

Sample project brief

Research manager
Sponsoring division manager
Brand(s)
Information needed
Decisions impacted by the research
Decision dates
Results of previous studies
Concurrent studies
Recommended methodology
Deliverables and circulation
Proposed budget

Sample screener

TEEN ENTERTAINMENT FOCUS GROUPS RESPONDENT SPECIFICATIONS

- All to be between the ages of 13 and 18 years old.
- All to be currently enrolled in school full time.
- All to have annual household earnings above $25,000.
- A mix of genders.
- A mix of racial and ethnic groups as defined by screener.
- All to be technologically sophisticated as evidenced by owning and using at least three or more electronics items from screener list.
- All to spend at least five (5) hours a week watching TV.
- All to spend an average of at least $20 per month purchasing music recordings either in CD or other format.
- All to go to movies at least three (3) times a month.

Security/past participation
- None to have family members employed in the following industries: market research, marketing, advertising, broadcasting, newspaper or magazines, music, video or film production, theatrical enterprises.
- None to have participated in more than five (5) focus groups ever.
- None to have participated in any focus groups in the past year.
- None to have participated in focus group research on the topic of teen entertainment ever.

RECRUIT SIX (6) GROUPS SEGMENTED BY GENDER AND SCHOOL YEAR – SEPARATE GROUPS OF 7-8, 9-10, 11-12

Screening questionnaire – teen focus groups

Interviewer	Date	Time

Name _____

Address_____

Day phone _____ Evening phone _____

Fax _____ E-mail_____

Part 1 – Initial screening

INTRODUCTION: Hello. My name is _____ and I'm calling from _____ a market research company here in _____. I'm not going to try to advertise or sell you anything – our only purpose is opinion research. We're putting together a study on teen entertainment. Participants who qualify for the focus group interviews we'll be conducting will be paid for their time and effort. All your responses during our phone conversation today and during the group interview will be kept strictly confidential. May I ask you a few questions.

S1. Are there any young people living in your household who are between ages 13 to 18.

      [ ] Yes
      [ ] No   (TERMINATE)

S2. May I get their name(s), gender(s) and age(s). (AT LAST BIRTHDAY)

First Name	M/F	Age
1. _____	_____	_____
2. _____	_____	_____
3. _____	_____	_____
4. _____	_____	_____

S3. Is each one currently enrolled in school as a full time student.

    (TERMINATE ANY NOT ENROLLED IN SCHOOL FULL TIME)

    (ONLY RECRUIT ONE RESPONDENT PER HOUSEHOLD – THANK AND TERMINATE IF NONE ARE QUALIFIED)

S4. Is the parent or guardian of this young person/these young people home.

      [ ] Yes   (ASK S5A)
      [ ] No   (ASK S5B)

S5A. May I speak with him/her.

      [ ] Yes   (GO TO PARENT INTRO)
      [ ] No   (ASK S5B)

S5B. What is a convenient time to call and speak with the teenager's parent or guardian.

Name _____ Call back times _____

Part 2 – Parental permission screener, when parent or guardian is on the line

Hello. We're putting together a series of focus group interviews with teenagers in ___(location)___ on behalf of a major producer of entertainment products. It's a well-known company but for confidentiality reasons I cannot disclose who it is right now. We'd like to ask both you and your son/daughter some questions. But, first, we want to make sure that it is okay with you for your son/daughter to participate in the focus group interview.

First, I need to ask whether anyone in your household works for any of the following types of companies: (CHECK IF YES)

Market research	
Marketing	
Advertising	
Broadcasting	
Newspaper or magazine	
Music/video/film production	
Theatrical enterprises	

(TERMINATE IF ANY OF THE ABOVE ARE CHECKED)

Do you know what I mean when I say 'focus group interview'?

(IF NO, DESCRIBE EXACTLY AS FOLLOWS)

A focus group interview is a roundtable discussion for research purposes. It is led by a professional moderator. Usually about 6-10 people participate in the group discussion. The moderator is there to present topics and try to get everyone to share their own attitudes and feelings with the group.

Do you think that your son/daughter could be a good participant in this kind of group discussion:

        [ ] Yes
        [ ] No   (TERMINATE)

(IF YES, CONTINUE)

Qualifying focus group participants will receive an incentive payment of $50 at the conclusion of the session. The interviews, again, are only for research purposes – no sales or advertising solicitations will be made at these sessions. All responses during our phone conversations today and with your son/daughter during the group discussions will be strictly confidential. Group interviews will last from 1 and a half to 2 hours. They will be audio/video taped and professional researchers working on this project will be observing the interview.

If you agree and your son/daughter qualifies, we will invite him/her to participate and, then, send a permission form for you to sign and return. Are you willing to allow your son/daughter to participate in this focus group study?

    [ ] Yes   (GO TO P1)
    [ ] No   (TERMINATE)

To ensure that we have the right mix of people in the focus groups, I need to ask you several questions.

P1.   First, could you please stop me when I hit the category that includes your household's total annual income from all sources.

    [ ] A. Under $25,000   (TERMINATE)
    [ ] B. More than $25,000 – less than $50,000
    [ ] C. More than $50,000 – less than $100,000
    [ ] D. More than $100,000 – less than $150,000
    [ ] E. More than $150,000

    (OBTAIN A MIX OF QUALIFYING INCOME BRACKETS)

P2.   Because it is important for us to recruit a diverse group of youngsters, could you please tell me if you identify your son/daughter as Hispanic or Latino.

    [ ] Yes
    [ ] No

P3.   Also, which racial group do you feel best identifies your son/daughter.

    [ ] Caucasian or white
    [ ] African American or black
    [ ] Asian/Pacific Islander
    [ ] Native American/American Indian
    [ ] Other or mixed race

    (OBTAIN A MIX OF ETHNIC/RACIAL GROUPS)

    (CONTINUE)

P4A. May I speak to your son/daughter now.

    [ ] Yes   (GO TO TEEN INTRO)
    [ ] No   (ASK P4B)

P4B.   What is a convenient time to call and speak with your son/daughter.

Name _____ Call back times _____

Part 3 – Teen screener

As I told your mom/dad/guardian/stepparent, we're putting together some focus groups with teenagers in the ____(location)____ area. You may already know what a focus group is but let me explain what we're trying to do. A focus group interview is a roundtable discussion for research purposes. It is led by a professional moderator. Usually about 6-10 people participate in the group discussion. The moderator is there to present topics and try to get everyone to share their own attitudes and feelings with the group.

Our focus group will be about teen entertainment and you will have a chance to discuss interests that you share with other people your age. Do you want to hear more?

Qualifying focus group participants will receive an incentive payment of $50 at the end of the session. The interviews, again, are only for research purposes – no one will try to sell or advertise anything to you at these sessions. Group interviews will last from one and a half to two hours. Are you interested in participating?

          (IF YES, CONTINUE)

To assure a good representation of respondents, I need to ask you some questions.

T1.   Have you ever participated in a focus group interview.

          [ ] Yes   (CONTINUE – ASK T2)
          [ ] No   (SKIP TO T3)

T2A. In how many focus groups have you ever participated. _____

          (TERMINATE IF MORE THAN 5)

T2B. What was/were the topic(s).

_____

          (TERMINATE IF RELATED TO TEEN ENTERTAINMENT)

T2C. When was the (most recent) focus group held. _____

          (TERMINATE IF LESS THAN 1 YEAR AGO)

T3.   Gender. (DO NOT ASK UNLESS UNCLEAR)

     [ ] Male   (RECRUIT TO MALE GROUPS)
     [ ] Female   (RECRUIT TO FEMALE GROUPS)

T4A. What was your age at your last birthday.

     [ ] 13
     [ ] 14
     [ ] 15
     [ ] 16
     [ ] 17
     [ ] 18

     (TERMINATE IF UNDER 13 OR OVER 19)

T4B.   What is your current grade in school.

     [ ] Seventh grade – middle school
          (RECRUIT TO GROUP 'A')
     [ ] Eighth grade – middle school
          (RECRUIT TO GROUP 'A')
     [ ] Ninth grade/freshman middle or high school
          (RECRUIT TO GROUP 'B')
     [ ] Tenth grade/sophomore – high school
          (RECRUIT TO GROUP 'B')
     [ ] Eleventh grade/junior – high school
          (RECRUIT TO GROUP 'C')
     [ ] Twelfth grade/senior – high school
          (RECRUIT TO GROUP 'C')

T5.   Which of the following devices do you own and how often do you use each item. (READ LIST – CHECK COLUMN 2 ONLY IF USED EVERY DAY)

	Own	Use daily
Cellular telephone	[ ]	[ ]
Laptop computer	[ ]	[ ]
Sub-laptop computer	[ ]	[ ]
2-way pager	[ ]	[ ]
PDA (personal digital assistant)	[ ]	[ ]
Personal minidisc player/recorder	[ ]	[ ]
MP3 player	[ ]	[ ]
High-end gaming system (e.g., Sega Dreamcast™, Nintendo 64™, Sony™ PlayStation)	[ ]	[ ]
Digital camera	[ ]	[ ]
Digital video (DVD) player	[ ]	[ ]

(ALL RESPONDENTS MUST OWN AND USE AT LEAST 3 OR MORE ITEMS FROM THIS LIST)

T6.   How much time do you spend watching TV during an average week.

[ ] less than 5 hours (TERMINATE)
[ ] between 5 and 10 hours
[ ] between 10 and 20 hours
[ ] more than 20 hours

(OBTAIN A MIX)

T7.   How much do you spend in an average month on purchasing music recordings - CDs, tapes or any other format.

[ ] less than $20 (TERMINATE)
[ ] between $20 and $50
[ ] between $50 and $100
[ ] more than$100

(OBTAIN A MIX)

T8.   How many times do you go to the movies in an average month.

[ ] None (TERMINATE)
[ ] Once or twice (TERMINATE)
[ ] Three to five times
[ ] Six to ten times
[ ] more than 11 times

(OBTAIN A MIX)

(INVITATION)

I'm happy to let you know that you qualify for one of the discussions. Here are the details.

Sample legal release form

This form is adapted from the Advertising Research Foundation (1992) *Understanding Qualitative Research*. New York: Advertising Research Foundation. These are listed for illustrative purposes only and do not represent the provision of legal services. Please do not use any legal form without consultation by competent counsel.

Research consent, release and assignment

For valuable consideration of _____(amount of payment)_____ to be distributed following completion of the Research Session, I give full permission to _____(name of research company)_____ and/or its clients, subsidiaries, affiliates, agents and assigns, hereafter called Grantees, to make or reproduce throughout the world, either alone or in conjunction with other material, any photographs, audio recordings, films and videotapes made in connection with the Research Session identified below without restriction. I further agree that the recording, incorporating my name, likeness and/or voice, may be used, in whole or in part, in material prepared for purposes of advertising, research and client presentation.

I understand that there will be observers at the meeting as well as those involved in recording and conducting the proceedings.

I grant to Grantees all rights, including the right to copyright, in any ideas, slogans, plans, suggestions, sketches, artwork or other material that I may produce during or in connection with the Research Session.

It is further understood that Grantees may use said material without mentioning any name and may make reasonable editorial or stylistic changes in the material.

I further waive any right of approval with respect to use of said material and hereby release and discharge Grantees from any claim or liability, including without limitation invasion of privacy or defamation of character based upon such use.

I hereby assign the Consideration to which I am entitled to:

(Fill in if applicable)_____

Research session identification _____

Name _____

Signature _____

Address _____

Date _____

Sample consent form

Parental consent agreement

I, the undersigned, am the parent or legal guardian of the below named minor and, as such, am fully authorized to enter into this agreement on her behalf.

For valuable consideration of _____(amount of payment)_____ to be distributed following completion of the Research Session, I give full permission for my child to participate in the Research Session on _____(date and time)_____.

I understand that audio and/or video recordings of the proceedings will be made and I give full permission to _____(name of research company)_____ and/or its clients, subsidiaries, affiliates, agents and assigns, hereafter called Grantees, to make or reproduce such audio and/or videotape without restriction. I further agree that the recording may be used, in whole or in part, in material prepared for purposes of advertising, research and client presentation.

I understand that there will be observers at the meeting as well as those involved in recording and conducting the proceedings.

I grant to Grantees all rights, including the right to copyright, in any ideas, slogans, plans, suggestions, sketches, artwork or other material produced by my child in connection with the Research Session.

It is further understood that Grantees may use said material without mentioning any name and may make reasonable editorial or stylistic changes in the material.

I further waive any right of approval with respect to use of said material and hereby release and discharge Grantees from any claim or liability, including without limitation invasion of privacy or defamation of character based upon such use.

Child's name _____

Parent's or guardian's name _____

Parent's or guardian's signature _____

Address _____

Date _____

Sample discussion guide – healthcare

PROJECT TITLE: Arthritis Pain Exploratory Study

PROJECT NUMBER: ZZ001

LOCATIONS: Detroit, Dallas, Jacksonville

DISCUSSION GUIDE

1. Case history
- How long have you had arthritis pain
- Has it been brought to a physician's attention
  - To another professional's attention
  - If so, how was it diagnosed
- What, in your opinion, caused it
- Any other significant problems, such as rheumatism, gout, etc.
- Regular care regimen

2. Arthritis pain experience
- Level of severity
- Perceptions of experience
- Do you have arthritis pain at that moment
  - PROBE: Sensations (open-ended)
  - Is it different/similar to other arthritis pain experiences
- Location of pain, such as shoulders, fingers, hands, wrist, back
- Sensations experienced
  - Analogies, similes
- Is it episodic or constant
  - How long does an episode last
  - What is associated with the onset, end of an episode
  - What are the first sensations experienced
- Sensory changes over the day
- Is it different by climate, locations, season
- Is it associated with taking medications
  - What is the lag/timing of the onset
- Is it associated with other activities or experiences
- Any differences in sensory experiences depending on source
  - Exercise
  - During stress
- Personal descriptors of the experience, such as texture or feelings
- Language used to describe – 'arthritis pain', other pains
  - A 'problem', a 'medical condition', a 'side effect'
  - 'healthy', 'unhealthy'

- Physical, emotional, social and medical consequences of arthritis pain
  - Pain, blistering, swelling, nodules
  - Embarrassment, inhibition
  - Difficulty walking, working, sleeping
  - Change in self concept

3. Remediation

- How often do you have arthritis pain
- How often do you seek relief
- Is there a need for a new product for arthritis pain
- Motivations for seeking relief
- Steps taken to obtain relief
- Steps taken to stimulate normal function
- Steps taken to restore sensation and well-being
- Steps attempted in the past but no longer used
- What remedies work best, worst
- Products or medications used
  - Advantages, disadvantages of each
  - How did you find out about them
  - Where and how obtained
  - Rx vs. OTC
  - If from a store, where is it located; how easy to find
- When are products used
- Time of day
- Trigger experiences
- Where are products used
- How fast is relief expected
- Consequences of usage, such as embarrassment, inconvenience, lack of privacy
- Have you sought advice about arthritis pain
- Who has the most knowledge about arthritis pain – chiropractors, nutritionists, physicians, pharmacists, other
- Do any friends/relatives, etc. have arthritis pain
  - Do they discuss symptoms, treatments, etc.

4. Remediation Experience

- Personal descriptors of well-being and relief from arthritis pain
  - How should your joints, hands, shoulders feel
  - What should be sensation in affected areas
  - Open-ended
- Likely consequences of relief – emotional, social, etc.

WORD ASSOCIATION EXERCISE
MIND MAPPING EXERCISE
COLLAGE EXERCISE

5. Product preferences

- Likelihood of purchasing an OTC remedy
- Desired characteristics of an OTC remedy
- Mode of administration preferences
  - Tablet
  - Gel cap
  - Lozenge
  - Capsule
  - Gel (form of application)
  - Liquid
  - Plaster
  - Appliance
- What would be implications, consequences of each format
- Is there any interest in a combination product
  - Analgesic with minerals
  - Minerals + gel
  - Plaster + vitamins
- Any interest in a regime with multiple products
- Should there be a standalone arthritis pain product
- Benefits wanted
- Desired sensations as product is taken/working
  - Texture
  - Effervescence
  - Foamy
  - Flavor/no flavor
  - Temperature
- Color
- Expected frequency of administration
  - How long lasting
  - Length of administration
- Which activities should it be associated with: walking, sleeping, working
- Preferred location of usage – public vs. private
- Packaging
  - Size, dimensions
  - Portability
  - Amount, frequency of refill
- Efficacy – what vocabulary describes an effective product
  - Does clinical efficacy need to be demonstrated
  - FDA, scholarly publication
- Information needs
  - What would you like to know about the product, for example, is it sugar-free
  - Where should it be provided

- How should it be promoted and advertised
  - Media
  - Credible spokespersons and endorsers
  - Recommendation from AMA
  - Recommendation by chiropractor/physician/other
- Expected pricing
- Merchandising parameters

6. Closing

WORD LIST EXERCISE
  A. Select the words that describe your arthritis pain when you experience it.
  B. Select the words that describe how you want your joints, hands, shoulders, etc. to feel.

- Concluding advice

Sample observation guide

Bathroom cleaning observation guide

- (look) Scan and map bathroom environment
  - Fixtures
  - Ventilation
  - Materials
  - Air and light

- (look) Product inventory
  - Exclusive bathroom use vs. shared with other spaces
  - Brand, Flavor, Size, Packaging
  - When purchased
  - Freshness

- (look) Where are products stored
  - Ease of access

- (ask) What is intended use of each product
- (ask) What are the biggest cleaning problems in the bathroom
- (look) Who is cleaning, watching, assisting, being taken care of while cleaning

- (look) Routine cleaning (as relevant)
  - Toilet bowl inside
  - Toilet bowl outside
  - Sink
  - Cabinetry, closets
  - Bathtub
  - Shower stall
  - Appliances
  - Mirror surfaces
  - Floor
  - Walls
  - Decorations

- (look) While cleaning
  - Product used
  - Quantity, dilution
  - Amount of effort, ease of use
  - Tools used
  - Combinations of products
  - Time allotted
  - Attention to detail

- Problems experienced
- Body language reflecting attitudes
- Results

- (listen) What is respondent thinking and saying while cleaning
- (ask) How are results described
- (ask) Areas of satisfaction/dissatisfaction with results
- (ask) Problems, issues, wishes

Sample introductory dialogue

Opening

Hello. My name is _____ and I'll be moderating tonight's discussion. This is what we call a 'focus group'. It's a form of market research conducted by just about every major company in the United States.

Companies conduct focus groups to learn from the people who are most important to them – their customers. No company can stay in business very long if it ignores the feelings and needs of its customers.

We'll be doing various things here tonight. (Pick these if appropriate or add others.)

- *Participating in a group discussion.*
- *Doing some writing.*
- *Evaluating some ideas and materials that I'll present later in the discussion.*

There are a few things I want to reassure you about.

First of all, I need you to say exactly what you think. There's no such thing as a right or wrong answer to any of the issues we'll be covering. Also, you may have positive or negative feelings about any of the things we'll be discussing and I want to assure you that we need to hear all sides. Please don't hold back even if everybody else in the room has a different opinion. We need to understand your point of view.

Anything you say here tonight is confidential. If we write memos or reports to summarize the discussion, no names will be used.

As the moderator, I'm not here to sell or to advertise anything to you. I'm not going to push a particular point of view. If I probe or ask you to explain your opinion later on, it's only because I want to understand you as thoroughly as possible.

I'm based in _____ and I'm part of a research group that will be talking to dozens of people across the country just like you.

I appreciate your coming in this evening to be an ambassador for your fellow customers. It takes a special person to say what he or she thinks in front of a group of strangers. Remember, I'm counting on you to be as open and honest as you can be.

Disclosures

There are a few features of this conference room I'd like to tell you about. You may have noticed microphones around the table. These have been set up to make a tape recording of tonight's discussion. Every word that you say is important and we don't want to miss anything when we analyze the discussion.

There is also a two-way mirror behind me with other members of the research team acting as observers on the other side of the mirror. They are just as interested in what you have to say as I am. It's just easier to have only one person leading the discussion, rather than three or four, and that's my job as a team member. During the discussion, I may leave the room at various points to review things in the back room with my colleagues or to pick up some things to show you. That is something normal to expect during tonight's session.

Again, I want to assure you that no one is here to evaluate or judge anything you say here. The folks behind the mirror are also here to listen.

Participation ground rules

Let me conclude this introduction with a few ground rules for participation.

First of all, I need to hear from everyone tonight and that means giving everyone in the room a chance to contribute.

You don't have to wait to be called upon to speak. Feel free to jump in and react to what somebody else in the room is saying. But, let's make sure that only one person at a time is talking. Let whoever is talking finish before you start because if there is more than one voice at a time on the tape, we won't be able to hear a thing. For that reason, I have to make another rule – no side conversations.

Please speak up when it's your turn because the tape recorder won't pick up if your voice is too weak.

Again, I want to say, 'Thank you' to everyone for coming out tonight and agreeing to participate. Your contributions are very important and I guarantee that they will make a difference.

So, let's get going – relax and have fun. Are there any questions?

Sample evaluation form

Date_____ Research manager_____

Consultant name/company_____

Project title_____

Primary methods used_____

Please respond to all questions on this form and provide sufficient detail in the comments to explain and clarify your judgment. Please use the following 4-point scale in making your ratings.

1. Truly exceptional – Within the top 5%
2. Outstanding – Distinctive and highly valued – Within the next 20%
3. Responsible and professional – Within expectations for most projects – Middle 50%
4. Performance below expectations – Bottom 25%

A. Responsiveness

A1. Understands business issues stimulating the research.				
1	2	3	4	
COMMENTS				

A2. Accepts management views in designing the study.				
1	2	3	4	
COMMENTS				

A3. Shows cooperative attitude toward changes and adjustments.				
1	2	3	4	
COMMENTS				

B. Process management

B1. Handles project execution responsibly.				
1	2	3	4	
COMMENTS				

B2. Appropriate selection of subcontractors.				
1	2	3	4	
COMMENTS				

B3. Appropriate screening of respondents.				
1	2	3	4	
COMMENTS				

B4. Prepares useful discussion/observation guide, exercises and tools.				
1	2	3	4	
COMMENTS				

B5. Supplies information and orientation of research managers and observers.				
1	2	3	4	
COMMENTS				

B6. Manages debrief session.				
1	2	3	4	
COMMENTS				

B7. Designs report appropriately.				
1	2	3	4	
COMMENTS				

C. Interpersonal skills

C1. Communicates well within a variety of statuses within the company.				
1	2	3	4	
COMMENTS				

C2. Behaves in a humane, professional and balanced manner toward clients, respondents and suppliers alike.				
	2	3	4	
COMMENTS				

D. Intellectual skills

D1. Makes an extra effort to learn about the category and its special marketing issues.				
1	2	3	4	
COMMENTS				

D2. Delivers added value through insights derived from professional experience as well as knowledge of human behavior, business trends and current affairs.				
1	2	3	4	
COMMENTS				

E. Moderation skills

E1. Uses interviewing skills and techniques that provoke insights into consumer attitudes.				
1	2	3	4	
COMMENTS				
E2. Explains the importance and significance of tools used during interviews.				
1	2	3	4	
COMMENTS				

F. Timeliness

F1. Accomplished all projects in a timely manner without unnecessary delays.				
1	2	3	4	
COMMENTS				

G. Value for fees

G1. Billing procedures are clear and understandable.				
1	2	3	4	
COMMENTS				
G2. Accounted for all billed items in the original budget.				
1	2	3	4	
COMMENTS				

G3. Charges appropriate fees for services.				
1	2	3	4	
COMMENTS				

H. Overall quality

H1. Rate the overall quality of the consultant's contribution on this assignment.				
1	2	3	4	
COMMENTS				

Sample limitations statement

Qualitative studies such as this one are largely exploratory and should be used for background information and for advice and guidance in developing marketing strategies. These data are <u>not</u> appropriate for decisions that require definitive marketplace projections. Since probability sampling procedures are not followed in the recruitment of subjects, these data do not provide for a valid statistical representation of consumer characteristics and behavior.

Conclusions drawn in this study are based upon intensive interviewing in which subjects are challenged and probed for the most accurate, precise and representative responses. Findings are reported when they appear to represent a consensus or clear tendency among participants. In cases where disagreements or varied opinions arise, the study's conclusions reflect that fact. Verbatim statements are presented in the text to 'flesh out' and illustrate subjects' viewpoints in their own language. Quotes sometimes are edited for clarity. These statements do not constitute the only evidence for points made in the analysis. Such evidence consists of the entire transcript of the sessions' proceedings including observations of gesture, body language and voice nuances communicated during the course of the interviews.

Endnotes

1. On guerilla marketing see Levinson (1989, 1994). For further discussion of word-of-mouth marketing, see Silverman (1996).
2. See also Slurzberg and Rettinger (1994).
3. See also Steinberg (1993), Atkinson (1998) and Riessman (1987).
4. See Manning (1993) and Barthes (1972).
5. A thorough review of the general problem of objectivity in qualitative research across several generations of practitioners is provided by Kirk and Miller (1986).
6. Material in this section is based upon a panel presentation delivered by the author at the 1998 annual conference of the Qualitative Research Consultants Association in Phoenix, AZ entitled, 'Global fieldwork: locating, selecting, orienting and working cooperatively with qualitative research suppliers around the world'. I am grateful to fellow panelists Gabi Antonescu, Jack Kravitz and Rachel Shuker for numerous insights and suggestions.
7. A review of up-to-date facility requirements is provided by a manager who polled qualitative research practitioners before expanding his business; see Meier (1993). For a research consultant's perspective see Langer and Miller (1985).
8. Ethnography tactics are reviewed at length in Mariampolski (1998).
9. See, for example, Greenbaum (1998).
10. See also Tuckel, Leppo and Kaplan (1993).
11. Several standard problems in developing effective screeners are reviewed by Schild (1995).
12. This issue is evolving and unsettled; see Newman (1995). It is best to follow local customs and practices.
13. See also Fuller (1995b).
14. Other related titles that offer guidance for creative conduct of focus groups include Harrington, Hoffherr and Reid, Jr. (1998), and Nadler and Hibino (1998).
15. See Kinzey (1993) and Crandall (1997).
16. An alternative introduction is provided by Fuller (1996).
17. See Huberty (1995).
18. Material in this section is adapted from Gorden (1975).
19. Henderson (1997) advocates the 'two-thirds' rule – if two-thirds of the group has responded and the moderator has not gotten additional reactions to a probe on other opinions, the discussion moves on.
20. Hall's stance on body language is elaborated in several works (1959, 1966, 1976). Other works which review body signals in a helpful way for researchers include Pease (1984) and Wainwright (1993).
21. Compare to Neal (1980).
22. A useful review of laddering in the context of projective techniques used in qualitative research is offered by Sampson (1998). A classic formulation on the process is by Reynolds and Gutman (1988).
23. Compare with Moore (1987).

24. Bob Harris, a well-respected senior consultant, reported that a respondent in one of his focus groups once drew a gun on a fellow participant who was being somewhat confrontational, but this case is too peculiar for our discussion.

25. For more on this point and other details on researching seniors, see Haller (1995) and Pranses (1996).

26. See Mariampolski (2000) and Maso-Fleischman (1997).

27. See Simon (1996).

28. See Mariampolski (1989).

29. See Feder and Mattimore (1996).

30. Details reported here are educated by a report of a survey conducted by the QRCA; see Good and Provost (1997).

31. This entire section has been immeasurably assisted by the wise insights of Judith Langer and Patricia Sabena.

32. See Greenbaum (1997).

References

Anastas, Michael (1994) 'Visuals stimulate richer response in focus groups and individual interviews', *Quirk's Marketing Research Review*, 8 (10): 15, 38 – 39.

Arnould, Eric J. and Wallendorf, Melanie (1994) 'Market-oriented ethnography: interpretation building and marketing strategy formulation', *Journal of Marketing Research*, 31 (4): 484 – 504.

Atkinson, Robert (1998) *The Life Story Interview (Qualitative Research Methods Series 44)*. Beverly Hills, CA: Sage.

Baldinger, Allen L., Faberman, Jay and Greenbaum, Thomas (1992) *The ARF Qualitative Research Market Study*. New York: Advertising Research Foundation.

Barthes, Roland (1972) *Mythologies*. New York: Hill and Wang.

Bartos, Rena, (1992) 'Qualitative research: what it is and where it came from', reprinted in *Understanding Qualitative Research*. New York: Advertising Research Foundation. pp. 7 – 14.

Belisle, Pierre (1993) 'From moderators to consultants', *Quirk's Marketing Research Review*, 7 (10): 34 – 37.

Clowes, Rusty (1993) 'Making storyboards work in focus groups', *Quirk's Marketing Research Review*, 7 (10): 30 – 32.

Cooper, Peter and Patterson, Simon (1999) 'The trickster: a theory of modern branding and advertising', paper presented at the ESOMAR Conference on Qualitative Research, Athens.

Crandall, Bruce (1997) 'Ten keys to defusing political land mines in the back room', *Quirk's Marketing Research Review*, 11 (10): 12 – 13, 60.

Day, Rebecca H. (1993) 'Moderating: when gender matters', *Quirk's Marketing Research Review*, 7 (10): 18, 47.

de Bono, Edward (1970) *Lateral Thinking*. New York: Harper and Row.

Deshpande, Rohit (1983) 'Paradigms lost: on theory and method in research in marketing', *Journal of Marketing*, 47 (4): 101 – 110.

Dichter, Ernest (1964) *Handbook of Consumer Motivations*. New York: McGraw-Hill.

Dichter, Ernest (1992) 'Do I still have to fight (after 47 years)?', reprinted in *Understanding Qualitative Research*. New York: Advertising Research Foundation.

Dickie, Walt (1997) 'Seven rules for observational research: how to watch people do stuff', *Quirk's Marketing Research Review*, 11 (10): 18, 61 – 63.

Douglas, Jack D. (1970) *Understanding Everyday Life*. Chicago: Aldine.

Durgee, Jeffrey F. (1992) 'Richer findings from qualitative research', reprinted in *Understanding Qualitative Research*. New York: Advertising Research Foundation, 26 (4): 36 – 44.

Feder, Richard A. and Mattimore, Bryan (1996) 'Rethinking focus group reporting: dynamic debriefing', *Quirk's Marketing Research Review*, 10 (10): 12 – 13, 41 – 43.

Fetterman, David M. (1989) *Ethnography Step by Step*. Vol. 17, *Applied Social Research Methods Series*. Beverly Hills, CA: Sage.

Forcade, Karen M. (1996) 'Focus groups with kids...imagine', *Quirk's Marketing Research Review*, 10 (10): 30 – 31.

Fuller, H. Grace (1995a) 'Recruiting problems: how much responsibility should moderators shoulder?', *Quirk's Marketing Research Review*, 9 (10): 16 – 17, 40.

Fuller, H. Grace (1995b) 'What respondents should expect: an open letter to qualitative research participants', *Quirk's Marketing Research Review*, 9 (10): 41 – 42.

Fuller, H. Grace (1996) 'Qualitative introductions: an annotated script for meeting and welcoming focus group respondents', *Quirk's Marketing Research Review*, 10 (10): 18, 48.

Fuller, H. Grace and Pampalone, Gerard (1995) 'Writing effective screeners.' *Quirk's Marketing Research Review*, 9 (10): 40 – 41.

Garfinkel, Harold (1967) *Studies in Ethnomethodology*. Englewood Cliffs, NJ: Prentice-Hall.

Glaser, Barney G. and Strauss, Anselm L. (1967) *The Discovery of Grounded Theory: Strategies for Qualitative Research*. Chicago: Aldine-Atherton.

Goffman, Erving (1959) *The Presentation of Self in Everyday Life*. New York: Anchor.

Goldman, Alfred E. and McDonald, Susan Schwartz (1987) *The Group Depth Interview: Principles and Practice*. Englewood Cliffs, NJ: Prentice-Hall.

Good, Ellen and Provost, Kathy (1997) 'Analyzing and reporting qualitative data', paper presented to the annual conference of the Qualitative Research Consultants Association, New York.

Gorden, Raymond L. (1975) *Interviewing: Strategy, Techniques and Tactics*. Revised edn. Homewood, IL: Dorsey Press. (1st edn, 1969.)

Greenbaum, Thomas L. (1992) 'Focus groups with physicians have different requirements than those with consumers', *Quirk's Marketing Research Review*, 6 (1): 14 – 15, 30.

Greenbaum, Thomas L. (1993) *The Handbook of Focus Group Research*. Revised and expanded edn based on *The Practical Handbook of Focus Group Research*. New York: Lexington Books. (1st edn, 1988.)

Greenbaum, Thomas L. (1995) 'Making it work for you behind the one-way mirror', *Quirk's Marketing Research Review*, 9 (10): 22, 50.

Greenbaum, Thomas L. (1997) 'The focus group report: what is the moderator's responsibility?' *Quirk's Marketing Research Review*, 11 (10): 46, 48.

Greenbaum, Thomas L. (1998) 'Internet focus groups are not focus groups – so don't call them that', *Quirk's Marketing Research Review*, 12 (7): 62 – 63.

Hall, Edward T. (1959) *The Silent Language*. Greenwich, CT: Fawcett Publications.

Hall, Edward T. (1966) *The Hidden Dimension*. Garden City, NY: Doubleday.

Hall, Edward T. (1976) *Beyond Culture*. Garden City, NY: Anchor Press.

Haller, Susan and Benedict, Dale (1994) 'Done with mirrors: qualitative research helps Stanley™ Hardware reposition its line of mirror doors', *Quirk's Marketing Research Review*, 8 (9): 8 – 9, 74 – 76.

Haller, Terence (1995) 'Observations on researching seniors', *Quirk's Marketing Research Review*, 9 (10): 24, 45.

Harrington, H. James, Hoffherr, Glen D. and Reid, Jr., Robert P. (1998) *The Creativity Toolkit: Provoking Creativity in Individuals and Organizations.* New York: McGraw-Hill.

Harris, Leslie M. (1996) 'Choosing the ideal focus group facility', *Quirk's Marketing Research Review*, 10 (10): 22, 49 – 50.

Henderson, Naomi (1991) 'The art of moderating: a blend of basic skills and qualities', *Quirk's Marketing Research Review*, 5 (10): 18 – 19, 39.

Henderson, Naomi (1997) 'The magic of eight', *Quirk's Marketing Research Review*, 11 (10): 22, 24 – 25.

Hirschman, Elizabeth C. (ed.) (1989) *Interpretive Consumer Research.* Provo, UT: Association for Consumer Research.

Huberty, Tim (1995) 'Sharing inside information: spending a little time getting to know respondents can improve your qualitative learning', *Quirk's Marketing Research Review*, 9 (3): 10, 30 – 33.

Jung, C.G. (1981) *The Archetypes and the Collective Unconscious/Archetypen und das kollective Unbewusste.* Tr. R.F.C. Hull. 2nd edn. Princeton, NJ: Princeton University Press. (1st edn, 1959.)

Kaladjian, Lynn (1996) 'Children's qualitative research past and present', *Quirk's Marketing Research Review,* 10 (10): 32 – 33, 53 – 54.

Kinzey, Reyn (1993) 'Faster is better when writing qualitative reports', *Quirk's Marketing Research Review*, 7 (10): 12, 44 – 45.

Kirk, Jerome and Miller, Mac L. (1986) *Reliability and Validity in Qualitative Research (Qualitative Research Methods Series 1).* Beverly Hills, CA: Sage.

Knoll, Toni (1992) 'Integration of the synectics creative-problem solving process into Warner-Lambert's corporate culture', reprinted in *Understanding Qualitative Research.* New York: Advertising Research Foundation. pp. 255 – 260.

Laflin, Lori and Hyatt, David E. (1999) 'Using focus groups to generate satisfaction questionnaire content', *Quirk's Marketing Research Review*, 13, (9): 18 – 19, 74 – 75.

Langer, Judith and Miller, Susan (1985) 'The ideal focus group facility', *Journal of Data Collection*, 25 (2): 34 – 37.

Langer, Judith and Sabena, Patricia (1997) 'Sharpening analysis: writing reports that get read and used', paper presented to the annual conference of the Qualitative Research Consultants Association, New York.

Lazarsfeld, Paul F. (1992) 'The art of asking why: three principles underlying the formulation of questionnaires', reprinted in *Understanding Qualitative Research.* New York: Advertising Research Foundation. pp. 15 – 32.

Levinson, Jay Conrad (1989) *Guerrilla Marketing Attack.* Boston: Houghton Mifflin.

Levinson, Jay Conrad (1994) *Guerrilla Advertising.* Boston: Houghton Mifflin.

Levitt, Theodore (1983) *The Marketing Imagination.* New York: Free Press.

Lofland, John (1976) *Doing Social Life: The Qualitative Study of Human Interaction in Natural Settings.* New York: Wiley-Interscience.

Manning, Peter K. (1993) *Semiotics and Fieldwork (Qualitative Research Methods Series 30).* Beverly Hills, CA: Sage.

Mariampolski, Hy (1989) 'Focus groups on sensitive topics: how to get subjects to open up and feel good about telling the truth', *Applied Marketing Research*, 29 (1): 6 – 11.

Mariampolski, Hy (1998) 'Ethnography as a market research tool: why, how, where and when', in Peter Sampson (ed.), *Qualitative Research: Through a Looking Glass*. Vol. 4, *New Monograph Series*. Amsterdam: ESOMAR.

Mariampolski, Hy (1999) 'The power of ethnography', *Journal of the Market Research Society*, 41 (1): 75 – 86.

Mariampolski, Hy (2000) 'Learning from ethnic market research in the USA: applying community-based approaches and ethnography', paper presented at the ESOMAR Worldwide Ethnic Marketing Conference, Paris.

Maso-Fleischman, Roberta (1997) 'Understanding Hispanic culture: a case for ethnographic research', *Quirk's Marketing Research Review*, 11 (4): 22, 24 – 25.

Masters, J. (1995) 'The history of action research', in I. Hughes (ed.), *Action Research Electronic Reader*. Sydney: The University of Sydney online. <http://www.behs.cchs.usyd.edu.au/arow/Reader/rmasters.htm> (Downloaded October 10, 2000.)

Meier, Harold (1993) 'Moderators know best: designing a focus group facility', *Quirk's Marketing Research Review*, 7 (10): 6 – 7, 35 – 37.

Merton, Robert K. (1987) 'The focussed interview and focus groups', *Public Opinion Quarterly*, 51 (4): 550 – 566.

Merton, Robert K., Coleman, James S. and Rossi, Peter H. (eds) (1979) *Qualitative and Quantitative Social Research: Papers in Honor of Paul F. Lazarsfeld*. New York: Free Press.

Merton, Robert K., Fiske, Marjorie and Kendall, Patricia L. (1990) *The Focused Interview: A Manual of Problems and Procedures*. 2nd edn. New York: Free Press. (1st edn, 1956.)

Moore, Carl M. (1987) *Group Techniques for Idea Building*. Vol. 9, *Applied Social Research Methods Series*. Newbury Park, CA: Sage.

Morgan, David L. (1988) *Focus Groups as Qualitative Research (Qualitative Research Methods Series 16)*. Beverly Hills, CA: Sage.

Nadler, Gerald, PhD and Hibino, Shozo, PhD (1998) *Breakthrough Thinking: The Seven Principles of Creative Problem Solving*. Revised 2nd edn. Rocklin, CA: Prima Publishing. (1st edn, 1990.)

Neal, William D. (1980) 'Strategic product positioning: a step-by-step guide', *Business*, 30 (3): 34 – 42.

Newman, Jan (1995) 'The visual language of focus groups and one-on-one interviewing', *Quirk's Marketing Research Review*, 9 (10): 32 – 33.

Norman, Donald A. (1990) *The Design of Everyday Things*. New York: Currency/Doubleday. Originally published as *The Psychology of Everyday Things*. New York: Basic Books. (1st edn, 1988.)

Odesky, Stanford and Kerger, Richard (1994) 'Using focus groups for a simulated trial process', *Quirk's Marketing Research Review*, 8 (4): 38 – 40, 53.

Ozanne, Julie L. and Hudson, Laurel Anderson (1989) 'Exploring diversity in consumer research', in Elizabeth C. Hirschman (ed.), *Interpretive Consumer Research*. Provo, UT: Association for Consumer Research. pp. 1 – 9.

Pearson, Tom and McCullough, Susan (1997) 'Overcoming the obstacles to conducting international qualitative research', *Quirk's Marketing Research Review*, 9 (9): 38 – 40.

Pease, Allan (1984) *Signals: How to Use Body Language for Power, Success and Love*. New York: Bantam.

Peñaloza, Lisa (1994) 'Atravesando fronteras/border crossings: a critical ethnographic exploration of the consumer acculturation of Mexican immigrants', *Journal of Consumer Research.* 21, 32 – 54.

Perry, James M. (1994) 'Clinton relies heavily on White House pollster to take words right out of the public's mouth', *Wall Street Journal*, 223 (57): A16.

Pranses, Terence J. (1996) 'Making new friends: how to optimize qualitative research with seniors', *Quirk's Marketing Research Review*, 10 (10): 26, 51 – 52.

QMRR staff (1992) 'Leaving nothing to chance: the Missouri lottery tests new games with focus groups', *Quirk's Marketing Research Review.*

Qualitative Research Council (1992) 'Focus groups: issues and approaches', *Understanding Qualitative Research.* New York: Advertising Research Foundation. pp. 33 – 68.

Reynolds, Thomas J. and Gutman, Jonathan (1988) 'Laddering theory, method, analysis, and interpretation', *Journal of Advertising Research*, 28 (1): 11 – 31.

Riessman, Catherine Kohler (1987) *Narrative Analysis (Qualitative Research Methods Series 7).* Beverly Hills, CA: Sage.

Rodgers, Alice (1992) 'Money isn't everything part III', *Quirk's Marketing Research Review*, 6 (6): 12 – 15, 32.

Rogers, Carl (1951) *Client-Centered Therapy.* Boston: Houghton-Mifflin.

Rogers, Carl (1961) *On Becoming a Person: A Therapist's View of Psychotherapy.* Boston: Houghton-Mifflin.

Rydholm, Joseph (1992a) 'Right on the mark: focus groups help Ethan Allen™', *Quirk's Marketing Research Review*, 6 (9): 6 – 7, 40.

Rydholm, Joseph (1992b) 'Personality in a glass: respondents in focus groups, one-on-ones endorse fun-loving Libbey™ Glass ad campaign', *Quirk's Marketing Research Review*, 6 (10): 6 – 7, 37.

Rydholm, Joseph (1994) 'Berry inspired: One-on-ones help Finlandia™ distill a winner', *Quirk's Marketing Research Review*, 8 (10): 6 – 7, 49 – 50.

Rydholm, Joseph (1995a) 'Igniting the Sunfire™: respondent collages help agency develop ads for new Pontiac™', *Quirk's Marketing Research Review*, 9 (3): 6 – 7, 51 – 52.

Rydholm, Joseph (1995b) 'Building a better brand: qualitative technique helps Scott™ Paper find out if consumers cotton to new Cottonelle™', *Quirk's Marketing Research Review*, 9 (9): 10 – 11, 46 – 47.

Rydholm, Joseph (1997a) 'A working vacation: agency uses a little R&R (research and relaxation) to develop ads for RV group', *Quirk's Marketing Research Review*, 11 (3): 12 – 13, 54 – 55.

Rydholm, Joseph (1997b) 'The people have spoken: customers improve Oregon utility's power outage reporting system', *Quirk's Marketing Research Review*, 11 (10): 10 – 11, 64.

Sabena, Patricia (1999a) 'Ten of the latest trends in qualitative research', *QRCA Views.* pp. 1, 6 – 8.

Sabena, Patricia (1999b) 'Contemporising brand equity: relaunching the Helena Rubinstein™ brand in the States', paper presented to the ESOMAR Conference on Qualitative Research, Athens.

Sampson, Peter (1998) 'Qualitative Research in Theory and Practice', in Sampson, Peter (ed.), *Qualitative Research Through a Looking Glass.* Vol. 4, *New Monograph Series.* Amsterdam: ESOMAR. pp. 15 – 81.

Schild, Rhoda (1995) 'So how tall do you want me to be?', *Quirk's Marketing Research Review*, 9 (2): 10, 33.

Schutz, Alfred (1970) *On Phenomenology and Social Relations*. Chicago: University of Chicago Press.

Shaffir, William B., Stebbins, Robert A. and Turowetz, Allan (1980) *Fieldwork Experience: Qualitative Approaches to Social Research*. New York: St. Martin's Press.

Silverman, George (1996) 'How and why to research word-of-mouth', *Quirk's Marketing Research Review*, 10 (10): 26, 51 – 52.

Simmel, Georg (1960) *The Sociology of Georg Simmel*. New York: Free Press.

Simon, Murray (1996) 'Physician focus groups revisited', *Quirk's Marketing Research Review*, 10 (6): 16, 38 – 39.

Slurzberg, Lee and Rettinger, Charlotte (1994) 'A review of focus groups for advertising agencies', *Quirk's Marketing Research Review*, 8 (3): 10, 51.

Spanier, Jim (1993) 'Focus group listening and hearing', *Quirk's Marketing Research Review*, 7 (10): 33.

Spier, Daisy (1993a) 'Qualitative ad research: walk like a researcher, think like a creative person', *Quirk's Marketing Research Review*, 7 (3): 6 – 7, 28 – 29.

Spier, Daisy (1993b) 'Serendipity happens: the element of surprise in qualitative research', *Quirk's Marketing Research Review*, 7 (10): 14 – 15, 48.

Spradley, James P. (1979) *The Ethnographic Interview*. New York: Holt Rinehart Winston.

Spradley, James P. (1980) *Participant Observation*. San Diego: Harcourt Brace Jovanovich.

Steinberg, Lois (1993) 'Story analysis in qualitative research', *Quirk's Marketing Research Review*, 7 (10): 16 – 17, 46.

Steinberg, Lois (1997) 'Learning from customers' stories', *Quirk's Marketing Research Review*, 11 (10): 38, 40 – 41.

Stewart, David W. and Shamdasani, Prem N. (1990) *Focus Groups: Theory and Practice*. Vol. 20, *Applied Social Research Methods Series*. Beverly Hills, CA: Sage.

Straus, Michael (1998) 'Mining a new mint: Charlotte art museum uses research to light path into 21st Century', *Quirk's Marketing Research Review*, 12 (2): 10 – 11, 49.

Tamler, Howard (1998) 'How (much) to intervene in a usability testing session', *Common Ground*, 8 (3): 11 – 15.

Taylor, Steven J. and Bogdan, Robert (1984) *Introduction to Qualitative Research Methods: The Search for Meanings*. 2nd edn. New York: Wiley. Originally published as Bogdan, Robert and Taylor, Steven J. (1975) *Introduction to Qualitative Research Methods: A Phenomenological Approach to the Social Sciences*. New York: Wiley.

Thompson, Fiona, Wernicke, Lucie and Barker, Andy (1999) 'Qualitative recruitment: advancing the state of the art', paper presented at ESOMAR Conference on Qualitative Research, Athens.

Tonneberger, Mary P. (1992) 'In search of the perfect plastic', *Quirk's Marketing Research Review*, 6 (5): 6 – 7, 37.

Tuckel, Peter, Leppo, Elaine and Kaplan, Barbara (1993) 'A view from the other side of the mirror: participants reveal their perspectives on focus groups', *Marketing Research*, 5 (4): 24 – 27.

Van Maanen, John (1983) *Qualitative Methodology*. Beverly Hills, CA: Sage.

von Oech, Roger, PhD (1983) *A Whack on the Side of the Head: How to Unlock Your Mind for Innovation.* New York: Warner Books.

Wainwright, Gordon R. (1993) *Body Language (Teach Yourself Books).* Chicago: NTC Publishing.

Weber, Jack (1994) 'Absorbing some changes: Brawny™ takes a giant step into research', *Quirk's Marketing Research Review*, 8 (9): 6 – 7, 28.

Weber, Max (1948) *The Protestant Ethic and the Spirit of Capitalism/ Protestantische Ethik und der Geist des Kapitalismus.* Tr. T. Parsons, foreword by R.H. Tawney. New York: Scribner.

Weber, Max (1949) *The Methodology of the Social Sciences.* Glencoe, IL: Free Press.

Whorf, Benjamin (1956) *Language, Thought, and Reality: Selected Writings of Benjamin Lee Whorf.* Cambridge, MA: MIT Press.

Wilson, Martha (1994) 'Setting the tone for effective observation', *Quirk's Marketing Research Review*, 8 (6): 16 – 17, 29.

Wirth, Louis (1956) *The Ghetto.* Chicago: University of Chicago Press.

Wright, Andrew and Fitkin, L.K. (1997) 'Focus group videos: a survival guide', *Quirk's Marketing Research Review*, 11 (10): 42, 44 – 45.

Zanes, Ruth L. (1992) 'Qualitative research professionals are more than just moderators', *Quirk's Marketing Research Review*, 6 (6): 24 – 27.

Zorbaugh, Harvey Warren (1976) *The Gold Coast and the Slum.* Chicago: University of Chicago Press.

INDEX